6-8-02

To all those from the "CC" who influenced my life. Too many to Name, but, none forgotten.

Please pass the word on. about VERPA and our certification to help all veterans and loved ones, dealing with denial of Service-Connected

Beyond the Scope of Justice

disability claims.

God Bless you all!

Tim

To see where our "VISION" has taken us, Please see WWW.VERPA.NET.

BEYOND
THE SCOPE OF
JUSTICE

JEFFREY A. TRUEMAN

Published by VERPA
Duluth, Minnesota

Printed in the United States of America
Published by VERPA, PO Box 3213, Duluth, MN 55803

Produced by Griffith Publishing, Caldwell, Idaho
Cover design by Griffith Anderson Design, Boise, Idaho

ISBN # 0-9677924-0-1

Dedication

*To my daughter Tiffany and son Gage.
If not for the both of you, I do not know where
I would be.
I love you both and forever will!*

*To all my family and friends in the Philadelphia
and the surrounding area, and my newly
"adopted" family in the Duluth, Minnesota and
Superior, Wisconsin areas—too many wonderful
people to name but whose love, affection, and
support has given me the strength to "fight the
good fight" in advocating the prevention of
human rights abuses in the military's mental
health system;*

*To all the wonderful people I met along the way
in my journey and those whose words of
encouragement will forever be remembered;*

*To all veterans and their families who have
suffered injustice or injury over the past fifty
years due to the unlawful or ill-advised actions
of our government officials in the wake of the
United States Supreme Court's wrong holding
regarding Feres;*

*To my wife Tina. I know this ordeal has destroyed
our bond as husband and wife. However, without
the love, attention, and support you provided to
the kids, I could have never made it this far for
the good of other military families such as ours
once was!*

In Loving Memory

of
Stephen C. Condi
and Douglas Hege
Two special people whose friendships
I will always cherish

Table of Contents

Preface

I have written *Beyond the Scope of Justice* to present to the American public and the millions of rank and file members in the active and reserve branches of the United States Armed Forces, the chilling effects of a devastating law entitled *The Feres Doctrine.*

In a nutshell, Feres allows for medical malpractice, abuse of power, and human rights violations to go unchecked within the Armed Forces of the United States of America. The ruling known as the Feres Doctrine allows military officers to dismiss legitimate complaints of gross mismanagement and abuse of power simply by relegating troublesome persons to the military's mental health or alcholism treatment program and then eliminating them from the military. Under the Feres Doctrine, military members in good standing watch helplessly as their military careers are destroyed for no reason except that they took reports of misconduct from their subordinates to the proper channels for review and appropriate action.

In this book I share my story showing how the Feres Doctrine allowed officials of the U.S. Military to violate their constitutional oaths and powers. The American Judicial system's legal position is that it is "inappropriate for a civilian court to second guess military decisions." I will show how this position has caused our government to turn its back on injustices arising out of the U.S. Armed Forces since 1950 when the *Feres Doctrine* became the "law of the land." When "military decisions" violate the United States Constitution, and the United States Congress condones such violations, the question must be asked: "Where are the checks and balances on military officials who abuse their powers?"

I share my story so that American service members and their families will not have to experience the hardships my family and I have endured. I am writing in protest of a system wherein the "rule of man" governs the "rule of law." I remind the reader that for this behavior our founding fathers declared independence against King George III of England in 1776.

The reality is that human and constitutional rights of honorable men and women are violated when they attempt to expose corruption and abuses that are allowed by the Feres Doctrine to go unchecked. For the first ten and one-half years of my career, the Navy Department considered me a 4.0 sailor and an asset to the team. Within weeks of presenting issues of fraud, waste and abuse, I watched helplessly as my years of dedicated service to my country were wiped out by false claims of mental illness to discredit my claims of improprieties. One year later I was "structurally discharged" without being afforded the right of due process of law that every American civilian is privileged to possess.

The Navy's legal position for discharging me was that my claims of abuse of power were "false and fantasy," that I made up false claims against superiors due to a paranoid thought process brought on by alcohol abuse. This position is not founded in fact. No alcohol-related incidents or other misconduct appear in my personnel record. I became but another victim of the chilling effect of Feres, another service member whose rights were destroyed with the stroke of a pen authorizing false claims of mental illness.

If one American can be destroyed by the military establishment without due process of law, it will happen to others. In this book I maintain that we owe those who serve our country the same protection that all private citizens enjoy under the Constitution. No one who wears the uniform of this country should ever be victim of unlawful retaliation by an abusive leader.

We will never achieve change unless we show our strength in numbers. If all veterans and families who have been victimized by these practices pull together with other Americans who see the dangers in Feres-sanctioned abuse of power and demand reform, we can send the message to Congress that—

"We who defend the Constitution should receive the same privileges of freedom as all American citizens!"

In November 1999, I registered a nonprofit organization with the State of Minnesota entitled *VERPA: Veterans' Equal Rights Protection Advocacy*. The primary goal of *VERPA* is to organize a nationwide petition drive to protect members of the military who report misconduct by their superior officers. We aim to compel the United States Congress to hold congressional hearings to reform or repeal the "incident to service bar" on intentional torts and medical malpractice within the United States Armed Forces. Additionally, *VERPA* advocates special legislation to compensate American service members and their families who have suffered injury or injustice due to false claims of mental illness. Such retaliatory actions are in violation of the 1992 Amendment to the Military Whistleblower Protection Act (Title 10 U.S.C. §1034), which makes mental health evaluations in the wake of "protected communications" unlawful. To achieve these goals, 50 percent of the proceeds from the sale of this book will go to fund *VERPA*.

I hope the facts and circumstances in this book will convince the reader that *The Feres Doctrine* is the most unjust law in this nation. Any law that accommodates abuse of power and of the constitutionally guaranteed rights of military men and women is a law that must be rendered unconstitutional. This is especially obvious when one law impedes the enforcement of another as is the case with the connection between *Feres* and §1034.

While my legal challenge that the Feres Doctrine is unconstitutional was denied review by the United States Supreme Court in June 1999, I have been vindicated in the court of public opinion. On October 23, 1998 ABC's PrimeTime LIVE (now 20/20) aired a story entitled, "An Abuse of Power?" I was interviewed extensively by Sam Donaldson for this report. The PrimeTime LIVE program exposed the unthinkable human right abuses taking place in the military's mental health system of the Clinton Administration, the very system used to destroy my career. In introducing the broadcast, Barbara Walters said the following:

> "You will find the story we are about to show you very hard to believe I think. Indeed we consider it explosive! It's about the U.S. Military and the awesome power it can use to strike back at personnel who are in any way critical, even when their criticism may be in the best interests of the country."

It is time to speak up about the atrocious practice of sending military members into mental hospitals to cover up corruption. Such conduct passes the boundaries of decency and is intolerable to a civilized nation.

I hope the lessons I've learned as stated in the Appendix will be beneficial to all honorable military members who face abuse of power during their careers. As Thomas Jefferson once said, *"The spirit to resistance of government is so valuable on certain occasions."* I believe my advocating the "evils" of The Feres Doctrine is one of those occasions.

Jeffrey A. Trueman

Disclaimer

The laws that I discuss in this book and my thoughts about them should not be construed as legal advice. I am not an attorney licensed to practice law. It is important for the reader who may be experiencing legal problems within the U.S. Armed Forces to seek competent legal assistance so that your rights, if any, can be explained to you by an attorney at law.

An open letter to the President of the United States of America

29 December 1999

Dear Mr. President,

Seven years ago you took command of a lean fighting outfit that had just busted Saddam Hussein's chops in a war that was over faster than you could say, "Oh, Monica."

Back in 1992, our warriors were combat-ready, battle-tested and bristling with magic spirit—that fire in the belly which is the most crucial of all the elements of war.

As this century closes, our military is 50 percent smaller than the armed forces George Bush placed in your trust, and their once-deadly edge has been dulled on the futile rocks of Iraq, Somalia, Haiti, Bosnia, and Kosovo.

The bumbled war with Serbia has only confirmed that today we simply don't have what it takes to replicate another Desert Storm.

Mr. Clinton, you've tasked our forces to do too much with too little for too long. Their combat ability is frayed, and they and their loved ones are weary and dispirited.

Daily, fine men and women from buck sergeant to bull colonel tell me, "I'm hanging it up. I can't take it anymore!"

In more than a half-century of being a soldier or a writer about soldiers, I've seldom seen lower morale.

Nor have I seen more self-serving senior leaders. From Secretary of Defense Bill Cohen in the bloated Pentagon to the generals and admirals who make up the most brass-heavy military bureaucracy in our country's history.

Perhaps you can take credit for our booming economy—of those sort of matters I'm ignorant. But you must also take responsibility for the weakening of our military—you are the person under whose command our forces went from STRAC to SLACK. As Harry Truman once said, the buck stops at your desk. And I hold you accountable.

Your feckless leadership and fickle policies began with your order that gays serve openly, followed by your policies earmarking the profession of arms as a place to provide females and minorities with equal opportunity. You and your advisors never got it straight that the U.S. military is not an equal job employer, but a finely honed sword forged only for the battlefield—where survival and winning are dependent on skill, sacrifice, spirit, unit cohesion and discipline.

These factors, mixed with total trust and caring leadership, allow a force to win. Battles are not won by how skin color or gender fits into a Pentagon personnel quota matrix, but by teams who've been sweated to perfection.

Every serving senior brass hat has been personally approved by you. The majority fit into the same go-along-to-get-along and don't-rock-the-boat-mold. None have challenged your reckless misuse of our military or your wrongheaded personnel policies.

Why should they? They weren't picked for stand-up leadership, but because they'd roll over. There's not a Patton, Nimitz or Puller-type in the lot of them, and few are trusted by the folks they lead.

But you can still redeem yourself—although don't think it can be by throwing more money at the Pentagon, even though the leading candidates hustling for your job say that's the fix.

The answer is leadership. You need to begin by sacking Cohen and replacing him with a person of the stature of George C. Marshall. A leader with the integrity, know-how and guts to turn the U.S. military around. Cohen's (1) allowing the forces to be weakened, (2) mishandling of the war with Serbia or (3) his Anthrax disaster—pick any one of the above—are more than sufficient justification.

At the beginning of World War II, our military's senior leadership was also sick. Marshall, then Army Chief of Staff, sacked the General Blimps and fast-promoted the Gavins, Ridgways, and Pattons. Leaders who weren't afraid to make the sweeping, visionary changes that reshaped our military and took it from trench to mobile warfare. These savvy leaders performed a miracle and won a war even though the early odds were on the enemy's side.

Besides sending Cohen packing, read Sun Tzu. There you'll learn the how vital the military is to the state and how a bad Commander-in-Chief can hobble an army.

You still have the time to turn things around. Marshall did the job in less than a year, and he was fighting a two-front war.

David H. Hackworth

Acknowledgments

I am indebted to the following for helping me through years of frustration in seeking justice:

To the Government Accountability Project, Washington D.C. and Seattle, Washington, for independent review of the evidence and assistance in helping me tell my story to ABC News;

To Dr. Andrew Wilkerson and Mr. William Shea, for honesty and integrity in upholding your duties to assure justice in my case. You have sustained my belief that there are decent and honorable people in our government. If not for the two of you two government officials and gentlemen, I would be a broken man!

To ABC News and the entire crew at *Prime*TIME Live (now 20/20) for kind words of support in my own struggle, and for broadcasting "An Abuse of Power?" exposing the tactic of psychological retaliation in the United States Armed Forces which is the predicate of this book;

To Joyce Griffith, Griffith Publishing, for believing in this project and for her work in editing my sometimes verbose proclamations to create a work that will be comprehensible to the reader;

To "Lars" Lasky, Stealth Productions Duluth, Minnesota and "Fitz" Fitizgibbons Photography for expedient efforts in producing the back cover of this book;

To Greg Gilbert, Attorney at Law for volunteering the time to review the necessary documents required to register *VERPA* as a nonprofit organization;

Abbreviations

§1034 Federal legislation enacted in 1989 granting military personnel the right to circumvent the military chain of command with "protected communications" —reports of fraud waste, and abuse to Members of Congress or military Inspectors Generals. Amended in 1992 to outlaw mental health referrals in the wake of protected communications.

ACDUTRA Active Duty for Training

AEC Aviation Electrician Chief

ARS Alcohol Rehabilitation Service

ASN Assistant Secretary of the Navy

BCNR Board for Correction of Naval Records

BPR Board on Professional Responsibility

CAAC Counseling and Assistance Center

CNARF Commander, Naval Air Reserve Force

CNO Chief of Naval Operations

CO Commanding Officer

DAPA Drug and Alcohol Program Advisor

DD-214 "Certificate of Release or Discharge from Active Duty"

DOD Department of Defense

DODIG Department of Defense Inspector General

FBI Federal Bureau of Investigation

FOIA Freedom of Information Act

FTCA Federal Tort Claim Act

GP Government Accountability Project

IDA Initial Denial Authority

IG Inspector General

JAG Judge Advocate General

JSTPS Joint Strategic Target Planning Staff

MEPS Military Entrance Processing Station

M&RA Manpower & Reserve Affairs

NAS Naval Air Station

NLSO Naval Legal Services Office

PA Privacy Act

PSD Personnel Support Detatchment

RPD Reserve Programs Department

TAMP Transition Assistance Management Program. A pre-separation program which provides counseling on relocation, medical and dental coverage, education assistance and other services to separating military personnel, by Public Law 101-510.

UCMJ Uniform Code of Military Justice

USN United States Navy

XO Executive Officer

YN1 Yeoman First Class

Introduction

On July 4, 1999, two hundred and twenty-three years after our Founding Fathers declared our independence from the King of England, I finished the first draft of this book. On television that day I saw reports of a poll taken to see how many Americans were familiar with the way our nation was created.

Surprisingly, 51 percent of all Americans do not know the history of this nation's birth. Since I am writing to average Americans who are in the military or thinking of joining, I open this book with a brief history lesson. This will help the reader understand my reasons for taking on the Clinton military establishment, the United States Congress and now, the United States Supreme Court. When I speak of "taking on" these three branches of government, I am referring to taking the fight into the only court whose doors are open, the "Court of Public Opinion!"

When the Founding Fathers decided that liberty was worth putting their lives on the line for freedom, the United States consisted of an estimated three million citizens. Out of those three million colonists, one million—or one-third of the total population—were loyal to King George III. In the same way, my views will not be accepted by all, and I will be criticized for writing this book. However, thousands of people around the country are supportive of my cause. In the end, I hope, this will become the cause of the majority. Of all the sectors of the American government, the United States Armed Forces represents serving in the public's trust in the most critical manner. "We the People" must take back our government and elect people who will serve in the public's trust, over that of their own personal agendas.

Where It All Began

On July 4, 1776 in Philadelphia, Pennsylvania, the Founding Fathers declared their independence from King George III of

England, and our country was born. The bold experiment we know as the United States of America was undertaken because of the colonists' desire to be free and their belief that government should be of the people and not of a tyrant.

After the Declaration of Independence of 1776 and America's winning the war against England, the next phase of our freedom was putting into place laws to prevent the newly established U.S. Government from repeating the same abuses that the King of England had placed on the American colonists. Hence, the Constitution of the United States of America was created and ratified in 1789. This document established the powers of the U.S. Government and a safety net—a three-branch government to ensure no one individual ever becomes powerful enough to control the majority of the people.

The three-branch system of checks and balances includes the Executive, Legislative and Judicial branches. The head of the Executive Branch is the President of the United States, who is also the Commander-in-Chief of the U.S. military. The Legislative branch is made up of both houses of Congress, the Senate and House of Representatives. Finally, to ensure that justice is administered equally in our society and that the U.S. Constitution is preserved, the United States Supreme Court was established. These three branches of government are designed with separate powers and an interrelated set of checks and balances to keep any one of the three branches from overpowering the others.

The United States Constitution is the ultimate controlling law of our nation. This document lays out the powers of our three branches of government and with the Bill of Rights protects individual liberties and prevents unlawful intrusion of government.

According to our Constitution, the U.S. Congress was provided with the power to establish and fund an Army and Navy to protect our national interests and to defend our borders from hostile nations. The overseers of the U.S. Armed Forces are thus our elected officials who serve in the U.S. Congress.

2

Because the federal judiciary will not intervene on military decisions, it is up to Congress to prevent abuses within the Armed Forces.

As I will show you in this book, Congress has failed to uphold its duty to address and correct corruption in the military's mental health system. We as a free people must hold them accountable.

Although I have been silenced by the political structure of our government, I remain steadfast in my fight to strengthen the laws on the books. From my standpoint as a U.S. Veteran and a private citizen, I believe the ultimate protectors of our freedom are the men and women who make up the rank and file in the United States Armed Forces.

If we do not support those who are honorable and serve in the public trust rather than individuals with ulterior motives, the price we pay could be American citizens refusing to serve their country in a time of national crisis. As the record reflects in 1999, the trend for manpower shortages is already being set. Navy recruitment is down by 7,000 sailors. All the services except for the Marine Corps struggle to recruit personnel to fill the billets. I believe, from listening to the young people and their parents, that sacrificing one's self for the politicians in the U.S. Government is no longer worth the price of their loved one's life because our so-called leaders cannot be trusted. This fact is clearly evident at the top of our government with respect to our Commander-in-Chief in 1999.

Following is the essential argument I am making pertaining to the protection of the constitutional rights of men and women in uniform who expose corruption:

"Should military members sacrifice their careers, jeopardize their families' security, and place themselves in harm's way to report fraud, waste, abuse or a potential harm to the public's safety for the benefit of the People of the United States of America... if the judicial system cannot protect these 'patriots' from false claims [of mental

3

shortcomings] and falsification of their official military records by officials of the U.S. Government?"

If you answer this question "no," read on! I think you will find the events and abuses that I have endured because of my patriotic beliefs in duty to country are outrageous. As you read, try to put yourself in my shoes and think of those you love. If you were singled out for retribution by the U.S. Government, what would you do? Who would you turn to?

If you have substantial amounts of money, you may be okay, but if you are in the poverty zone such as I was for years after my discharge, the war is a tough one.

Throughout my legal struggles in the administrative remedy process in the Department of Defense and throughout the federal judicial system after a false arrest by the United States Navy when I was a private citizen, I have been amazed at the failure of justice and accountability within all three branches of government.

In an argument I made at the Third Circuit Court of Appeals in Philadelphia, Pennsylvania, in the case of Trueman v. United States of America, Lekberg, Powell *et al*, I presented the Court with this question:

> "... in February 1993, if [Trueman] 'knew' that a Navy pilot was going to steal an aircraft with a nuclear weapon on board and was going to drop it on this Court, would [Trueman] be obligated to report this event to the proper authorities? The short answer is *absolutely!* And if this scenario truly took place, and [Trueman] prevented a major injustice, [Trueman] would be a national hero! Now, if [Trueman] knew that reporting this event would lead to the destruction of his career, and follow on retaliation initiated against him as a "private citizen." knowing no legal recourse was available to protect his constitutional rights, rest assured, [Trueman] would choose protecting his career and family over that of protecting this Court. Hence, would this be considered justice in the eyes of the Court's own family and friends when [Trueman]

4

had the opportunity to head off a potential threat to the very system he took an 'oath' to defend? Would the United States Government hesitate in holding [Trueman] accountable for 'turning the blind eye' and for his failure to report a hostile action against the United States of America?..."

The above hypothetical question goes to the heart of my argument: "If we don't protect the rights of our men and women in uniform from unlawful reprisals and the manpower numbers continue to drop, who will protect *your* rights?" Think about it.

I have been asked many times why I consume my life with taking on the largest bureaucracy in the world. I can only say that being from the Philadelphia area has had a tremendous influence on me as an American. Also, I served with many wonderful and caring people. I don't think that any service member should be treated like a second-class citizen with no legal right to protection from abusive government officials.

General George Washington knew he must treat the soldiers of the Continental Army with respect and dignity. He provided genuine leadership and concern for the well-being of his men. Why should the present-day warrior be willing to sacrifice himself or herself for political leaders such as Bill Clinton (a man who has used the military to deflect corruption in his administration), when the Courts do not protect the constitutional rights of its military members?

When ABC's 20/20 program announced to the world that the United States Armed Forces retaliates against its members as Hitler's Nazis once did, no reason was given to explain why this unthinkable tactic could take place in our military. From my research, I have concluded that this type of egregious conduct resulted from the 1950 Supreme Court ruling known as the *Feres Doctrine*. Hence, before I tell you my story, I must brief you as to what this law represents.

In 1950, a landmark court decision took place which essentially states that anything that happens to a member of the Armed Forces incident to his or her service in the military—so be it. For example, if a military member goes into surgery for a knee injury and the doctor cuts of the veteran's arm, so be it!

Furthermore, because of the "incident to service" holding, decisions of military leaders are given great deference by the Courts. This allows for abuse of power and corruption to go unchecked. For example, in the 20/20 broadcast, it was reported that military commanders asked military psychiatrists to grease the wheels to support military commanders who want to silence those they perceived to be a threat to their commands. A law such as the *Feres Doctrine* that allows this conduct to take place is simply bad law that must be challenged.

In my eleven and one-half years in the military, I have known many wonderful and honorable people who would lay down their lives to keep this country free. However, when a military member who speaks up legally for the good of the nation is retaliated against by the misuse of the psychological evaluation in the U.S. Armed Forces, I think the cry for justice and accountability must be sounded.

As Ben Franklin stated to John Hancock at the signing of the Declaration of Independence on July 4, 1776: "We must indeed all hang together, or, most assuredly we shall all hang separately." This statement rings true today. Good, honest and dedicated service members must stand together to prevent fraud, waste, abuse and retaliation in the U.S. Armed Forces.

I have always held the belief that no government official should ever have the power to destroy a citizen without affording the citizen due process of law. I believe due process is the essence of our existence as a free people and that we can never let even one American be deprived this inalienable right. The Feres Doctrine and other legal technicalities such as "qualified immunity" deprive the military member of due process.

If we are truly a "government of the people" it is time for the "People" (as jury), to decide on matters of justice if military officials who abuse their powers are not held accountable by the Department of Defense and United States Congress!

6

In 1951, Supreme Court Justice Frankfurter made his thoughts about due process known as follows:

"The requirement of 'due process' is not a fair-weather or timid assurance. It must be respected in periods of calm and in times of trouble; it protects aliens as well as citizens. But 'due process,' unlike some legal rules, is not a technical conception with a fixed content unrelated to time, place and circumstances. Expressing as it does... 'due process' cannot be imprisoned within the treacherous limits of any formula. Representing a profound attitude of fairness between man and man, and more particularly between the *individual and government*, 'due process' is compounded of history, reason, the past course of decisions, and stout confidence in the strength of the democratic faith in which we profess. Due process is not a mechanical instrument. It is not a yardstick... It is a delicate process of adjustment inescapably involving the Constitution entrusted with the unfolding of the process."

What it comes down to is fair play and decency. What more can there be in a free society as we Americans truly believe we live in!

Although I was cheated of my liberty in many ways during my experience with the military, on October 23, 1998 with the help of ABC's 20/20 and many other wonderful people I met in my journey, I became free once again. I have been vindicated. Now I have a story to tell. I hope it will forever change the way the U.S. Government treats its military members and their families.

Speaking as a veteran and father of two beautiful children, I hope this book paves the way for positive change in our government and the laws that govern the U.S. Armed Forces so that our future young men and women will never face the chilling effects of authority gone bad in the United States Government!

Because of the Feres Doctrine, my career was destroyed by a simple "stroke of a pen." I have documented outrageous official conduct and intentional violations of federal laws from the lowest level of my former chain of command, all the way to William Jefferson Clinton, Commander-in-Chief of the U.S. Armed Forces. Because the U.S. Congress and Federal Judiciary will not intervene, writing this book is the only way I will get my story in the public's eye.

I hope my story will interest you and teach you about the way justice or the lack thereof is administered in the U.S. Armed Forces. Most of all, I hope this book helps prevent a repeat of the emotional and financial hardships that were placed on myself and my family for upholding my military oath.

Chapter 1

I've Got a Name

"I'm not a number, I'm an American citizen"

I am simply an American citizen attempting to convince the reader that my story is bona fide and credible and that the U.S. Government is covering up intentional wrongs and human right abuses in our military.

My life as an American began on January 17, 1964 when I was born the son of Robert Trueman and Rosemary Macellaro-Trueman, in Upper Darby, Pennsylvania. Upper Darby sits on a hilltop which overlooks a valley wherein is seated the City of Philadelphia. For the next eighteen years, I grew up in a town named Ridley Park, ten minutes south of the Birthplace of Freedom—Philadelphia, Pennsylvania.

Ridley Park, for the most part, was a typical American small town of thirty thousand people. I was lucky to grow up in a neighborhood where violent crime was non-existent, and the most feared human beings in our town were the ones who were supposed to protect us—the Ridley Park police. My friends and I were for the most part typical good kids of the full-sized G.I. Joe action figure generation who ran around the neighborhood playing army and fighting to the end until victory or until our mothers called us in for dinner.

Located at the end of Board Street next to the home of the Philadelphia Flyers, Eagles, Phillies and Sixers was the former home of the oldest naval base in the country. The Philadelphia Naval Station/Shipyard housed both the Navy and Marine Corps. Because I lived so close to this military installation and had a father who was a Marine, I had many opportunities at a young age to be exposed to the men and women who defended the United States of America.

9

I can remember my father taking me to the base to watch the Marines drill on the parade grounds. I vividly recall the feeling of excitement I had in my stomach as a young boy watching them. I can also remember seeing in my dad's face the patriotism he had for this country. My exposure to the military as a youngster played an essential part in my decision to join the Armed Forces later. Furthermore, because relatives on both my mother's and father's sides of the family had served this country over the generations, I felt I should keep the tradition running. (Unfortunately, I may be the last Trueman to serve this nation unless reforms are made.) I am proud to say that my family has always contributed to the freedoms we enjoy, and I always sensed that one day I, too, would be wearing the uniform of this great country.

Each Thanksgiving my father took us to visit his sister Marion and her family in Doylestown, Pennsylvania. On the way there I always looked forward to driving past a Navy installation five minutes from my aunt and uncle's home. I would fight for the seat behind my father because it gave me the best view of the planes and the guards who stood watch at the main gate. On the return trip home I would fight for the seat behind my mother to catch a final glimpse of the base at night, knowing I would not see it for another year.

I thought that the guards at the gate looked so cool! As kids, we admire those who wear a uniform and protect us from the evils of the world. I remember dreaming of being like those guards myself one day. Little did I know that my dream would one day come true. The military installation that I would be assigned to and that would change my life forever was the same base that my family and I used to ride by on the way to Thanksgiving dinner each year—Naval Air Station, Willow Grove, Pennsylvania.

Growing Up Where Our Country Began Influenced My Patriotic Beliefs

Growing up in Delaware County and living ten minutes from Philadelphia was interesting for me. As a young child in elemen-

10

tary school, I can remember going on field trips to see the historic sites in Philadelphia (an everlasting impression). These sites included the Betsy Ross house where the "first" American flag (by tradition) had been stitched, the Pennsylvania State House (Independence Hall), the site of the signing of the Declaration of Independence and United States Constitution, and most familiar to all Americans—the Liberty Bell.

Missing Out on an Education

School to me was a bore, probably because I was tremendously shy except on a football field. I had a difficult time talking in front of large groups of people. I never completed a book report in school, knowing that I would have to get in front of the class and discuss it. Trying to express myself in front of a classroom of kids was the most chilling part of going to school. When I tell this to friends who didn't know me when I was in school, they can't believe me. For my first seven years in the military I was still shy when it came to speaking in front of groups of people.

Because of my lack of confidence in myself, I barely passed high school. I was allowed to graduate, and one of the officials at the school district office told my parents I had the potential to achieve whatever I wanted. I was allowed to graduate on time in 1981, one year prior to joining the U.S. Navy.

Doing the Right Thing is not Always Painful

One thing that has always been a part of me is my love for my country and my loyalty to it. One of my favorite moments during my school years was in the morning when we recited the "Pledge of Allegiance."

One evening my best buddy Steve Gav and I went to meet some friends at our elementary school. While we were waiting for them, we saw an older kid stealing the American flag. Both Steve and I yelled at this kid and chased him, but we were unable to retrieve the flag. The next day Steve and I went voluntarily to the principal's office and told him what we had seen. From our description of where the kid ran with the flag, school officials found the flag in a bush that day. We were treated like heroes for an entire week and received free pretzels for our good deed. Steve and I thought that standing up for our flag and being rewarded for our efforts was cool! Even as little kids, Steve and I both knew that the flag stood for something special and that citizens such as Steve's father, a Marine, served this nation to protect the flag, our symbol of freedom.

Finding a Mentor Made All the Difference in the World

I was fortunate to have been raised by two wonderful parents and to have an older sister, Marion, who has always been there for me. I also had fine friends and parents who influenced us kids, especially in athletics. What I learned from a very young age is that although we as individuals had our own responsibilities to the team, it took teamwork to achieve the many victories we enjoyed in all the sports we played. I also learned that finding a mentor is important.

After I graduated from high school at age seventeen, I began work as a busboy and dishwasher at various Italian restaurants in the Philadelphia area. I met the man who became my mentor, friend, and adopted big brother, Stephen C. Condi.

When I met Steve, I was unsure as to what my life had in store for me. Although my parents were full of love for me during my teen years in the 70s and early 80s, talking with them about my innermost thoughts and feelings did not come easily for me. When I met Steve and started to talk to him like a big brother, he always had an ear to listen. This made a tremendous impact on my life. After about a year working at the restaurant, I told Steve I intended to join the military.

We sat down and had a long talk. Steve spoke to me about being drafted and serving a tour of duty in the Central Highlands of Vietnam. He gave me some insight as to what military life was all about and shared the pros and cons with me. At the conclusion of our conversation, Steve told me something that would shape

12

the type of leader I would eventually believe myself to have been in the Navy. The words he spoke to me I carried in the back of my mind throughout my career:

> "You don't have to be a tough guy or a hero. Go in and learn something you can take back into civilian life if you decide to leave the military. But remember one thing: If you are ever in a position of leadership, always take care of the people under your direction."

At the time Steve told me this in 1982, it did not seem to apply to me as I was going in at the bottom of the heap. However, ten years later I would have to make a decision pertaining to Steve's advice!

Throughout my military career, I stayed in touch with my adopted big brother and was always proud to see him. When I was confronted with my dilemma of whether to address the problems on the base or not, I went to see him. When I told him of the difficulties I was facing as a leading petty officer, he said to me, "Jeff, you have an excellent military record. However, you do know you are still in the military. I can only say that if what you are telling me is the truth, and it can be backed by evidence and personnel, then it is up to you to decide from your heart whether or not to proceed up the chain of command."

Steve knew that I was in for a possible conflict with military authorities, but he let me make the decision. I know he was concerned for my well-being although he believed I was doing the right thing.

Deciding to Take my First Major Step on My Own in Life

On a summer evening in June 1982, while I was sitting around with my friends at Steve Gav's home watching them work on cars, I knew it was time to move on in life. I knew at that moment that the military was my only chance to make something of my life. I told my friends I would be back in a half hour. "Where are you going?" Steve asked me. I responded, "I have to take care of something."

I jumped in my "69" Charger and headed to the Military Recruiting Station in Folsom, Pennsylvania, about five minutes from our neighborhood.

As I walked down the hallway, I thought that joining the Coast Guard was the right choice. When I arrived at the Coast Guard Recruiter's office the door was closed and no one was present. Just as I was ready to walk out of the building, the Navy recruiter stopped me and asked if I needed help. I said, "Do you know where the Coast Guard recruiter is?"

He said, "He is not here, and, as a matter of fact, the Coast Guard is going out of business. Come on in my office and I can explain to you the opportunities in the Navy."

My recruiter was a decent guy, and it is my understanding that in 1982 termination of the Coast Guard was being considered. Not all recruiters are honest and forthright, but I have no complaints about Petty Officer Second Class (PO2) Rossi.

After Rossi asked me to come into his office, we sat down and discussed my options. I explained to him my shortcomings and signed some preliminary entry papers. I asked Rossi, "How fast can I get into the Navy?"

"We'll find out tomorrow when I take you to MEPS (Military Entrance Processing Station), in Philadelphia," he said.

When I left the office, I had a weird feeling inside me, the same feeling I've had many times just prior to a big game.

One important reality I learned from childhood is that nobody can make it through life by one's self. It takes teamwork and upholding one's responsibility to fellow team members in order to achieve the common goals for the good of the entire team. Many people have asked me how in the world could I have fought what appears to be a futile battle against government officials in the American government.

It's like this. Playing quarterback does not take great size or strength, but the ability to convince ten other guys that "heart," "determination," and "selflessness" can result in victory against

14

any opponent who might appear more powerful and better equipped.

On the afternoon of July 12, 1982, when I took the military oath to "protect and defend the Constitution of the United States against all enemies, foreign and domestic..." I became part of a special team. I understood that selfless service rather than pushing my own personal agenda was the way the game was supposed to be played. On that day my life in the real world began. I stepped onto an airplane for the first time in my life for an all expense taxpayer-funded vacation to boot camp to begin my Navy journey, a journey that I loved dearly, even though it ended prematurely.

Chapter 2

A Free People Must Always Criticize Abuse of Power

How the Feres Doctrine allows human and constitutional rights violations to go unchecked in the U.S. Armed Forces

I n 1983 at the age of nineteen I sailed out of Norfolk, Virginia, with 124 other individuals heading for the Mediterranean Sea under orders to provide gunfire support to 241 U.S. Marines who would ultimately sacrifice their lives as "peacekeepers" in support of a government policy that we now know went terribly wrong. The eight and one-half month cruise gave me my first taste of what being an American stood for.

Although we did some patrolling off the coast of Beirut, Lebanon, for most of our tour of duty we were in the Mediterranean Sea. We also had an opportunity to see other countries and experience different cultures and listen to foreigners' opinions of the United States from countries such as Turkey, Spain, France, Italy, and Romania.

Our ship pulled into Taranto, Italy, for a couple days of liberty. A few buddies and I hit the beach, and, as true blue Navy men, searched for the first bar we could find! In those days if you didn't drink, you lived a pretty dull life.

After we had ordered a couple of beers an elderly gentleman approached us and started saying things to us in broken English. His first comment was, "We don't like your government!" Being a nineteen-year-old American wearing a Navy uniform, I felt like I was in a situation. So I responded by saying, "Neither do we!"

Ten or fifteen Italians stood around while he translated to them what he was saying and what I was saying. The old man said, "If you don't like your government, then why are you wearing that uniform?"

"We in the Navy trust that our political leaders will do the right thing, but unfortunately, sometimes they do not. This reflects negatively on the ordinary people in our country." I added, "We in the Navy come from all parts of the United States, and each one of us served our country to protect our friends and families. We work to ensure the safety and security of our homeland."

I must have convinced the Italians that we were not that bad because for next several hours, the Italians paid for all our drinks. At the end, we all shook hands and wished each other well.

After we left Taranto, we performed various duties off the coast of Beirut, awaiting our next port of call. The most compelling and profound nation I saw with my own eyes was Romania. My experience there helped me understand why America is the greatest nation on earth, even though we have corrupt politicians, mass murderers, and child molesters. What we don't have, yet, is a tyrannical government.

I was told that every six or seven years, the then-Communist nation of Romania invited an American ship and its sailors onto their soil. I was fortunate enough to be on my ship when the invitation was sent. It was a port of call that I will never forget. When we docked in Constanta, we were briefed about the customs. We were told that Romania was a communist country and that we were not allowed to talk with the general population, or they could be arrested.

When the liberty call sounded on ship, my buddy Shady Grady and I hit the beach and started our adventure into the unknown. We spent about a week in Romania, and never in my life have I seen poverty and slavery as I did there.

It was bizarre to me to see young soldiers walking the streets with AK-47s. For the local folks, it was just another day. Shady and I decided to take a bus ride, not knowing that since the country and its people were so poor, almost everyone rode the bus. The bus we boarded was packed with people, and all eyes focused on us. It was an eery feeling.

I was making about three dollars an hour, but in Romania I was a rich man. We ate, drank, and bought souvenirs for a week, and I spent maybe fifty dollars. In America, that fifty dollars would have been gone in a couple of hours. The most shocking thing I saw in Romania was a little old lady, probably in her eighties. She appeared to be homeless and was holding out a cup begging for money to survive. The look of helplessness on the face of that poor old woman and the poverty all around made me feel proud to be an American. For the first time in my life I began to understand how good we have it in our country.

Seeing the ways that Cheausscu the tyrant made the lives of the Romanian people miserable reinforced my unconditional belief in the principles our founding fathers set forth to prevent that type of tyranny from happening here. I vowed that I would rather die with honor than to turn my back on government officials who abuse the powers vested them by the American people!

The Condoning of Abuse of Power at the Grove Cost the Taxpayer Big Time!

Before I explain the event that began my challenge of *The Feres Doctrine*, I must jump ahead and explain some important facts and circumstances to provide credence to issues that are relevant to why "We the People" must criticize abuse of power in our government.

In September 1993, I received a call from Tony Keller, a civilian employee at the Grove. Tony spoke to me about problems he was facing for filing a racial discrimination complaint against the same command leaders who destroyed my career: Captains Broyles, Lekberg, and Commanders Powell and Gumpright. Both

18

our cases mirrored the same *modi operandi* of retaliation, so I agreed to help Tony. I assisted him in his fight for justice and in February 1996, Tony won an out-of-court settlement in the amount of a whopping $200,000!

Considering had he'd had only four years of civil service, I would have to say that Tony was vindicated! However, the hidden cost such as attorneys' fees, costs, and the defense of these people at taxpayers' expense could reasonably be estimated over $350,000. Once Tony prevailed in the summary judgment phase for retaliation in his case, the government folded. Its attorneys knew that if they put the defendants on the witness stand, the corruption at the Grove would have made the national spotlight. Spending half a million dollars to cover up the same type of corruption I'd exposed at the Grove by settling out of court was worth the price to keep the "hand off the Bible" in court.

Our cases were similar both in facts and circumstances, but because of the Feres Doctrine, my day in court would never come! Even with the facts readily available in the public record, the government would still have you believe that because I am the one speaking, these facts are "false and fantasy"!

This is just one example of the chilling effect the Feres Doctrine. Members of the military are deprived of protection of law that other American citizens enjoy.

Statistics Don't Lie Especially When They Are the Government's!

In addition to the Keller settlement, at the time I proceeded with protected communications I had no idea that the Navy Inspector General already knew of serious problems on the base. Following are some statistics reflecting the corruption at NAS Willow Grove while I was stationed there.

In an attempt to obtain background information on the personnel at NAS Willow Grove who claimed reprisals during my duty there, I requested statistical data for the three-years from 1989 to 1991 prior to the tenures of Broyles, Powell and Lekberg as command leaders. I found a total of 84 complaints of

19

reprisals at NAS Willow Grove over that three-year period. However, once these individuals took control of the base in 1992 the total number of reprisal complaints reached a whopping 122 for the two years of 1992 and 1993. These numbers are extremely disturbing, showing an increase from 28 complaints per year to 61 per year. If I had requested statistics for 1994, the year both Keller and I lost our careers with the Navy Department, I probably would have found that the numbers had skyrocketed.

I find it ironic that the Pentagon relies on numbers to do business every day, but never considered the numbers of claims of abuse of power and reprisals when I pointed out the fact that I was suffering reprisals by rampant misuse of the mental health system. The manpower figures on base show approximately 1,200 active duty personnel during this time. On average, then, 1 in every 100 members of this command complained of some type of abuse!

To me these numbers, especially in light of the Keller settlement, are evidence that I did not imagine abuse of power. The issues I presented related to drill pay and accounting fraud, falsification of official documents, gross mismanagement, and favoritism. They were supported by the Navy's own statistics. The Navy Department knew that prior to my grievance there were serious problems at NAS Willow Grove and failed to act to correct those abuses under the Inspectors General Act of 1978 and § 1034.[1] This lack of action goes to the heart of my claim that the Feres Doctrine allows for incredible things to happen to those who are perceived a threat to the "good ole boy network."

No matter how messed up Broyles' command was, the integrity of the system was deemed more worth of protection than were the rights of the military members. The Navy Department knew of the problems before I decided that I would not be party to the corruption.

---

1. The Military Whistleblower Protection Act, Public Law Title 10, U.S.C.§1034. This law and the Inspectors General Act of 1978 were enacted to stamp out corruption and reprisals in the Armed Forces.

It is amazing that one percent of the personnel on base complained of abuse of power during the years I stated there was a severe problem with corruption on Willow Grove. I did not know the problems were severe and widespread when I proceeded with my grievance in February 1993. Knowing that later, it was no wonder to me why the leaders of my former command did everything possible to discredit my claims. Because I chose not to remain silent, because I placed my duty and loyalty to country over that of few corrupt military officials, my record of mental stability was attacked and destroyed—on paper!

Here is one more tidbit showing how outrageous my orders for mental health examinations due to an alleged paranoid thought process truly are.

On February 26, 1993, two days before my request mast meeting with Broyles, an article appeared in Willow Grove's base paper entitled: "Philadelphia Vietnam Veteran Remembered."

The following article was published and it reads verbatim:

Petty Officer First Class Jeff Trueman of the station's Reserve Programs Department was 2 years old when Stephen Condi returned from Vietnam in 1966 at the height of the war. Neither one knew at the time the effect that this action would have on the other years in the future. At age 22, native Philadelphian Stephen Condi was drafted and shipped over to the Central Highlands, An Khe, Vietnam, right about the time that Trueman was born in Philadelphia. For the next two years Condi served his country with no definite assurance he would ever get back home. But, he did.

Just about two months ago, more than 27 years after serving his country, Condi received the military decorations he earned for that dedicated and faithful service to his country. "I was down to see Steve two months ago," said Trueman, who says Condi played a major factor in his joining the Navy 11 years ago. "When he showed me the medals

21

he received, I could see how much they meant to him. Even though he's always been good hiding his feelings, when he put them back into his desk drawer, I felt a sadness in my heart. At that moment, I was not going to see another Vietnam Veteran go unrecognized and the reasons why are simple."

Trueman explained that when he was about 17 years old his parents divorced. "I was out on my own," he said. I applied for work at an Italian restaurant and was hired as a dishwasher. This is where I met Steve."

During the first year the two worked together, the two men became as close as brothers. "He was like a big brother to me, and I took every piece of advice he gave me and applied it to my daily life," said the 29-year-old yeoman. "It was at a time in my life when I was unsure of what I had ahead for me. I knew things weren't always easy, but Steve was always there to listen." It wasn't until Trueman decided to join the U.S. Navy, that Condi shared with Trueman his experiences from Vietnam and the military. "Steve gave me some insight into what joining the military could do for me. I took his advice, and to this day, 11 years later, I am still serving," Trueman said. "When I think back, I believe that last conversation we had before I joined really set the tone for the type of individual I wanted to be in life."

Because of the love Trueman felt for his adopted big brother, and the respect he has for him and what he stands for, he presented Condi with a shadow box on the evening of January 24, 1993. "I wanted to recognize his faithful service to our country and all his brothers that served together during the Vietnam War," he said.

During this night a Vietnam Veteran finally got his just recognition. "He was so touched by the American Flag that was flown over the air station on December 7, 1992, in his honor. There were only a few good friends watching

22

him get his recognition, but all of us knew, it really touched his heart," Trueman added.

To this day, Trueman gives Condi much of the credit for his being in the Navy. "Even with everything that he went through in Vietnam, I've never heard him say a bad thing about serving his country in one of the most unfortunate wars of our times," Trueman said. "When I think about how bad things sometimes do get in life, I always remember a Vietnam Veteran and what he scarified for us, and then maybe my problems won't seem so big," (sic) Trueman concluded. "To all Vietnam Vets, God bless you all, you are not forgotten!"

I include this article to show that only two days prior to my protected communications to Broyles on February 28, 1993, no allegations of an alleged paranoid thought process existed. A reasonable person would probably conclude that the attacks against my mental stability were malicious and violated federal law. I also include the article to recognize Chief Flake for his skillful work in making my adopted big brother his shadow box. I also appreciated Petty Officer Dave Lanham (now retired), for his efforts in obtaining an authentic American Flag for the shadow box that was flown over our base in Steve's honor on December 7, 1992.

Broyles signed the official authentication documenting the fact that the American flag in Steve's box was flown in his honor over a U.S. Military installation. He also said to me, "I am proud of you Petty Officer Trueman for recognizing a fellow veteran in this fashion."

For a military commander to have the power of God, to one day say that a member of his command is one of his best and then the next day claim that the same person suffers from mental illness is the most credible argument I can make about the "chilling effect of the Feres Doctrine."

Thank God there are Good People in Government

I feel it is important to share the opinions of two distinguished people who played a key role in helping me formulate my concepts for this book: Dr. Andrew Wilkerson and William Shea.

I first met Dr. Wilkerson one month prior to my administrative discharge board in October 1993, when Captain Lekberg ordered me to obtain a psychological evaluation to further support his false claim that I was detrimental to good order and discipline due to mental illness.

During our consultation, Dr. Wilkerson asked me; "Are you crazy, Petty Officer Trueman?"

I responded, "Sir, I'm half nuts; I grew up ten minutes from this Naval base!"

At the conclusion of the psychological consultation, Dr. Wilkerson stated to me: "Off the record, I hope you beat these sons-of-bitches, because I am tired of seeing good people sent to me to cover up the dirt at other commands. Furthermore, you have the best military record I have ever seen."

I felt betrayed and degraded as a human being when I was sent to see the doctor, but meeting the doctor turned out to be a major turning point that helped me make it through nine years of hell to tell you this story. If Dr. Wilkerson had placed any false or detrimental information into my medical record, I probably would have received another all-expenses-paid vacation to a mental hospital. However, the doctor upheld his professional integrity and placed nothing detrimental in his consultation findings. He stated he would not make a diagnosis until my claims of improprieties were fully investigated.

I appreciated Dr. Wilkerson's professionalism. Fortunately, after Dr. Wilkerson's findings were released to my command, no further attempt to misuse a mental health diagnosis was undertaken in my case. Instead, the tactic switched to accusations of alcohol abuse.

I believe that if Dr. Wilkerson was called to testify, his testimony would be devastating to the U.S. Government's position that I was no longer fit to serve my country due to an alleged paranoid thought process.

The day following my interview with Mr. Donaldson, *Prime*TIME contacted Dr. Wilkerson by telephone. ABC News reported that the doctor, now in civilian employment, was hesitant to talk on national TV. He did, however, state for the record: "What happened to Jeff should not have happened."

I believe the testimony of Dr. Wilkerson in a federal courtroom would blow the lid off the military's practices of misusing psychological evaluations to discredit honorable men and women who report fraud, waste and abuse.

Another witness who would corroborate the military's practice of abusing its mental health system was William Shea, investigator, at the Office of Special Inquires, Department of Defense Inspector General (DODIG).

Mr. Shea took over the investigation after the DODIG's "first" preliminary (13-month) investigation found that all my communications of reprisals to Members of Congress and the Navy Inspector General, claiming corruption at the Grove and abuse of the mental health system "occurred after [my] discharge from the Navy."

I immediately challenged that decision, and Mr. Shea received a fax from me containing over thirty pages of evidence to contradict the DODIG's findings. I did not expect a response. I'd seen too many other investigators failing to act on credible evidence of retaliation. To my surprise, Mr. Shea obtained my protection under public law for engaging in protected communications. This event was a major victory for me. Nevertheless, the Navy Department, Members of Congress and the U.S. Federal Courts, continue to refuse to consider this explosive issue because of the Feres Doctrine. This supports my contention that the obstruction of §1034 by Feres produces a serious conflict in Federal laws and that therefore it should be rendered unconstitutional.

I believe that in the long run the DODIG did not investigate my claims of human right abuses in the military's mental health system because the repercussions would have been too costly. Millions of dollars in public funds and time-consuming courts martial of high-ranking officers for intentional violations of federal law would have been too bothersome to consider.

At the close of the DODIG inquiry, I wanted to thank Mr. Shea personally for his efforts on my behalf. In December 1996, I sent Mr. Shea a Christmas card with a picture of my family to give him an idea of the "military family" the U.S. Navy had betrayed. In January 1997, I received a personal letter from him which states:

"Dear Mr. Trueman,

Thanks for your Christmas card and very kind words. I sincerely wish you and that wonderful family of yours, a truly great year in 1997. I'm sorry that our relationship wasn't more beneficial for you. I hope your future endeavors are more rewarding and light years less frustrating. Please let me know when your manuscript for "system shortfalls" is complete. I would be happy to provide comments. The 'system' that I am part of, is by no means perfect or consistently just. It's the best one I've seen to date, but, it sure could be improved. I don't have any brilliant fixes though; I hope you come up with some."

Destroying One's Mental Stability Has Serious Consequences

Some military members who experience reprisals after reporting abuse of the mental health system to cover up wrongdoings and corruption cannot deal with the injustices on an emotional level and strike back. Officials are mandated to stop injustice and should realize that there are severe consequences to those who engage in political retaliation.

An example involves the case of a young Air Force member named Dean Mellberg. On June 20, 1994, Mellberg killed the doctor at Fairchild Air Force Base who discharged him from the service for an alleged personality disorder. Mike Tuffaurillo, president of the Wounded Eagles, told me the story of this terrible incident in a letter. I first became acquainted with Mike after I saw him on national television when he told his story of being sent to a mental hospital for exposing the fact that reserve units were being paid at a Naval Air Station in Dallas, Texas, even when the units did not show up for their drills. Mike's point was, "Yes, one would say that Mellberg had to be nuts, but does one have to be crazy to kill someone? No, no, and hell no!"

Mike obtained Mellberg's records as well as a written transcript of an interview between Mellberg and the doctor. Mike wrote to me, "Let me tell you, the s___ on that audio was and is devastating to the Air Force. The Air Force is attempting to totally discredit this guy and simply say he was a nut case, but I reviewed the file (660 pages) and although Dean Mellberg pulled the trigger, the military loaded the magazine and I can prove it."

The Mellberg incident shows what happens when military officials who abuse the mental health system are not held accountable. The Air Force apparently destroyed a young mind, and in that case, the outcome was deadly.

I have explained some important factors to establish a *prima facie* case of mental health retaliation for engaging in protected communications. Let me now begin the story.

The Event That Began It All

The beginning of the end for my naval career arrived one day when I was sitting at my desk in the ACDUTRA (Active Duty for Training) office on a Saturday drill weekend in October 1991. My assistant, Petty Officer Serkleski ("Ski") answered an incoming phone call from a reservist named Fireman Jones. After a few minutes Ski said to me "Jeff, I think we may have a problem."

"What do you mean?" I said.

Ski told me that Fireman Jones was on the phone and was explaining that he had just received a call from his unit informing him that he was scheduled to depart Fort Dix, New Jersey, for orders to his ship that very day. Jones had protested, saying

27

that he did not sign the unit application form and should not have had orders in the first place. When I heard this, I knew a potentially serious problem was about to arise because if Jones did not sign his name, who did?

I asked Ski to tell Jones we would look into the matter and would get back with him as soon as possible. In an attempt to verify whether or not Jones was on the up and up, we investigated his record and compared his previous signatures on unit applications to the one in question. The signature did not match, and I knew I had a problem on my hands.

I asked Ski to inform the unit's program manager, an active duty officer, who was responsible for coordinating all aspects of a unit's training objectives of the problem. I also instructed Ski to tell Jones that I would discuss the issue with Senior Chief Feener and get back to him. Although the names and actions of many government officials are referenced in my Supreme Court challenge against Feres (see Chapter 6), Feener is the individual I hold accountable for the massive corruption that will be explained in this book.

Before I had a chance to discuss the issue with Feener, Jones called back and stated that he had been threatened with a court martial if he did not report for orders.

This astonished me. First of all, reservists who are not on active duty cannot be court martialed and secondly, a reservist *must* clear with his employer the period of time one expects to be issued orders for a two-week active duty training period. Jones had not spoken with his employer, so I asked Ski to tell Jones he did not have to report for the orders and that I would rectify the situation.

As soon as Jones stated that he had been threatened with a court martial, I understood that the reason for the pressure was that the unit wanted to make their training numbers look good. I also realized that cancelling orders for any active duty training period is a costly thing involving airline tickets, berthing, transportation, and other expenses. Money wasn't the whole story. A unit commander's record of orders being modified or canceled is a reflection on that commander's ability to lead. The commander wanted to look good to qualify for advancement.

After Jones had been told that he did not have to depart on orders, I went to Feener's office and discussed the problem with him. Feener's reaction was essentially, "So what?" I thought that fudging active duty training numbers and forgery were serious issues, but obviously I was wrong.

Over the next two weeks, the Jones matter snowballed into political nightmare, especially for Ski and me. Jones' command continued to harass him and make empty threats. Ski and I refused to back off because we felt it was our duty to protect Jones' interests and uphold our own integrity.

Finally Jones' orders were cancelled, and he was allowed to perform his two weeks of active duty training at the Grove. The case, however, was a turning point in the perception of those in authority about myself and Ski. From that moment on we were both seen as boat rockers. Mind games were about to begin.

The incident with Jones took place near the end of 1991. For the next nine years of my life, doing the right thing in the Jones' matter consumed my life and took me through a journey of unbelievable corruption within our government. At times, they almost did break me mentally.

The Jones' matter was only the first revelation of the most grossly mismanaged military unit I have ever been assigned to. From favoritism to downright violations of public laws (fraud in the drill pay/training division), the abuses at NAS Willow Grove were many. Although I attempted over and over to address and correct the problems at the lowest possible level of my chain of command, I was continually told to "not worry about it." However, on the morning of February 7, 1993, after a year of outrageous conduct and incompetent leadership, I took my stand.

I was informed by my division chief (AEC Rumery) that if I proceeded up the chain of command with my claims and the claims of my subordinates regarding alleged improprieties in our department, my career would be over.

The issues of improprieties and other abuses included fraud in drill pay and training, falsification of official documents, dereliction of duty, and favoritism resulting in a hostile work environment. NAS Willow Grove was filled with corruption. As a resident of Pennsylvania, I was determined not to be party to it.

According to *Black's Law Dictionary*, corruption is "illegality; a vicious and fraudulent intention to evade the prohibitions of the law; something against or forbidden by law; moral turpitude or exactly opposite of honesty involving intentional disregard of law from improper motives."

In the wake of that threat to my career, I decided it was my duty to inform my commanding officer (CO) of the improprieties which were taking place under his direction. I told Rumery to "run the chit." (In the Navy Department, the proper protocol to request a meeting with the commanding officer is to submit the request on a form known as a "special request chit" to inform the chain of command of the request.) Little did I know at that time that the collusion to attack my mental stability had already been set in motion.

The Meeting Which Set the Tone for Psychological Retaliation in My Case

I submitted my chit to Rumery and was summoned to Commander Bresnahan's office, my department head at that time. I attempted to explain the issues that my subordinates felt needed to be addressed in the Training Department. I asked him to speak directly to those under my direction as requested by my subordinates.

Although the issues of fraud, waste and abuse had been accumulating since the Jones incident, the favoritism factor between Rumery and his buddy, PO1 Scaffidi (the lowest ranking E-6 in the department) concerned me the most. Their friendship outside of work resulted in favoritism at work. This double standard compelled me to voice the concerns of my subordinates to Rumery's supervisors.

It was well known that Scaffidi was given special work hours. He did not have to stand duty and was provided direct access to the division chief and division officer while all others, even those with higher rank than Scaffidi, had to report up the chain of command through me. I felt this was a problem and made it known to Rumery. He did not want to hear it!

Meanwhile Rumery's buddy was failing to instruct his classes properly. I received many complaints about his presentations, his appearance and his body stench. Some practices bordered on fraud or abuse of power. For example, Rumery allowed Scaffidi to be absent from his place of duty in order to perform functions as a "volunteer fire fighter" on the public's clock. Other departmental personnel had to pull his load, and this cut deeply into the morale. I believe it is safe to say on behalf of all honorable men and women in the military that double standards destroy a military unit's cohesion.

In addition, training numbers were not recorded with headquarters, and inaccurate training numbers that were being passed to unit training coordinators reflected negatively on the department. An incident that set off a long train of abuses within the military medical and legal system occurred when E-6 annual performance evaluations were released in December 1992.

When the evaluations were released, Scaffidi was ranked number one. It was a military decision per se, so nothing could be done. However, a problem with his high ranking and 4.0 evaluation was the fact that he measured at 32% body fat, according to the Physical Readiness Coordinator, PO1 Riggins. The cutoff for participation in a mandatory weight control program was 22%. Chief Rumery had no problem with that. He just falsified an "official" document to take care of his buddy!

This incident—on top of Scaffidi's failure to uphold his duties—put me over the edge! When I addressed the issue with Rumery, I was told to mind my own business or else. When

Feener condoned the falsification of Scaffidi's evaluation, I knew the time to speak to my CO had finally arrived.

Before proceeding to Broyles, I afforded my Department Head Commander, Breshahan the opportunity to address and correct the Scaffidi issue. Instead, Breshahan replied, "I'm not talking with anyone."

Bresnahan made his position clear. He was not going to investigate claims of falsification of official records, dereliction of duty, etc. I was then subjected to a verbal attack by Commander Mayeau, including being told that I was *"disloyal to the chain of command."* Mayeau was an overweight, unfit, and buying-his-time type of leader. His type was otherwise known in the Navy as a "ROAD Sailor" (Retired On Active Duty)! For many military personnel and former members, the "body fat" requirement is a touchy issue. Good people have been discharged because of this so-called "readiness standard." To give a slacker a 22% rating when he was 32% is wrong!

In light of the personal threat of Rumery, the comment by the Commander that I was "disloyal," and the failure of our department head to intervene and address the concerns of his subordinates, I decided it was time for me to formally request a meeting with Captain Broyles. I was hopeful that the issues could be rectified by Bresnahan, but it soon became obvious that Bresnahan knew the problems existed and wanted to cover them up. At the conclusion of our meeting, Bresnahan informed me that he was ordering me to attend a "stress management" seminar, an unfavorable personnel action that I found outrageous and offensive. This was ironic, since prior to my discussions with him, he had considered me to be an asset to his department as reflected in my December 23, 1992 evaluation.

I decided to take the issues to a higher level. I was totally confident that Captain Broyles would see to it that corrective action would be taken on all issues of concern to many of us in our department. I also felt that since he recognized me as one of his best sailors on base, he would be fair in dealing with the issues I was going to present him. Unfortunately, I did not know that Captain Broyles was set to retire in July 1993. Projecting total integrity of his status as a commanding officer and protecting his cronies were more important tasks than upholding his responsibilities to ensure that the "inactive reserve program" was being properly administered. Due to the many problems at the Grove and in light of his upcoming retirement date, Captain Broyles knew it would be easier to destroy my credibility by attacking my mental stability than it would be to initiate an investigation to correct the problems on base. Remember, he had Feres on his side.

The Conspiracy to Silence and Discredit Trueman

The first sign of collusion to destroy my mental stability in order to discredit my claims of improprieties was the delay in my request chit from being "expeditiously handled" up the chain of command. Even though there were only seven personnel in my upper chain of command before reaching Captain Broyles, this chit took over two weeks to reach its final destination—Captain Broyles—for approval.

I believe the delay in my chit being approved was a calculated move to allow for a "damage control" mode involving abuse of the mental health system to be planned and incorporated. At that juncture, in February 1993, Mr. Broyles and my departmental leaders apparently planned to exercise undue command influence that would infest my case from that moment forward within the Department of the Navy.

On the afternoon of February 25, 1993, after several attempts to determine the status of my request to speak with Broyles, I was informed by Rumery that Broyles had approved the chit for me to speak with him. Rumery then told me to follow him to his office. As I walked into Rumery's office he told me to close the door and sit down and then proceeded to say: "You are being counselled for insubordination... "

I almost fell out of my chair. I had not been given a reason for any unfavorable personnel actions to be taken against me.

Although the counseling sheet resulting from my meeting with Rumery was bogus, I found out that it was the only document needed to advance the "false and fantasy" defense. It was used to set the tone for determining my status as "disruptive to good order and discipline," a classification equivalent to the "death order" to any military member.

For the record, the counseling of February 25, 1993 was the *only* formal counseling sheet during my Navy career. This is documented in my official microfiche file held in St. Louis, Missouri. On that day the conspiracy to destroy my mental stability using intentional violations of Navy Grievance Procedures and federal law (i.e. Title 10 U.S.C. §1034, Military Whistleblower Protection Act) was set into motion.

Undue Command Influence

I will explain the difference between true and false leaders and by telling about an incident that took place during my assignment with the Joint Chiefs of Staff, Offutt Air Force Base, Omaha, Nebraska. This was a top secret, independent duty assignment whereby I worked for the "best of the best" in the entire United States Armed Forces, and the situation occurred just prior to my assignment to the Grove.

One day I was picking up some documents for the most influential officer I have ever worked for during my active duty service, Colonel Robert Ames. I overheard my Captain, Admiral and General discussing a potential breach in security in a very highly sensitive area within the nuclear war planning directorate. Although I was only a Second Class Petty Officer, I proceeded to tell these outstanding military officers that I could fix the problem within 90 days!

I could feel my knees shaking as I spoke, and my Captain, another fine American by the name of Captain Robert Smith, just looked at me and smiled. Several days later my top secret clearance was upgraded to a much higher status, and I was informed I was being reassigned to a very sensitive position.

34

To make a long story short, I undertook the tedious task of reviewing over 500 top secret documents line by line to identify enclosures and other information mentioned in the these documents. During my investigation, a meeting was called by the General's executive officer, and I was directed to sit in on the meeting. Being the only enlisted man in a room full of high ranking officials with hundreds of total years of service was somewhat intimidating. I did not expect to say much, except to describe my progress at that point.

When the executive officer asked the security manager I was working for as to the progress of the investigation, he responded, "We are almost complete."

Since I was the one with hands-on knowledge of what was being undertaken, I simply shook my head slowly back and forth in the negative.

The executive officer saw me, flipped, and said, "Jeff, why in the hell are you shaking your head No?"

"Sir, I believe the job will not be complete for a few more weeks if not more."

"God damn it," he said. "There is no rank in this room at this time. Now, Jeff, you tell us what needs to be done to achieve completion." I could see that the security manager was annoyed, but I explained what I thought needed to be done to ensure that all documents were accounted for. At that point the exec told the security manager to sit down with me and go over what remained to be accomplished, and he dismissed all of us. All the officers departed and said nothing to me.

The next day, the security manager pulled up a chair and said, "Okay Jeff, you are in charge. Tell me where we are."

As it worked out in the end, after only 93 days, I presented to my superiors a stack of "memoranda for the record" confirming either the destruction or existence of all the documents I had identified. Additionally, I drafted document security procedures to prevent a repeat of the problem. I did this voluntarily out of my sense of loyalty to my superiors because I completely respected them. They were the best of the best in the United States Military!

I share this story because if shows that true leaders are firm but fair, while poor leaders would rather cover up gross misman- agement and other issues reflecting poor leadership to protect their own status rather than doing the right thing on behalf of the public's trust.

To my surprise, I was awarded the "Joint Service Achieve- ment Medal" for my dedication to duty and loyalty to my superi- ors in bring closure to the identified problems. In addition, I received the same day the "Joint Service Commendation Medal." On its back this medal states, "For Military Merit" for my service to the Secretary of Defense and the Joint Chiefs of Staff while assigned at Headquarters Strategic Air Command. This award received in my short military career was higher than any awards the officers and enlisted staff who destroyed my career at the Grove ever achieved in theirs!

This brings me to an important point I must make about people who serve with honor and those who serve for their own personal gain.

Throughout my career I served under many great leaders, but Colonel Robert Ames was my favorite. The Colonel left the military for retirement shortly before I left my third duty station, Joint Strategic Target Planning Staff (JSTPS) in Omaha, Nebraska, for orders to the Naval Air Station (NAS) at Willow Grove. On his last day at JSTPS, I asked him why he was leaving the Air Force. He told me that had been ordered to the Pentagon did not want to go there. He wanted to keep flying, so he was leaving the military to fly commercial.

I happened to run into the Colonel on his way out of the headquarters for the last time. I told him that he should stay because there was no doubt in my mind that he would become a four-star general one day. He thanked me for the comment and said, "Trueman, you will go a long way in the Navy!" I thanked him, and he gave me firm hug and said, "Take care, Trueman!"

I still wonder why the Colonel did not want to go to the Pen- tagon. After experiencing the abuses and condoning of abuses by the Pentagon in my case and the others as mentioned on Prime-

TIME Live by ABC-TV, I can only speculate that he did not want to "sell his soul" by obtaining orders to the Pentagon where human beings are considered only as numbers!

When a person such as Colonel Ames leaves the service before his time and people like Feener, Rummey, Broyles, Powell and Lekberg remain in uniform it is an indicator that the system definitely needs to be reformed!

Many individuals in my story either willingly participated in the reprisals I faced for exposing corruption at NAS Willow Grove or just turned the blind eye in fear for their own careers. It comes down to true leadership. Now that I have explained the positive influence of Colonel Ames on me as a subordinate, I must tell about a poor leader who places personal beliefs and agendas first—over duty to country. I speak of Master Chief Donald Feener, the author of the Navy Department's "false and fantasy" legal defense used to discredit my claims of corruption at the Grove.

I estimate that 99 percent of the personnel I was stationed with at NAS Willow Grove disliked Feener and the way he placed his religious extremist personal beliefs on others and his lack of concern for those under his direction. Feener seemed to enjoy manipulating others and seeing people suffer psychologically and that he definitely did not enjoy seeing others having more fun than himself. From the moment I first saw Feener, I had that gut feeling that there was something I couldn't trust about him.

My first encounter with Feener occurred upon my return from lunch one afternoon. As I entered the building and turned the corner, I saw this guy walking toward me wearing a New York Giants jacket. I nodded and said, "Hi." He just looked at me and kept on walking. I thought this was weird, but not knowing him I assumed he was having a bad day. When I walked into the administrative office, several of my peers were standing around chatting. I asked the question: "Who the hell was that guy?"

That is our new departmental leading chief petty officer," one of them said.

37

The evil that would consume our department began the day Feener walked into our lives. Little did we know that day that this guy would turn upside down the lives of many of us at the Grove. Our working conditions went from a place where people enjoyed coming to work to a place filled with anger, rumors, incompetence and manipulation once Feener took control of the department as the senior enlisted advisor.

From the beginning of Feener's reign as senior enlisted advisor, I was warned by Ski, who had worked in Washington D.C. when Feener was there. He told me that Feener was a Bible-thumping maniac. A man like that gives a bad name to all true Christians.

One day Ski came busting out of the ACDUTRA office in a fury. Although Ski was a "big dude" he was always pleasant to be around. He is a big teddy bear! On that day, I could see in Ski's eyes that Feener had pushed Petty Officer Serkleski to his breaking point. I did not get out of Ski exactly what had happened, but Ski was looking for blood!

A couple of years after both of us had been discharged, I called Ski to see how he was doing and asked him about that day. "Were you going to hurt Feener?" I said.

"If you hadn't told me to take the remainder of the day off, I probably would have killed him."

If not for my intervention and telling Ski to take the remainder of the day off, I am sure that Feener would have been severely hurt that day. Now, after years of betrayal in the U.S. judicial system, if I could do it all over, I think I would let Ski have a field day with Feener!

Feener was our connection between management and the rank and file. In his position, his responsibilities included, but were not limited to, liaison between enlisted personnel and their leaders, ensuring we were kept up to date on changing regulations, taking appropriate action to preserve the morale and well-being of departmental enlisted personnel, and other tasks. Cutting to the chase, Feener upheld none of his responsibilities to his subordinates, and because of this, he was despised.

38

All of us in the department picked up on Feener's leadership style quickly. We observed his eagerness to take all the credit when things went well but to pass off to his subordinates the blame if anything did not go as planned. Every true military leader knows that giving credit to subordinates for a job well done and taking the heat for problems encountered is the only way to do business. I recall Feener speaking in front of the department in a meeting pertaining to the breakdown of morale in our department. Instead of listening to our concerns, he told us that he looked out for "number one," meaning himself. We were all stunned that he could be so blatant about his feelings towards his subordinates.

The most obvious prejudice Feener had was against those people who smoked or drank alcohol. He especially did not like drinking. I know his feelings about alcohol because he told me that he almost killed himself drinking vodka one night during his early days in the Navy. After that episode he quit drinking. In my opinion he became what is known as a "dry drunk."

If a person has a drinking problem or emotional problems and works to address them, more power to the individual. Too often people despise those who try to impose their own beliefs and hatred of alcohol on those who enjoy partying and being with friends and associates—and can handle it. I believe that because Feener could not socialize in an atmosphere of partying, his personal beliefs crossed the line into his professional life. If not for a $3.50 insignia which represented a higher rank than mine, Feener would have never gotten away with his repeated abuse of power.

One day our department went out for a luncheon. The event was to recognize the promotion of several of our former First Class Petty Officers to Chief Petty Officer. While we all sat around shooting the bull, no one was drinking. This was unusual because all my shipmates were fun people to be with in the partying atmosphere.

There were a couple of pitchers of beer on the table. However, with Feener present, none of the chiefs, and only a few or the rest of us consumed any. When Feener left the luncheon, the new chiefs said, "Now that he is gone, let's party!"

Feener was also a rascal when it came to pitching in money when our department on occasion would send out for food. One day we ordered about six pizzas, and everyone pitched in except Feener. As we were all standing around eating and joking, Feener sat in his office alone, eating his usual peanut butter and jelly sandwiches. I felt bad for the guy as he was an extremely lonely and even pathetic soul. I asked him if he would like to join us and he did. He didn't offer to pitch in for the pizzas that day, although one would think that he would show some sort of gratitude. Not only that, but he was quick to offer our food to another chief who came to see him! Feener may have told the chief that he bought the entire department pizzas that day for all our hard work and dedication to duty! I think we all know this type of predator.

The Meeting That Resulted in the End of This Veteran's Career

On February 28, 1993, I finally met with Broyles and discussed with him every issue of impropriety presented to me by my subordinates and all issues of falsification of official documents and other improprieties I had observed during my duty at the Reserve Programs Department.

After the meeting, word was passed on to all personnel in our department that an investigation would be conducted with respect to claims of abuse of power in our department. The official notification of the investigation came during departmental quarters on March 3, 1993.

Bresnahan announced to all personnel that Broyles would be down to speak with all my peers and subordinates individually about their concerns and the issues I raised on their behalf. Those meetings never took place.

The notification was necessary to provide a false sense of belief that corrective action would be taken. It amounted to a delay tactic as well as undue command influence and obstruction of the administration of justice.

After Bresnahan informed personnel at quarters of the pending inquiry and meeting with Broyles, I was subjected to an arrogant glare from Feener, the man most responsible for the below-zero morale and gross-mismanagement in the department. I never forgot that look. If looks could kill, I'd be six feet under. The intimidation factor had been set into motion, but I was not going to let it stop me from doing what I believed was in the best interests of the Navy and our people.

The Conspiracy to Obstruct the Administration of Justice Commences

On March 3, 1993 an internal investigation was ordered by Broyles. The investigator assigned was Lieutenant Commander Smedberg, the goofiest officer on board NAS Willow Grove and a direct subordinate in Broyles' chain of command. According to military investigative procedures, investigations are to be "independent" and "unbiased." The official position of the government is that "even the appearance of improprieties" will not be tolerated.

Broyles' assignment of Smedberg violated the ethical requirement of independence of the investigation. I believe Smedberg was instructed to tailor his findings to fit the command's position that my claims were "false and fantasy."

During the three-week bogus inquiry, I was approached by my subordinates who kept telling me, "They are not looking into the issues we raise, they are going after you!" The case to build a psychological defense to protect Broyles' command and discredit my issues was being achieved by the investigator himself!

On the afternoon of March 26, 1993, I was in my office sitting at my desk preparing matters for our upcoming triennial command inspection when Bresnahan walked in and stated in front of the six instructors under my direction: "Petty Officer Trueman, pack your belongings. You no longer work in this department."

41

I was speechless. The reality that my days in the military were numbered hit me like a ton of bricks! I was told to report to my home and await further orders. Never before in my entire career, had I heard of someone being sent home to await orders when no judicial or medical reasons applied to the situation. The long train of abuses of power and the intentional and deliberate violations of federal law with respect to §1034's prohibition of mental health evaluations had been set in stone!

As I packed my belongings and said good-bye to my peers and subordinates, I could see the shock on their faces. They knew that the way to silence those under my direction was to make an example of me. The message was sent to all—"Keep your mouths shut!" For me, departing the building for the last time and saying good-bye to those I had come close to, was almost too much to bear. However, I had to remain strong as to not break down and lose the faith of those whom I had attempted to help. My last words to everyone was, "Are you with me in the end?" They all responded, "Yes!"

On my drive home, I was shocked and angry about how easily the retaliatory actions against me and violations of my military rights were taking place even before the "official findings" of Broyles were released. I should not have been surprised, considering the pattern of abuse which had taken place in the wake of my outstanding annual performance evaluation stating no detrimental behaviors whatsoever.

When I walked into my home before the end of the work day, my wife asked me, "What are you doing here?" I told her that I had just been fired and had been ordered to report home until further notice. I started to wonder at that point if placing the best interests of my country over that of my family's was truly the right thing to do.

At approximately 4:30 on the afternoon of March 26, 1993, I received a call from Rumery who notified me that Broyles wanted to see me at 7:30 the next morning. I was not sure what the next retaliatory action against me would be. I never could have dreamed what was in store for me that next morning.

Setting in Motion the Intentional Violations of Federal Law

The next morning, March 27, 1993, I woke to a new day, after only a few hours of sleep, wondering what lay ahead of that day. As I arrived at the CO building, I could feel the tension in the air as I walked past fellow shipmates who apparently knew something bad was going to take place.

I stood at attention as Broyles entered the room and was told to sit down. His voice took on a commanding tone, notifying me that my request mast issues "had no merit." Hence, he proceeded to tell me he was "concerned for my well-being" and that I was to report to the base medical facility where a Dr. Huh was waiting to interview me to determine if I was suffering from a paranoid thought process, brought on by alcohol abuse. I knew the orders were bullshit and unjustified besides being illegal and in violation of federal law since I had not engaged in any alcohol-related incident or displayed any psychological shortcomings. Nevertheless, I followed the orders.

Even Foot Doctors Qualify as Mental Health Experts in the U.S. Military

At approximately 1300 hours, (1 p.m. civilian time), I arrived for my appointment with Navy Lieutenant Dr. Huh. At the conclusion of our fifteen-minute conversation, he informed me that he had found me alcohol dependent and that he felt I should be placed in a five-week inpatient treatment program. I vigorously protested his findings, pointing out to him that I had not been involved in any alcohol-related incident and not engaged in or been convicted of wrongdoing.

Obviously, the stench of "undue command influence" had reached Dr. Huh. He willingly violated his medical ethics even though not qualified as a mental health expert to "grease the wheels" in assisting Broyles' plan to cover up the corruption at the Grove.

I demanded an answer from Dr. Huh as to how he could classify me alcohol dependent when I had committed no alcohol related incidents. I also pointed out to him the exemplary evaluation of Mr. Broyles issued in December 1992, three months prior. Huh ignored these important factors and many others in coming to the conclusion after a fifteen-minute conversation that I was "psychologically" dependent on alcohol. His conclusion was based on allegations of verbal abuse of my wife, failure to pay my bills, lateness to work, and the claim that my alleged psychological dependence on alcohol endangered the public—all claims made by Feener.

None of these claims could be substantiated, and my annual performance evaluation covering the period of alleged detrimental behavior reflect behavior completely contrary to these allegations. In addition, my credit history at the time of my discharge showed my credit to be excellent.

Huh's findings were supported by false and misleading statements that he placed in my medical records. That was all the Navy Department brass needed to unlawfully place me in a medical facility for treatment.

The power of *The Feres Doctrine* to destroy American military members is crystal clear!

As stated in ABC's 20/20 telecast, military mental health personnel will help "grease the wheels" to assist a commander take down an individual by false reports of mental illness. Although I objected to Huh's findings, even more bizarre was the fact that I was referred for screening not because of an alcohol-related incident or evidence of alcohol abuse, but due to "currently multiple administrative issues."

Whatever the connection between administrative issues and alleged alcohol abuse could possibly be, as you will see, the United States Supreme Court condoned this nonsense and left the door open to the continual abuse of this process in the future. My referral to mental health care mentioned no incidents of alcohol abuse, something you might think would be necessary for a person to be sent for an alcohol abuse screening!

Imagine what would happen if the military condoned referrals for alcohol dependency screening every time there were disputes of internal departmental administrative problems. Nothing would ever get done. If everyone was sent for an alcohol dependency screening for "administrative issues," the military would go out of business!

Until I was ordered to submit to the mental health examination and Huh's diagnosis, I had never heard of the Feres Doctrine. I was totally unaware that false information could be placed in a military record, and that there is nothing that a military member can do if the Inspectors Generals or Members of Congress fail to act to prevent this outrageous conduct.

Although Huh "played the game" and went along with Broyles' version of the story and reasons for the referral, his findings raised doubt as to the integrity of his diagnosis. In addition to the fact that no alcohol incident had ever occurred, Huh also compromised his findings by stating, "feel member is fit for full duty!"

As I told Sam Donaldson during my 20/20 interview, "I would be a liar to say I never abused alcohol in the sense of partying hard with the boys and gals. However, it never once interfered with my performance on duty or with my responsibilities as a father. I learned never to mix alcohol with anger because it will lead to self-destruction."

In the military, there are three levels of treatment to assist a member who suffers from alcohol abuse or alcoholism. Level I is a one-week classroom training course. Level II is a three-week outpatient treatment program, and Level III is the most severe treatment that consists of five weeks of inpatient treatment. In all, it is estimated that Level III costs the taxpayers on average, $30,000 to bed and treat one military member.

My orders to Level III were ludicrous and because of the cost could be considered defrauding the American taxpayer. In that case, the orders were criminal!

I was on my way to rehab before I ever walked into Huh's office because of undue command influence on the part of Broyles.

Although Dr. Huh abused his medical ethics and should therefore never be allowed to practice medicine in civilian life, the most chilling factor in all of this is that he was not even a psychiatric professional. His findings are highly suspect. This type of situation is a real problem within our Armed Forces and an issue all America should be made aware of, especially, those who have young children thinking of going into the military.

Later in that day—March 27—I asked Broyles, "How can you do this when you just issued me a perfect evaluation?" Broyles said nothing. The next phase of the "intimidation" process to break my pride and dignity was undertaken by Gary Lee Powell.

On March 31, 1993, four days after Dr. Huh violated my rights, I was ordered to report to Broyles' office once again. At that meeting, I was officially informed that I had been found to be psychologically dependent on alcohol and would be admitted to a five-week inpatient treatment facility at Alcohol Rehabilitation Service (ARS), in Newport, Rhode Island.

Powell then ordered me in a forceful tone of voice to follow him into his office. When we arrived Powell told me to "Sit down!" He then proceeded to pressure me to sign an alcohol rehabilitation entry statement on the pain of "immediate discharge" if I failed to do so. In response, I attempted to ask one simple question: "What detrimental behaviors and alcohol abuse did I display to have to sign this statement?"

This infuriated Powell. He yelled at me that if I did not sign the administrative remarks page he would immediately process me for discharge. With no other choice but to let my position be known, I wrote on the statement; "I sign under intimidation." With that Powell went ballistic! He told me I had four days to decide if I was going to rehab and to find an attorney. He then dismissed me. As I was leaving I could see the hatred in his face which he had against me. If he could have ordered me dead at that moment and gotten away with it, he would have! At this point in the conflict, I knew I was in deep trouble, but I could have never of dreamed of the legal nightmare I was about to face.

Most of us on the base agreed that Powell was an arrogant prick, and most enlisted members and civilians on base hated that guy and for good reason! Powell yelled at his brother and sister officers in front of subordinates, whenever he felt the need to do this. If anyone truly needed psychiatric help for anger management, in the eyes of many—officers and enlisted alike—it was Powell! This former officer in the U.S. Navy, who was forced to retire after the Keller settlement, is now flying commercial aircraft in the civilian world—a time bomb ready to explode. (Would you place your life in his control?)

After I was told by Powell that I should find a lawyer if I disputed the recommendation to be sent to a five-week inpatient treatment facility, I searched the Philadelphia area for an attorney who could help me. I eventually spoke to Donald Bowman, Esquire, by phone. I told him that in the wake of a commanding officer's request mast where I presented issues of abuse that I had been retaliated against and that my mental stability was being attacked to discredit my claims. He told me to come see him so we could discuss the facts of the matter.

When I first met Mr. Bowman he seemed like a kind elderly gentleman, and he truly is, I came to find out. As I tried to explain the predicament I was in with NAS Willow Grove, I was nervous and I felt my world was collapsing around me. After listening to my issues Mr. Bowman stated in a very forceful voice, "My men never went against me in World War II when I was in command." This caught me off guard, and I responded, "Well, sir, your men must have respected you!" After that comment from him I figured there was no sense in attempting to obtain his help and was about to get up and leave his office when he said, "I will take your case!"

His willingness to take on my case caught me by surprise. I'd figured he was one of those "good ole boys" from the past who believed in the theory "Do as I say, not as I do!" It was wrong thinking!

Although our attorney-client relationship ended after my discharge and my return to Minnesota, I respected Mr. Bowman and his wonderful secretary Beverly. In a time of my life where it would have been easier to retaliate against Broyles, Powell and the others to ease the pain of the entire situation, the kindness of Mr. Bowman and Bev gave me hope.

I found it somewhat ironic that Mr. Bowman commented, "You are going to the Supreme Court, aren't you, kid?" I did not know what he meant, and he did not go into detail, but he was right! I had no legal recourse because of Feres, but he knew that I had it in me to fight as far as I could to obtain vindication, and that the road would end at the United States Supreme Court and a challenge against the constitutionality of Feres, as I discuss in detail in Chapter Six.

The arbitrary actions of Broyles and Powell made it virtually impossible for me to obtain legal assistance prior to my departure to ARS. I needed more time to prepare a motion to file a federal injunction to prevent my retaliatory orders to Newport. So I pretty much just went with the flow.

Manipulation of the Alcohol Rehabilitation Process

To give the reader another idea as to how I was set up for the fall for claiming abuse of power at the Grove, let me take a moment to explain the rehabilitation process. According to the Navy's alcohol abuse screening procedures, once an alcohol incident or self-referral takes place, the member is sent to the command's Drug and Alcohol Program Advisor (DAPA), a non-mental health expert who is responsible for coordinating a member's progression through the program. From that point on, an appointment is set up with the Counseling And Assistance Center (CAAC) at a Level II outpatient treatment facility. After a non-mental health expert at the CAAC interviews the client, a recommendation is made as to the level of treatment needed to fulfill the goal of restoring a member to a "fit for full duty" status.

The final process is the client's interview with a medical doctor for a professional opinion as to whether alcohol rehabilitation treatment is necessary. As the record reflects, in my case the first two phrases as described above were ignored. A direct call was made to ARS Newport seeking a bed. This was for one reason only: the triennial command inspection was quickly approaching, and Broyles and the boys knew if I remained on base, I and those who worked for me would have taken them down.

The Feeling of Helplessness

The emotional strain and pressure of everything that was taking place in March 1993 plus my fear that I would be discharged led me to make the decision to go to the rehab. I believed that the medical personnel there would see that my orders were reprisals for my February 1993 grievance. No other conclusion could be made since there was no alcohol incident or other documented abuses of any kind on my part. Or could it?

On the morning of April 4, 1993, I was informed that Broyles' private aircraft was awaiting my arrival for my flight to Newport, R.I. I was under a tremendous state of emotional distress, especially not knowing what new reprisals the "boys" had up their sleeves or what was waiting for me. It was a very trying time, to say the least.

Although my world was crumbling all around me, I was fortunate to have a true friend on my side, a fellow petty officer by the name of Kim Fox. Although other caring people have also stuck by me, Kim has been the number one positive support I've received out of all the negatives in my journey. If not for this special person, I don't know if I could have dealt with this entire situation without taking retaliatory strikes myself.

Kim reassured me that I had done nothing wrong and was doing was the right thing. If I learned anything positive through my struggle against my former command leaders is that when you are being unjustly wronged, find a person who will listen to you and support you. I am very lucky to know that Kim is on my team. Although I have not seen nor heard from her in a long time, I believe she is still with me in heart, and I miss her dearly!

Facing the Unknown

After I said good-bye to Kim before flying to Newport, I walked over to base operations to check in for my flight. I could see the CO's aircraft on the tarmac awaiting my departure. I did not know what I was about to get myself into, and weird thoughts crossed my mind about the many bad things that do happen behind the fences of military installations.

Realizing that unthinkable acts take place because of "evil people in uniform," I thought that perhaps maybe my life was in danger. It passed through my mind that since my command was so aggressive in destroying my mental stability, that perhaps I was being set up for the ultimate fall, and my flight would end prematurely somewhere over the Atlantic ocean!

Before you start thinking that maybe I am off my rocker, you should be aware that deaths in the military that are classified as suicides don't add up when the facts are considered by independent sources outside the scope of the military power structure.

You may be wondering how I would know of such things, so I will tell you. Just prior to my discharge in December 1993, I went to the *Philadelphia Inquirer* to seek help in exposing the corruption at the Grove. I spoke to a reporter by the name of David Zucchino, who was preparing to publish a report of an investigation into the deaths of 40 military members in a four-part series from December 20-24, 1993. The series was entitled *"The Suicide Files; The suspicious deaths of 40 service members deserve an independent investigation."*

The investigative report found the military's findings in these deaths to be *"outrageous and unacceptable."* You can find this chilling investigation report by logging on the internet at www.phillynews.com.

Since the military had destroyed my mental stability on paper, they could have followed up by claiming I went nuts and jumped out of the aircraft. When I boarded the plane I placed my life in the hands of the only one who would protect me—God. However, when I walked up the ladder and entered the plane I immediately looked to see who the pilot was. Fortunately, it was not Powell, but Lieutenant Moore.

When the pilot turned toward me and our eyes met, he nodded. My mind was at rest, and I knew I would be okay. Lieutenant Moore and I had worked together on many occasions because of his position as a program manager and mine as Leading Petty Officer in the Reserve Programs Department in support of his unit.

The two-hour flight to Newport was beautiful; the sky was clear and blue. As I was departing the plane, I was wished good luck by all the crew who knew a severe injustice was taking place.

In summary, on December 23, 1992, Broyles considered me one of his best, and less than eight weeks later he was attacking my mental stability to cover up for the "documented" corruption that was taking place under his command. No matter what my request mast issues were, reprisals are illegal, but on March 27, 1993, when he ordered me for mental health examinations, Broyles broke Federal law!

This infraction of fundamental law is the underlying issue in this entire ordeal. Broyles knew he had Feres on his side and from the moment I attempted to uphold my military oath, my fate in the Navy was sealed.

Now that I have spoken about the "undue command influence" that took place at NAS Willow Grove to cover up the corruption under Broyles and Powell's leadership, I will explain how the military's medical system was also abused to continue to discredit my grievance issues and my mental stability.

51

Military commanders who step over the line and destroy the reputations and mental stability of American citizens who uphold their constitutional responsibilities must be held accountable for their actions. In all, no matter if my issues of February 1993, had merit or did not, the simple fact of the matter is that in 1992, Congress passed legislation that makes it a punishable offense to send military members for mental health examinations in the wake of protected communications and the statute reads:

> "No person may refer a member of the Armed Forces for a mental health examination or evaluation as a reprisal for making or preparing a lawful communication to a Member of Congress; an Inspector General; a member of DOD audit, inspection, investigation, or law enforcement organization; *or to any appropriate authority in the chain of command."* (emphasis added).

Therefore, the following retaliatory factors are illegal, according to federal law, and Broyles should have been held accountable under the provisions of the Uniform Code of Military Justice (UCMJ).

Chapter 3

Military Medical Malpractice

The unethical and unlawful practice of evil medicine

O n ABC's 20/20 program aired in October of 1998, a civilian medical doctor was questioned regarding the alleged mental illness of Major Tim Scholfield. The major reported improprieties at the hospital where he was stationed. In return the Army sent this once vibrant soldier to a mental hospital for 90 days to break his pride and dignity. Unfortunately, the Army succeeded. On national television the civilian doctor who reviewed his records stated that what the military did to Major Scofield was "an outrage to the profession of medicine"

Malpractice: Any professional misconduct, unreasonable lack of skill or fidelity in professional or fiduciary duties, evil practice, or illegal or immoral conduct.

Obtaining a "bed" for a military member suffering from severe alcoholism is very difficult as they are hard to come by. However, in my case my bed was reserved in less than a week.

In the military there are three levels of treatment to address a member's problems with alcohol. Level 1 is a one-week classroom training program; Level II is a three-week outpatient treatment plan; and Level III is a five-week inpatient treatment plan. According to regulations, Level III is strictly reserved for personal with verified alcohol problems. The ARS program is

Level III; only eight weeks prior to my receiving orders to report to this program, my annual performance evaluation stated no substance abuse of any kind.

The objective of the military's alcohol rehabilitation program is to restore a member to "full-duty status" and as a "productive member of the community." Dr. Huh found me "fit for full duty," and I had not been involved in any alcohol-related incident. So why was I there?

When I walked into the Alcohol Rehabilitation Service (ARS) facility in Newport, Rhode Island, the first comment I made to the receptionist was, "I am here due to reprisals for filing a grievance at my command."

That comment fell on deaf ears. Throughout my five-week stay, I repeated many times that I was there for reprisal, but the position of my counselor always was that I was in denial. One would think a claim by an enlisted man that the mental health system was being abused to cover up claims of improprieties would be closely reviewed to be sure that any orders to send the person issuing the complaint to rehab were not retaliatory. It is the ethical responsibility of medical personnel who work in the military's alcohol rehabilitation program to ensure that alcohol is a contributing factor to a service member's problems, and if it is not, other avenues of counseling should be recommended such as stress management or marriage counselling. These are two major areas for alcohol abuse to surface.

Recall that Dr. Huh stated I was "fit for full duty." My performance evaluation reflected nothing but a physically fit 4.0 sailor with no detrimental behaviors. This record should have raised red flags for any ethical medical official with a sense of professional duty to put a halt to the abuse of the alcohol abuse process.

Unfortunately, in the U.S. Military's mental health system, once a person is placed into the system by a "command referral," any expression of dissatisfaction with being placed in the program is countered by the word "denial." Little credence is due counselors with only a few months of training or general practitioners such as Huh, who diagnosed me as psychological dependent. Simply stated, there are no checks and balances in the system!

The Mental Health Test

After the initial paperwork shuffle, I was informed that I had to take a psychological test consisting of over three hundred questions. I quickly found out that this was the "ice breaker" for conversation among other "rehabers."

Although it is impossible for me to remember all the questions that were posed, one stands out: "Do you fantasize about having sex with animals?" To me that question was almost as outrageous as a foot doctor making a mental health diagnosis. Of course, I answered "no" to the question. Thinking back about the sheer arrogance and incompetence of all those counselors, especially Lieutenant Commander Parker (the staff psychiatrist), I wondered what would have happened if I had answered "yes." Maybe I would have become just like them, and they would have released me!

I make light of this test, but one must realize when psychological warfare is the name of the game, it is important to keep a sense of humor. It's the only way you can overcome the tremendous mental anguish you will experience when the United States Military is your adversary.

Day 1 of the Psychological Games

On the morning of May 5, 1993, one day after my arrival, I met for the first time with my group counselor, Petty Officer First Class Chrisman. I told him I had been sent to his facility by my command without just medical cause in retaliation to cover up and discredit my grievance issues at Willow Grove. I also informed Chrisman that the alleged disease of alcoholism was being used to discredit my mental stability and to shed doubt on the merits of my issues.

Although I pointed out that only eight weeks prior to my request mast my performance evaluation stated no alcohol abuse, Chrisman refused to look into these disclosures and told me I was in "denial." From that moment on, Chrisman controlled my destiny.

The course Chrisman took in trying to brainwash me into believing that I was in Level III treatment mode due to alcohol abuse and my continued refusal to accept his position led to several close encounters wherein I wanted to physical attack him. Our relationship heightened to a point of verbal hostility over the five weeks that I was falsely imprisoned, a violation of my Fourth Amendment Constitutional Rights.

Every time I tried to explain the facts to my fellow groupies that I had been retaliated against, and my command used the mental health system to discredit my request mast issues, Chrisman continued to say that I was in denial. He never produced evidence.

The next official I met was Director Bobbie Smith. He seemed to be a decent individual and at least listened to my side of the story. Although I did not have access to my records during my stay at Newport, on my last day I found out that Mr. Smith upheld his ethical responsibilities and stated the following in his notes:

"Based on the information available, probably could not defend them if called upon to do so."

In context, what Director Smith was saying is that if I were ever to have the opportunity to challenge my orders to Level III in a court of law, he believed the Navy could not defend their placement of me in the program! This was the Director of the rehabilitation. However, Chrisman's word carried more weight than the Director! Hence, another compelling piece of evidence which the Inspector General should have acted on to raise doubt about my admittance in the program was ignored. Chrisman made many false statements such as stating that I continued to drink, even with adverse family, social and financial results.

All of these claims are false. The most important document in my entire ordeal, the annual performance evaluation of December 23, 1992, mentions no issues of any kind which were detrimental. As a matter of fact, my record showed I paid my bills, fed, clothed and housed my family, made it to work each day and stayed physically fit by working out in the gym and playing football and softball for most of the year.

If not for Feres, the medical malpractice of placing false information in my records would not have happened! One would think that an individual not qualified in the field of mental health would never be given so much power to take a guess at an individual's mental stability. This is another prime example why Feres must be challenged.

After my interview with Mr. Smith, I was confident that when I finally had an opportunity to speak with the staff psychiatrist and show him the evidence, I would finally be sent on my way back to my command. I was in for even a bigger shock!

Military Medical Ethics at its Finest

When it was finally "show time," the moment when I would speak with the staff psychiatrist, I believed that the nonsense and my retaliatory placement in the program would finally cease.

The staff psychiatrist who would give true meaning to the "evil practice of medicine" was Lieutenant Commander Parker. He told me to explain why I felt I was in his hospital. I of course proceeded to explained to him that prior to my grievance, I was recognized as one of the best at NAS Willow Grove and was never written up for any alleged abuse of alcohol. I again pointed out my performance evaluation which reflected no detrimental behaviors, let alone alcohol abuse. In conclusion I told him "If I had not proceeded with a grievance, I would not be here!"

Parker stated, "I had a chief like you, Petty Officer Trueman, who could not take 'no' for an answer and I fired him, too!"

I was shocked to hear this come from a so-called doctor, but it is fact that military doctors grease the wheels to further a

57

command's wishes and obviously, the fix was in before I ever met Parker.

At that point in the ordeal, the anger and frustration building inside me was coming to a boiling point! I had nothing to lose, so I could have probably gotten away with whatever action I decided to take against him. Once again, I bit my lip and faced the fact that I was being held for the five-week duration.

The Beginning of Five Weeks of Mental Torment

From the moment Parker abused his medical ethics, I was mentally challenged by Chrisman in the hopes that I would break down and admit that I was psychologically dependent on alcohol. I refused. I could have said, "Screw it," and returned to my command to face immediate discharge, but for some crazy reason, I still believed that someone in the Navy's medical system would end the retaliation. However, Chrisman was in charge and took the position that I was in "denial" and that I was failing to face my alleged demons!

Over the five-week period I was at ARS, I was simply amazed at the stories of others in the program. Some truly needed help with their alcoholism, but most argued that they were sent to ARS for ulterior motives from their commands.

The Double Standard in the Military's Alcohol Abuse Program

On my third day at ARS the word was around that I was placed in the program to cover up abuse of power at NAS Willow Grove. This generated a lot of support from many guys I did not even know, simply because we all knew that the Navy uses its alcohol rehab program as a disciplinary tool.

I will never forget one conversation I had, with a Petty Officer named Dave. He told me that prior to my arrival was chief had been sent for his third trip through the program. After receiving his third DWI he was ordered into ARS for the third time. From this you might think that the guy had bad luck or that maybe life's problems combined with alcohol were not a good mixture for him.

The chief worked for the Admiral at the War College across the river from ARS in an administrative position. I was told that because the Admiral wanted him back to do his job, he was released! Justice in the military is not by "rule of law" but by "rule of man." Whoever has the "higher rank" wins every time.

Although I obtained this information from a third person, which makes it *hearsay*, my instincts and gut feeling tell me that the story would be found credible if investigated.

Another disturbing case that I have first hand knowledge about involves a chief named Joe. Throughout my five-week stay, I had the opportunity to talk with Joe on numerous occasions in the smoking area, the only place we could openly talk about how screwed the system truly was because the walls did not have ears.

The first time Joe and I spoke, he told me that he was having difficulties with alcohol and that he didn't want to lose his wife because of alcoholism. I felt that Joe was courageous to face his problem; however, he almost did not get the help he sought because he was a chief. The double standard within the program almost prevented him from obtaining the help he felt he needed.

It worked like this. Because Joe was a chief, his command Drug and Alcohol Advisor (DAPA) gave him the option as to whether or not he would go into the program. As Joe was telling me about his DAPA's comments to him, I can remember the anger in his face directed towards his DAPA. When Joe started to pull himself up and realize that maybe alcohol and himself did not mix very well, he was pissed off at the fact that the help he needed within the system was almost bypassed because of his DAPA.

I wonder to this day how Joe is doing. To me, he is a very special man I only knew for five weeks. Joe will always be a friend in "heart," and I'll never forget him.

Another instance of mind control and manipulation is the case of a Navy Lieutenant who was assigned in our group. This individual was concerned about why he had to have a beer when he worked in his garden! From his own admission this man stated that he drank alcohol maybe once a month, usually when he was working outside.

Most of us were puzzled at his placement in the program and felt that he was not an alcoholic. However, Chrisman with his several months of training convinced this man he was alcoholic. Because of Chrisman, this man was led to believe he had a drinking problem, one of the most despicable situations I have ever seen. It was the first time in my career that I actually watched an enlisted man manipulating the mind of an officer!

I firmly believe that the Lieutenant's problems resulted from low self esteem and maybe depression, but by no means was alcohol the problem. Maybe he was using the program to get out of the Navy. I am no mental health expert, but if I were Chrisman, I would have sent this guy back to his command!

During my five weeks at ARS, as I listened to others tell their story, I became enraged. Of the people admitted to ARS, only a few appeared to be suitable for placement in an inpatient treatment facility; they could have received the necessary awareness of alcohol abuse in a classroom setting or in an out-patient treatment setting.

The truth is that many true alcoholics in the military need help but do not seek it because it can be used as a black mark on one's record, especially if one is targeted by an abusive commander!

Manipulation of Your Mind

One thing that infuriated me throughout my stay at ARS was the way Chrisman kept telling me that my command was "sincerely concerned for my well-being." Like clockwork, I continually disputed Chrisman's comment. Here's my proof. After I was led onto Broyles' aircraft and flown out of Pennsylvania to Rhode Island and for the entire time I was imprisoned at ARS, no one from my command called or checked in person on my family while I was gone!

How in the world could my command have been seriously concerned for my well-being when I only lived five minutes from the base and no one ever checked on my family! I believe this is a pretty good indicator that my best interests were not a priority. Courtesy and compassion for my family's well-being should have been automatic. It never happened because those at my command responsible for administering this program, knew their actions were illegal.

I can still feel my blood pressure rising when I think of that situation and how unsavory some people can be in the military when they play games with peoples' lives!

Getting Even With Chrisman

One day while in our "big group" (all rehabers, about fifty guys, in one session in a classroom setting), Chrisman was giving a lecture on "turning the other cheek and forgiving people for their mistakes." I kept my mouth shut during the big group but found that discussion rather interesting and was waiting for an opportunity to speak up. Finally a prime opportunity to challenge Chrisman and his lecture came along, and I asked him, "What do you do after you turn your cheek the first time, and it happens again?" He responded "Turn the cheek once again." I then asked, "What if it happens a third time" and before he could answer, a fellow reaper yelled out "Kick his ass!" The entire class erupted into spontaneous laughter, and Chrisman stood there like an idiot!

It was no secret that I totally objected to being at ARS, especially considering I had engaged in no alcohol related incident. I believe the comment was made on my behalf because most of the guys in ARS who heard the reasons why I was sent to ARS, believed that I was reprised against for filing a grievance. I am still smiling about this because although Chrisman had the upper hand at ARS, he was laughed at by the entire group.

Will the Boys Come and Show Their Support for My Well-Being?

On the final afternoon of the day before my group was to be released back into the real world, I was informed by Chrisman in our small group that my command officials who sent me to rehab, the same one's who were "concerned" for my well-being, would not be coming.

When I asked Chrisman in front of the group why my command leaders were not coming, he said that the command had called and stated that the CO's aircraft was down for maintenance.

My newly acquired friends and I knew that my command was not coming because I would have made known to all in attendance that they abused the mental health system to cover up their abuses of power. It is possible that CO's aircraft was down for maintenance, but they still have cars in the Navy and could have driven to ARS in about six hours. (I have not had the opportunity to subpoena the maintenance records, but I am almost positive that there will be no records to prove the aircraft was down at that time they said it was.)

Let's face the facts. If a person is truly alcoholic and one of the best members at a military command, a good commanding officer would find a way to show his support. The truth of the matter in my case was that Broyles deliberately used this program to cover up for the corruption I reported to him on February 28, 1993 to save his own hide!

The Most Moving Event of My Entire Military Career

On the morning of our last day, we had a final small group session wherein we exchanged our good-byes and closed out the records. In this final session, Chief Joe focused his closing moments on me for some reason. He made it known to Chrisman that he felt I was not suffering from alcoholism. I glared at Chrisman to see what his reaction would be; Chrisman did not acknowledge the statement.

During my five weeks at ARS, Joe and I got to know each other as people rather than as superior and subordinate. We listened to each other's reasons for being and discovered we had much in common. At the conclusion of his "good-byes" to the small group, he caught me off guard when he took off his "anchors" from his collars, placed them in my hand and said, "You will be wearing these one day."

Someone who had known me only five weeks handed me something precious to him because he truly believed that this young sailor—myself—had leadership potential although being destroyed by the system that I loved!

Chrisman attempted to break me mentally for the five weeks of treatment. He wanted me to admit that I was alcoholic, but the only admission he got from me was that I like to party! Prohibition has been dead in this country for almost seventy years, and alcoholism is considered a "disease"—not a crime.

After Joe's kindness it took me several minutes to regain my composure.

Chrisman determined with his so called "professional opinion" that: (1) I was an over achiever who had to be first in everything; (2) that I had to drink alcohol to function psychologically, and (3) that I was in denial and refused to face the fact that I was alcoholic. Nevertheless, he decided to release me back into the real world and, he said, if I remained sober, I possibly could resume a normal life!

My life would never be the same again.

It was Now my Time to Speak About How I Arrived at ARS

At the conclusion of our final meeting with my drunken Navy buddies, we all gathered in the main classroom in preparation for our "big step" ceremony. Once we all gave a speech, we would be let loose to roam the streets of the USA once again!

63

As I walked into the classroom, several of my fellow rehabers came up to me and told me to point out my DAPA when he arrived.

"Why?"

"If you'd like us to, we will kick the shit out of him for you!"

I smiled. Then one of them said, "We're all considered nuts anyway and we are already here, so what can they do to us?"

The comments of those guys was a show of support that they too, after listening to my claims of being reprised against within the mental health system to discredit corruption at my command, was believable. They were not surprised because they knew that questioning the word of a superior could have devastating consequences to anyone's military career.

I just laughed. Little did Cassidy know that just one row in front of him were several guys who wanted to inflict pain on him on my behalf! Although the offer was hard to resist, Cassidy was only a small fish in a sea of corruption within the Navy's mental health system. At this point, there were much larger fish to catch (i.e. Parker) and all the other boys from the Grove who abused the mental health system to cover up their wrongdoing.

I firmly believe is that "what comes around, goes around" and one day in their own pathetic lives, they will pay a price for their evil deeds.

The Moment of Truth

When it was finally my time to speak in front of a room full of approximately 70 people I did not know, I felt nervous. I had no idea what I was going to say. Approaching the podium, I focused directly at Cassidy and stared him straight in the eyes.

He seem nervous, perhaps unsure about whether I would open up my speech with relentless claims of his abuses of duty. Although I knew my career was essentially over at that moment I kept my integrity. I did not retaliate because I was preparing to fight for my constitutional and human rights when I returned to

Willow Grove. I eyed Cassidy, and if my recollection serves me correctly, I proceeded to speak the following words:

When I arrived here five weeks ago and walked through these doors, I did not agree and strongly objected to the reason I was sent here. However, I must say that I did learn a lot and have met some great people here.

Although I do not believe I am alcoholic, I believe there should be a course set up in the Navy, for all senior enlisted members to go through, to identify the signs of alcoholism to help those who do need such help, but who fear that exposing their problems will be a black mark on their records.

I understand now that alcohol is just a symptom of alcoholism, as all other life factors and stressors must be taken into consideration to fully understand the disease. However, what I don't understand is that Mr. Smith, the Director, told me that 'you can drink alcohol every day of your life and not be alcoholic, and you can drink once a year and be an alcoholic.'

Again, I do not agree with how I got here, but I did learn a lot, and met some great people. I wish you all the best. (Speaking to my fellow rehabers.)

With respect to Chief Joe's turning over his anchors to me, I went on to say:

This morning, when we were in our individual groups saying our farewells, I was handed a set of anchors from my friend, Chief Joe. He told me that one day I would be wearing these. (I had to pause for a few moments as the tears would not stop flowing from my eyes.)

This act of compassion is what we as military members must show for each other, and I just want everyone to know, what Joe did was the kindest act that anyone has ever done for me in my military career.

In closing, I want to thank all those with whom I shared the last five weeks of my life with here, and I hope you all work out your problems.

As we all stood in line to meet the guests, everyone who shook my hand—enlisted, officer, and civilian alike—wished me well with apparent sincerity. A few told me that my speech was moving and that they hoped my troubles would end soon.

That day was one of the most emotional times in my life. The experience helped me realize that even though there are people who will use and abuse you, there are more good, caring and compassionate people who walk this earth and make life worth living.

At the conclusion of the "big step" program, I exchanged hugs and well wishes with my newly acquired friends from Newport, Rhode Island. I felt sad saying good-bye. I knew that I would continue to serve out my contract, but my belief in "duty, honor, country" was overridden by my concern as to how I was going to protect my family's interests when I returned to Willow Grove to begin my long fight for justice.

As I got in the car my Command Career Counselor, Chief Flake and DAPA Cassidy drove from Willow Grove to pick me up, I saw my friends taking their afternoon smoke break. I told Chief Flake to wait a minute, because I wanted to say a final good-bye. Chief Flake had no objection to my request but Cassidy said "hurry up." I proceeded to the smoking area. As I approached again, the guys were smiling and said, "Go home, Jeff."

After one last embrace and show of respect, I told the guys I would take their memories with me throughout my life. To all my friends from Newport who truly cared for me, I thank you all, and who knows, just maybe we will all meet again and I wish you all well!

Finally, I Was on the Road to Reunite with My Children

When Chief Flake pointed the car south and we started the long drive from Newport R.I. to Willow Grove, Pennsylvania, many things were going through my mind. I wondered whether the damage to my marriage for placing the needs of the Navy over the needs of my wife could ever be reconciled. I thought about whether or not was I really going to take on Broyles' abuse of power and his unlawful use of the Navy's mental health system, chancing possible continued retaliation. Above these concerns, however, my first objective was to get home and give my two beautiful kids big hugs and kisses!

I was sitting directly behind Cassidy and was listening to him ramble on about everything under the sun. That was almost enough for me to take some frustration out on him, but I didn't. If I was truly mentally unstable, I probably would have!

When I arrived home early that evening, I did not feel like the same guy I'd been when I left five weeks earlier. I knew my relationship with my wife was at the end of its road. It was nice to see our children and be with them, and this took the serious issues I had to face out of my mind. If not for my children, I don't know where I would be.

On the morning after my return, I immediately undertook preparations to redress the failure of my request mast issues to be investigated, and further planned to seek an investigation into new issue of abuse of the mental health and alcohol rehabilitation process that took place in my case.

Chapter 4

Outrageous and Egregious Conduct

Obstruction of justice in the military's investigative and legal processes

Obstruction of Justice: "Impeding or obstructing those who seek justice in a court, or those who have duties or powers of administering justice therein."

I t is outrageous that the U.S. Military's mental health system could be so easily abused. I wonder how many others from around the United States have fallen victims to this Nazi-style tactic? Military medical malpractice is commonplace because there are no safety nets to prevent abuses in the system from taking place due to Feres and it has got to end!

Two other stories reflect the need for reforms to prevent medical malpractice and other unethical behaviors in the military medical system. The first story is about my buddy Ski, Donald Serkleski, who is now finally rated at 100 percent disability for the medical malpractice he was subjected to in the Navy Department.

Ski had to go for a biopsy for a raised mole on his back and was informed by the Navy doctor that there was only a small percentage of cancer under the mole. Ski was informed that the surgery was not difficult and that it would not leave any obvious scar. The Navy doctor ended up cutting a circular hole in this man, approximately 8 inches by 8 inches in diameter and about one-fourth inch deep. Since that surgery, Ski has lost the strength in his right arm and is forever scarred both mentally and physically because of this medical incompetence.

Another disturbing story I heard was from a civilian doctor who worked for the Department of the Army. I met this man in Ridley Park after my discharge. I told him I had just lost my Navy career due to unlawful reprisals and false claims of mental illness. He replied that he lost his career as a doctor after an incident in which an infant was brought into the emergency room while he was on duty. Another doctor wanted to give the baby some type of medication and he objected, concerned that it could kill her. However, the medication was administered, and the child died. One would think that the doctor who killed the baby would be held accountable. However, the doctor who tried to intervene and save the baby's life was blackballed, and he lost his career with the military.

Many other former American service members and civilians have lost their careers for simply doing their jobs. In this case someone's baby is dead, a doctor is blackballed, and the doctor who killed the baby is probably still serving the Department of the Army or practicing medicine in the civilian world.

If the system does not police itself and if military doctors are not required to be fully trained in their profession, then American lives will continue to be destroyed by "evil" doctors such as Parker as well as the simply incompetent.

Although the acts of abusive leaders and incompetent doctors are chilling, injustice is compounded when military investigators turned a blind eye to obvious wrongdoing to please the upper echelon at the Pentagon.

When I returned from Newport, I knew in my heart that I would pursue justice not only for those who served under my direction and were victimized, but also to clear my records of false information stating that I suffered from mental illness. In the wake of the swift retaliation I faced for simply alleging improprieties, I knew I would not get a fair shake. I also knew that to make a compelling argument for true reforms in the laws to protect military members from abuse of power and reprisals, I had to use my chain of command from the very bottom at NAS Willow Grove to the very top—William Jefferson Clinton, Commander-in-Chief, United States Armed Forces.

On the second day upon my return home from ARS, I thought it would be good for me to go and watch some softball games on base in order to ease my mind, and begin to refocus on where I was going in all of this.

Walking up to ballfield, I was approached by several civilians who I had played ball with over the past couple of years. Gumby (a great hitter) said, "Hey Trueman! We understand you got f---ed over."

I said, "At this point, I don't known what is going to happen to me, but I am confident that my Navy career is over!"

As I was watching the game Drew, a civilian I'd played against in our base league, approached me. Drew said, "How are you doing?"

I told him I was attempting to deal with the attacks against my mental stability the best that I could. Drew then went on to say, "Jeff, I was a Navy SEAL!" This disclosure caught me off guard, because I was not sure as to what Drew may have heard about my situation. Knowing he was once part of the "elite" special forces units in the United States Armed Forces, I said nothing and awaited his comments.

Although I had watched the SEALS practice maneuvers off my ship when I was in Beirut, I had never personally met a SEAL or had opportunity to speak "heart to heart" with the elite fighting men in our military service. Drew proceeded to tell me a story about how he jumped from an aircraft in 1976 and hurt his legs pretty bad. Essentially, it ended his SEAL career, but he shared his thoughts about all of us being considered numbers when no longer of use to those who run our government. He said that after his injuries, he attempted to receive treatment and benefits within the military's medical system through the Veterans Administration. After a futile attempt he gave up!

This is a Navy SEAL we are talking about! Drew said he got tired of dealing with the hassles within the bureaucracy. He moved on with his life and obtained a college degree. I could hear the sense of betrayal in his voice. He was willing to die for his government, but it turned its back on him when he most needed its help!

At that moment, I realized that it doesn't matter who you are or what you do in the military. When your time is up, and you're of no further use to the military establishment, your time is up!

Drew went on to say, "Jeff, hang in there and do what you know is right for the benefit of others. Don't give up like I did because of frustration, and I am with you! Make a change for the better of all military members because I know you can!"

The words of my adopted big brother Steve combined with Drew's perceptions of betrayal told me from that moment that I would take the fight as far as I had to go. I would do all I could to prevent future abuses of military men and women who uphold their military oaths.

The statement Drew made to me moved me tremendously and I responded: "With support from people like you, Drew, I will fight until the end!"

Drew's words were a major encouragement for me to keep on keeping on, from the very early stages of the psychological warfare the government took against this veteran.

Although many years passed since that conversation with Drew on a summer's evening in May 1993, I was fortunate to reach him on December 29, 1997, when I called and wished him a belated Merry Christmas and a Happy New Year. We talked for about forty-five minutes. I briefed him on the events that occurred since we'd last spoken and told him that finally the national media was investigating the military's practice of psychological retaliation within its mental health system.

So much time had passed that I wasn't sure how he would react to my call. Again, I was moved by this patriot's comments about his support for my family, and my goal to make a change to protect our average military members and their families from injustice within the Armed Forces.

My Return to Duty

On my first day back to duty after being fired as the Leading Petty Officer of the Training Department, I was notified that I was being reassigned to the Environment Department. The Environment Department was located in the Public Works building where the majority of personnel were civilian employees and many Navy Sea Bees were assigned there. I knew that I had to go into my new department with a positive attitude and I did just that.

When I arrived at the Environmental Department and informed those in the office as to who I was and that I was reporting for duty as the Administrative Assistant to the Environment Officer, a civilian employee yelled out, "Who did you piss off to get assigned in this department?"

I smiled, but I knew that my final eight months on Willow Grove would be interesting to say the least!

The civilian who posed the question to me was the base Energy Coordinator, Jim Edmonds, who became a good friend.

To Jim I said, "What do you mean?"

"All perceived boat rockers and the throwaways from other departments are assigned to Environmental," he said.

All of those "throwaways" I worked with turned out to be decent people, and we became friends. The guys I met who were reassigned to Environmental for many different reasons were some of the most squared away sailors I've met in the Navy.

On that first day back to work, I decided to go to the Flight Line Inn, a small canteen which served cheese steaks and other pretty good food. The Flight Line Inn was located across the parking lot from my former Department, Reserve Programs. As I was about to walk in and grab some chow, my buddy "Commander Powell" happened to be going to lunch himself and we met face-to-face at the door! Because his rank was higher than mine, I held the door for him out of a show of respect for the uniform. With a big smile he said to me, "Welcome back!"

It was the last time Powell would address me with non-hostile words until my discharge. I acknowledged his greeting.

72

For the first two weeks of duty in the Environmental Department, I familiarized myself with the departmental personnel. I was assigned to work under the direction of Lieutenant Commander Welsh. I knew him from the Grove where he was a Program Manager and one of my favorite officers. My Leading Petty Officer and Division chief were also decent individuals and definitely not the "good ole boy" types.

I was accepted in my new department and treated with respect.

Round Two of the Retaliatory Phase Begins

On May 21, 1993, approximately three weeks after my return from ARS, I submitted what is known as a "Request for Redress" under the provisions of Article 138 of the Uniform Code of Military Justice (UCMJ). However, prior to proceeding with my request, I spoke to Lieutenant Inserra, a Navy lawyer stationed at the Philadelphia Naval Shipyard. Mr. Inserra was a very nice man, but he was not impressed by the seriousness of the situation I was encountering.

Later I learned from Mr. Bowman that Mr. Inserra had told him that I should give up the fight because there was no possible way to prevail in the matter. I assume he was referring to the chilling effects of the Feres Doctrine, and if so, he was right!

After I reviewed Article 138 (Redress of Wrongs by Superiors) of the UCMJ, I wanted to confirm whether or not I needed to send my request through my chain of command or if I could legally direct it to Broyles. Mr. Inserra advised me to submit my request for redress under the provisions of Article 138 of the UCMJ directly to the CO, and I followed his advice.

On May 21, 1993 I hand delivered my request to Broyles' Administrative Secretary and returned to my office. Within hours, I received the first threat from Powell. The second intimidation phase had begun. This time I was prepared for Powell's tactics and was determined to stand my ground and remain professional. I knew if I failed to show Powell any signs of weakness or fright, that would infuriate him, and it surely did!

73

When the Powell phone call came in, I answered the phone. He started to threaten me, implying that I had violated the chain of command by submitting my redress directly to the CO. He said, "Trueman, don't create the problems in the Environmental Department that you did in the Reserve Programs Department."

I tried to tell him that my attorney had directed me to submit my request for redress directly to the CO, but Powell did not want to hear it. I listened to Powell go on and on and in the end, he warned me that I better follow the chain of command or I would be written up! Although the investigative reports of the Navy Inspector General (IG), reflect that I circumvented the chain of command, I was never written up for this alleged insubordination.

After I hung up, Greg, my Leading Petty officer, asked me, "Who was that?" He'd seen how angry I looked during the phone conversation.

"It was the XO (Executive Officer)," I said. "He tried to tell me I'd jumped the chain of command."

"What did you do to be accused of jumping the chain of command?" Greg asked.

"I submitted a request for redress—according to my attorney's advice."

Greg already knew there was tremendous hostilities between Powell and myself. He said, "Just hang in there."

The Undue Delays Continue

Powell reviewed my May 21 request for redress and explanation about why my grievance issues were not addressed, why those who worked for me were not questioned, and why my request for an independent investigation into abuses of the mental health system had not been carried out. After this review the hostilities between Powell and myself heightened although they could not write me up and discipline me on any false charge because I could have requested a court martial.

If the "boys" attempted to file bogus charges against me, I would have the legal right to bring in witnesses to corroborate my grievance issues and the reprisals I faced. In this way I could have destroyed their "false and fantasy" defense in ruling that my issues had no merit.

Several weeks passed, and I did not hear anything about my request for redress. One day I asked my Division Chief Wolfe to speak with Command Master Chief Moore about the unlawful delay in the request being processed. Chief Wolfe did just that and arranged a meeting with all three of us—Wolfe, Moore, and myself.

Chief Wolfe did not know any of the circumstances of abuse of the military's mental health system that were taking place, so I knew he would be an unbiased witness to the events that were about to transpire between myself and the Command Master Chief. Additionally, he was not one to play games with me. If I was barking up the wrong tree, he would make that known to me. This meeting would be the first—and only—time that an outsider not familiar with the facts, would listen to my pleas for justice.

When the meeting began, I pointed out to Moore that I was concerned about the failure of my request for redress to be expeditiously processed. According to Navy Regulations, any request to higher authority must be proceeded immediately. I argued that it was in my opinion that my request was being unlawfully held by Powell. I requested Command Master Chief Moore to help me get my chit to Broyles. (The Command Master Chief position is designed as a liaison person providing a direct link between concerns of enlisted personnel and the commanding officer).

Although Moore knew that there was tension between my former department and myself, I told him the circumstances of the entire situation and reasons for my redress request in front of Chief Wolfe—so that there was a witness to the conversation. I also asked Moore, "How could Captain Broyles send me to Level III when I did not even commit an alcohol related incident?"

This question caught the ears of Chief Wolfe, and he waited for an answer from Master Chief Moore, who said, "You were sent to rehab without committing an alcohol related incident?"

I looked over at my Chief, and he shook his head in aston-ishment. I said, "That's right, Master Chief. I was sent to rehab without probable cause."

Wolfe responded in words to this effect: "I don't know what the circumstance were for Petty Officer Trueman to be sent to rehab, but from listening to both of you for the last forty-five minutes, I believe Trueman was reprised against for filing a request to speak with the CO."

At the conclusion of the meeting, my Chief told the Master Chief to make sure that my request for redress reached the CO. As we left the meeting, I commented to Wolfe how outrageous the entire situation was. He agreed. He also said I'd gotten myself into a predicament. "If you can get the big boys here," he said, "I will speak about the abuses on base."

I thanked Chief Wolfe for his support. I understood that although he was a Chief Petty Officer, if he pushed the issue of retaliation and other abuses, he would probably face reprisals as well, since Broyles and Powell were out of control and felt invin-cible because of the Feres Doctrine. For 49 years Feres has allowed the federal courts to rubber stamp unjust decisions of military commanders.

On July 12, 1993, almost seven weeks after I applied for redress, I received notification from Broyles that he had denied my request. I was not surprised. I immediately proceeded to my next available administrative remedy. I filed a formal complaint against Broyles under the provision of Article 138 of the UCMJ. According to the regulation, a complaint against a CO can be sub-mitted to *any* senior ranking officer from any of the military ser-vices to be served upon the Respondent's superior officer. I forwarded the complaint to the Admiral at the Philadelphia Naval Shipyard. It took over two months for my request for redress to be denied.

On July 17, 1993, the day of Broyles' retirement ceremony and change of command, my 138 complaint was forwarded to Broyles' superior officer, Admiral J. D. Olson, III, Commander, Naval Air Reserve Force, New Orleans, LA. Olson essentially had the final say as to whether the 138 complaint would be prosecuted or not. Ironically, on the day the complaint was forwarded to Olson, he was at the Grove partying with Broyles and Lekberg, the new CO. From the pattern of abuses that I have documented, I am confident that the complaint was denied redress by Olson at the bar that evening!

The Final Straw That Broke My Loyalty to the U.S. Navy

In response to my Article 138 complaint, Powell was apparently more determined than ever before to find a way to destroy my career or push me past my breaking point. He not only wanted me off the base for good but booted out of the Navy also. He initiated his first tangible reprisals on July 29, 1993 when he ordered his Manpower officer to interfere with top-secret transfer orders I had already been granted for my second "independent duty" of my career at the Space and Warfare Command, Washington, D.C.

Powell had a logical reason to initiate an unlawful interference with my transfer orders. A major problem that would have arisen because I would have been questioned once again by the FBI to obtain an upgrade to my top secret security clearance so that I could be granted permission to handle highly sensitive information once again. My being placed in the military mental health system for a paranoid thought process without just cause would have been reviewed by the FBI. The attempts by Broyles, Powell and Lekberg to conceal their unlawful conduct at the premises of Willow Grove would thus have been exposed. Both Lekberg and Powell knew that my gaining access to an FBI agent could have blown the lid off all their unlawful conduct. There was no way in hell they were going to take that chance and allow my transfer orders to go through.

In the wake of Powell's continued attacks against my career and interference with my transfer orders, I decided that it was time to take a stand and fight the injustice and abuse of power he was displaying. I thought the best avenue to defend myself was to proceed through the administrative remedy process. This was a

77

big mistake. I learned that in the U.S. Armed Forces the "administrative discharge" process is designed to quickly remove less desirable personnel from the service without having to court martial them. However, the method can also be used to destroy honorable persons.

As with the abuse of the grievance investigation in which Broyles hand picked Smedberg to cover up and violate the independence of the investigation, the administrative discharge process is also easily manipulated. Board members are hand picked by the Executive Officer and approved by the Commanding Officer. If a member is having problems with his or her Executive or Commanding Officer, this process can easily be abused by the assignment of biased board members—Gumpright (Keller's former boss) in my case. Additionally, the rules of evidence for an administrative discharge are substantially less rigorous than those a trial. The Board President and hand-picked members can prevent evidence from being introduced that would be relevant to a trial and favorable to the Respondent, the person being separated by administrative processes.

Finally, the administrative discharge board is not conduct by a military judge. Determinations of whether a member should be retained or discharged are thus in the hands of nonlegal experts— a recipe for a tragedy.

After Olson's actions (to be discussed shortly) and the Navy Department's failure to stop the retaliation I was facing in the medical system, I decided to enlist in the U.S. Army at the end of my enlisted contract with the Navy in May of 1994 and attempt a new start. That plan never materialized because the administrative discharge process was invoked by Powell and Lekberg. Although their attempts to discharge me with a personality disorder failed, they knew they could railroad me out the back door by claiming that I'd refused alcohol rehabilitation.

Powell claimed to the Navy Inspector General that the command did not need my services any longer at the Grove. The truth of the matter is that on July 31, 1992 (six months prior to my grievance), Broyles approved an extension request with a transfer in May 1994. In his recommendation he stated that I was an "asset" to his command. This is another piece of evidence to establish a *prima facie* case for unlawful reprisal under §1034. *Primae facie* is a Latin term meaning "at first sight; on first appearance" and with respect to the case at hand, "such as will suffice until contradicted and overcome by other evidence"). Remember that I had been granted permission to remain on board until May 1994, but I was not allowed to do so after my communications regarding improprieties at the Grove. The evidence was ignored by investigators. If I had not proceeded with the grievance and had complied with the Rumery threat, no unfavorable personnel actions would have ever been taken against me, and I would still be in the Navy.

I think it is appropriate to clarify the facts at this point.

1. From the period of July 12, 1982 through December 23, 1992, I was graded 4.0 with no detrimental behaviors noted in any of my performance evaluation for 10½ years.

2. On February 7, 1993, I proceeded with my grievance issues and received the threat that proceeding with such issues would result in the end of my career.

3. On February 25, 1993, my request to speak with Broyles was approved, and I received my first and only formal counseling of my career for alleged insubordination.

4. On February 28, 1993 I discussed my issues with Broyles.

5. On March 3, 1993, Smedberg investigated the case.

6. On March 26, 1993, I was fired as Leading Petty Officer and ordered to report to my home.

7. On March 27, 1993, Broyles found no merit to my issues and ordered me for mental health examinations, in violation of federal law.

8. On March 27, 1993, I was classified as psychological dependent on alcohol although "fit for full duty" by Dr.

Huh in a fifteen-minute consultation and placed into the
Navy Level III treatment program without being charged
or convicted of any wrongdoing. Remember, I was
ordered to alcohol dependency screening for "administrative issues" only.

Broyles managed to destroy me on paper with false claims
of mental health problems and denied redress to my request under
Article 138. On August 17, 1993, the condoning of violations of
my human rights as guaranteed by the U.S. Constitution made it
to the "flag officer" level under Admiral J. D. Olson, III, Commander, Naval Air Reserve Force, New Orleans, LA.

On that day the ball game changed. Olson denied redress of
my Article 138 issues. Under Broyles' direction, corruption had
reached the upper echelon of the command and control structure
in the Navy Department. The legal and medical systems would
now be placed on trial.

Olson decided to ignore the facts that prior to my grievance
issues I was a top-notch performer and an asset to Broyles—in his
own words—but that immediately following my discussion with
him, I became a liability! It does not take a rocket scientist to figure out that unlawful reprisals in violation of military and federal
laws were undertaken and then covered up by Olson. This was
possible only because the "rule of man" continues to control the
"rule of law" within the Navy Department command structure.

My First Protected Communication to
Congress is Initiated

After Olson's decision to cover up for his buddy Broyles, I knew
I had to start researching other avenues to protect my career from
further reprisals. I felt that communicating with my Senator from
Pennsylvania, Arlen Specter, could put an end to the nonsense
and blatant abuses of federal law by Broyles. I fooled myself into
believing that a politician would help in this matter.

Congress passed a law in 1992 prohibiting mental health
referrals when protected speech was the issue. In my case, Senator Specter did not care, nor did other Members of Congress such

as Representative Curt Weldon. Although I told members of Congress about the situation, they did not think that Nazi-style psychological retaliatory tactics in the U.S. Armed Forces were worth investigating. In other words, they condoned deliberate violations of their own statutes.

The lesson I learned from this is, first, that unless you or someone close to you knows a Member of the United States Congress, you won't get the attention of your elected leaders. Second, I learned that your elected officials will not risk any political ramifications that could adversely affect their power in Washington. No matter how egregious an issue is in the military, Congress can turn a blind eye to any injustice, due to the Feres Doctrine. One way that military personnel can take progressive steps to combat Feres is to write to their elected representatives and demand that Congress reform or repeal the law. If enough people speak up, the message will be heard.

The Obstruction of Justice in Violation of Public Law Begins

As previously stated, on August 30, 1993 I filed my first protective communication under federal law with Senator Specter. I informed him in this document that the military leaders at Willow Grove were abusive and had failed to uphold their duties to ensure the well-being of base personnel. I added that hundreds of personnel were willing to testify to these facts. I believed that Specter might think that just possibly the problems at the Grove were real.

The Navy IG must submit a semiannual report to Congress about their activities. Statistics reflecting that 1 out of 100 personnel on base complained of abuse of power would seem to indicate that Specter was knowledgeable of the problems. He turned a blind eye for political reasons. It was easier for him to sweep the situation under the carpet, allowing a few people to suffer great damage rather than to do the right thing and correcting the problems at the Grove.

81

As a result of Specter and Weldon's failure to address the corruption at the Grove, Powell's abuses against me escalated. Unfavorable personnel actions included interference with my transfer orders and a rewrite of my 4.0 evaluation to 2.8. I countered Powell by filing an abuse of power and retaliation complaint against him with the Navy IG on September 14, 1993 in accordance with §1034.

The complaint focused on Powell's intimidation, threats, and interference with pre-approved top secret independent duty transfer orders. I believe that this complaint was the final straw. From that point on Powell would do anything no matter how unconstitutional to see that I was terminated from my employment with the Navy Department.

If Looks Could Kill

On September 24, 1994, ten days after I faxed the Powell Complaint to the Navy IG, I was subjected to the final intimidating glare and smirk from Powell.

The event took place while I was performing my duties in the CO's administrative office. As Powell walked by me with squinted eyes and an evil glare, something snapped in me. I was not going to sit idle while Powell toyed with my mind. I decided it was time to challenge all the unfavorable personnel actions and reprisals that had occurred since my initial grievance. The thought crossed my mind several times that I was setting myself up to retaliate against Powell! I had to do something to defuse these thoughts.

Immediately after the Powell look, I happened to run into Cassidy. I ripped into him. I attacked his unethical handling of my case and told him that continuing to participate in the aftercare program was not of a benefit to myself nor my family. In response, he stated words to this effect: "You are the one who brought the situation on yourself. If you'd said nothing, no action would have been taken against you." His comments again made it clear to me that nothing would have happened to me if I had remained silent and played the game.

82

After our confrontation, Cassidy went to Command Master Chief Moore's office and told him what I had said. Cassidy asked me to wait while he told Commander Moore about the situation. Moore then called me in and asked me if I had stated that I would not follow the aftercare program. I repeated the same words I had shared with Cassidy concerning the unethical behavior by the leadership. I added that if it meant being sent to an administrative discharge board in order for the evidence and witnesses on my behalf to be heard, that is what I would do. Cassidy was then ordered to file an incident report with the base police although no criminal conduct took place.

On the next day, September 25, 1993, I received notification from Lekberg that if I failed to follow the aftercare program I would be processed for discharge for failing to comply. For the next week, I fought with the anger inside me. I felt they had finally broken me as a person and that no longer did rank, pay, duty, honor, country matter. The belief that serving my country was an honor was in my heart no longer. Now I was going to take control of my destiny and legally and peacefully defeat my opponents. The most important game of my life began in earnest that day. My own government had destroyed everything good in my life simply because I upheld my military oath.

I knew my aftercare contract stated that two (2) unauthorized absences would lead to termination of the aftercare program. I had two weeks to decide if this ploy on my part was the right one.

My next aftercare meeting was quickly approaching, and the entire week was emotionally straining. My anger and hatred towards the boys reached an all-time high! My anger was no longer with Feener, Cassidy, Parker, Christman, Huh *et al*, but with Powell. Again, I figured that if I was sent to an administrative discharge board, I would finally have a chance to vindicate myself. I was not prepared for the obstruction of justice that took place at that hearing.

On the day I was supposed to attend my weekly aftercare meeting in Philadelphia, I remained at work and finished out the day. The next morning I was informed that I was being processed for administrative discharge for failure to participate in the after-care regimen for alcoholism treatment. The command's long awaited opportunity to complete my structured discharge was at hand, and now the boys were going to abuse the administrative discharge process just as they did the mental health system. Due to Feres no evidence was required to abuse the process—only word of mouth. It is a chilling reality that nothing more is needed to destroy an honorable American in uniform.

Teaming up with Keller and Others to Expose Abuse of Power

While I was waiting for my administrative separation board to meet, I knew it was imperative that I continue to obtain the help of Senator Specter or I would be discharged on false pretenses that I was unfit to serve my country. Although Specter did nothing to help me, I must explain the nexus between myself and Tony Keller because that connection justifies the serious charges of obstruction of justice I will discuss later in this book.

I met Tony Keller in September of 1993. We decided that a congressional meeting with other members of the base, with Senator Specter, and with then-Senator Wolford in Philadelphia was our only remaining protective avenue to stop Lekberg and Powell from continuing their unlawful conduct.

The next month a meeting took place in Philadelphia between seven base personnel and an aide of Wolford. As a result of that congressional meeting, the "buzz" around the base was that an investigation was going to take place on board the air station. As fast as the word got around that a congressional inquiry could soon be initiated, the word also got around that getting involved with Trueman and Keller was not a wise thing to do.

Many of the inactive reserve sailors for whom I had placed my career in jeopardy, unfortunately backed off from wanting to file their own complaints to me about wrongs against them. This upset me because I had put my career on the line for them. When the time came to step up to the plate, they had decided to sit on the bench, leaving me hanging.

I was upset with people backing out when the heat was turned up. While thinking about this, I was approached by a female petty officer who stated, "We support you Jeff; however, we are fearful of retaliation." She said she had a family and bills to pay and relied on her reserve paycheck to make ends meet.

I appreciated her candor and concerns for her family. Then I asked her, "In the end, will you be there if I subpoena your testimony?"

"Yes, I will," she said, "and so will many others."

After the October 1993 whistleblower meeting Powell and Lekberg had had enough of both Keller and myself. They were starting to feel a lot of pressure and knew that if a congressional investigation were to be conducted and all of us on base stood firm, they would be taken down.

The solution to their problem was to terminate Keller and me without further delay. False claims had to be made immediately in order to achieve our unlawful terminations. Keller was alleged to have made a death threat, and I, of course, was alleged to have failed to participate in my aftercare program.

In many ways, as I have pointed out, my case and Tony's mirror each other. The primary difference was that because of Feres I had no legal protection within our judicial system. Tony, who was subjected to the same *modus operandi* that I was, received a settlement of $200,000 because he had civil rights and constitutional protections that military members simply don't have. With this fact known, who would want to serve in the military? Why enlist knowing that it takes only a stroke of a pen to destroy a person's liberty and rights under the U.S. Constitution.

Obstruction of Justice in the Navy's Administrative Discharge Process

When I was informed that I was being discharged for failure to participate in the aftercare program, I made it known to congressional and officials in the Inspectors General office that the administrative discharge process was being abused.

On November 9, 1993, I had still not received confirmation from Lekberg that I would be processed for administrative separation. I met with my military attorney, Inserra, and discussed briefly the issues of how I was being railroaded out of the Navy. He prepared a request for release of documents which would further support my Article 138 complaint and provide evidence needed to convince the administrative board that I was being separated in retaliation for my protected communications. I provided this request for release of documents to the station Legal Petty Officer McGugin for issuance to the command.

Failure to Release Evidence Relevant to My Defense

I received permission from the Office of the Judge Advocate General (JAG) Washington, by letter via Lekberg that I had been granted additional time to retrieve evidence to support my Article 138 issues. This notification by JAG was approved by Lekberg. However, when I attempted to retrieve pay and training records and other documents to support my claim of gross-mismanagement and falsification of official documents, the RPD Commander said he would not grant me permission until he spoke to the CO, even though the CO had already endorsed the letter. Everyone was stonewalling.

As a result of the stonewalling, on November 10, 1993 I placed a call to Mary Clark at Specter's Philadelphia office and informed her of my difficulties in obtaining documents to corroborate my claims of corruption. Mary contacted the Navy Department in Washington, who placed a call to Powell. The fireworks were about to begin!

On the afternoon of November 10, I checked back with Mary. She asked me if I was still on the on base and I responded "yes." She told me that Powell wanted to see me in his office. I knew then that Powell's hostility toward me was going to reach its peak.

Later I figured out that the boys could not take a chance on my requesting a court martial. But at the moment, because I was concerned about being written up for alleged insubordination or worse, I called a friend of mine and asked him if I could use his tape recorder. My intention was to get this meeting on tape to protect myself and hopefully get some evidence that Powell was abusing his powers. Specter and Weldon could then use the tape to prove that Powell was truly out of control.

After I obtained the recorder, I called Powell at about 1615 (4:15 civilian time). When Powell got on the phone, he ordered me to report to his office immediately. As I sat outside his office waiting for him to call me in, I wondered what was going to happen.

Powell approached me, and I could feel my temperature rising. My hands were sweaty. He said, "Follow me." In addition to Powell and myself was the acting Command Master Chief. Moore was not present because—apparently as a special favor— he had been given transfer orders to his home area in Washington State while awaiting his retirement.

I was directed to sit down. As I did so, I placed my white hat and the tape recorder under it on the floor.

Powell said, "I called you here because you got us confused as to what you want. What do you want, Petty Officer Trueman?" His voice sounded very hostile.

I told him I needed to obtain documents from my last department which would prove that my request mast issues and Article 138 issues had merit. He said, "The Article 138 is out of the command and no longer under our jurisdiction, so tell us what you want!"

I told him that I had received a letter from Senator Specter. He interrupted. "What letter from Specter? I have no letter from Specter, I have no letter from Joe Blow!"

I could tell that my persistence in obtaining relevant evidence that reflected misconduct was touching a raw nerve.

During the meeting I felt Powell's contempt. To me seeing a lowly commander refuse to comply with a Congressional inquiry was a disgrace since military officers work for Congress, as do we all. His attitude was to me a prime example of how Feres allows people like the Powells of the military to act as they do!

Although I attempted to speak in a professional manner throughout the meeting to make Powell understand what my request entailed, he kept interrupting me. I documented six interruptions after he asked me what information I was trying to obtain. This can be confirmed by ABC News, who were provided a copy of the tape to corroborate my allegations of his hostility.

The congressional inquiry by Mary Clark on November 10, 1993 truly set Powell off. The most intense moment of the meeting occurred when I pointed out that the Article 138 had not been properly investigated. Powell almost flew out of his chair in a rage. "That is in your mind," he roared.

Once again, it was the Navy Department's legal position that the claims I brought forth of corruption were "false and fantasy." They were pushing the mental health issue for all it was worth because Feres allowed them to do so.

Although I had faced many acts of retaliation from Powell, this comment was an insult to me. I was defiant and stood up to leave. Powell yelled at me, "You sit down petty officer. You are not dismissed and you are still in the United States Navy."

I responded "No, Sir, I am not in the Navy any longer, and you have destroyed my career!"

Powell started whining like a child to the acting Command Master Chief that I was showing borderline insubordination. I bit my lip and allowed Powell's arrogance to flow.

At the conclusion of the meeting, I received official notification that my administrative board was being convened on November 18, 1993. I was also directed that any information I sought with respect to JAG Washington's grant of approval to obtain evidence to support my claims had to be submitted in writing directly to Powell for forwarding to Lekberg for approval or disapproval.

The following morning, November 11, 1993, I provided my document request to Powell. The next day, November 12, 1993,

Lekberg denied my request in its entirety, stating that the documents I sought were irrelevant for my defense at the upcoming administrative board.

Although I reminded both Specter and Inserra about the "due process" factor, nothing was done. I would go into the administrative board without any evidence to prove that my orders for mental health examinations were retaliatory for exposing the abuses which were documented at that time.

After Lekberg refused to release the information I requested, I notified JAG of this problem. I told them that although Lekberg had endorsed their authorization for me to obtain additional evidence, he had turned around and denied me access. This was a clear violation of a directive from higher authority.

I heard nothing further from JAG in Washington, D.C., the headquarters for all Navy lawyers in the service. The failure of its lawyers to compel Lekberg and Powell to comply with their own directive severely hurt my chances for a fair hearing.

During the eight-day period between the official notification and my Board, I prepared a witness list consisting of over 75 people who could have corroborated my claims of improprieties from my former department and reserve units attached to the base. However, until I was issued the appointment letter of the Board President after its approval by Lekberg, I could not submit my witnesses list.

On the afternoon of November 17, 1993, I found on my desk an undated copy of the appointment letter. I immediately proceeded to submit my witness list to the Board President, but she was nowhere to be found. Without her approval or disapproval of the witness list and her submission of said list to Lekberg for his approval or disapproval, I was in limbo—just where the boys wanted me to be! The long train of constitutional right abuses continued.

My Destiny in The Navy is Decided by Kangaroo Court

On the morning of November 18, 1993, I finally met with my defense attorney, Lieutenant Daniel Inserra. Until that day he had not reviewed the issues of fact or evidence. We had about one hour to go over nine months of evidentiary documentation which reflected that the Navy's mental health system was unlawfully abused.

With such a short time preparing for the hearing, I don't believe that I received an adequate defense. No one can prepare for a hearing in one hour. Knowing this, I informed Inserra that if the questioning required recall of specific facts, I would act as co-counsel on my own behalf.

There are no formal "rules of evidence" for an administrative hearing. In addition, Board members were hand picked by Powell and approved by Lekberg. A reasonable person probably would have concluded from this even before the Board convened that I was going to be recommended for discharge. I never stood a chance within the administrative discharge system. It is too easy to manipulate and abuse.

Even the Appearance of Improprieties Will Not be Tolerated in the Military

The Board was convened at 1300 on the afternoon of November 18, 1993. All sitting members were all from NAS Willow Grove. The prosecutor for the government was Timothy McGugin, the station's legal petty officer. He had no formal legal education, was the same rank as I was, and had never before prosecuted an administrative discharge Board.

McGugin may have been offered a promotion or medal for conducting the kangaroo court and doing the dirty work for Lekberg and Powell. It was a court that no lawyer with integrity would have ever permitted. Just as Dr. Huh's fifteen-minute diagnosis violated medical ethics, the military's legal system was also manipulated with ease because of the chilling effects of Feres.

90

The board began by dealing with several procedural due process issues such as the government's appointment letter of Board members. The government's copy bore the date of September 13, 1993, although I did not receive my undated copy until November 17. This detail showed that procedural due process had been manipulated. The appointment order was falsified and back-dated. This in itself could possibly be considered obstruction of justice.

In a sworn affidavit provided by Chief Fox, she testifies that she observed McGugin on the evening of November 16, 1993, preparing the notification on a computer in her office. This corroborating fact has never been considered by anyone in the Department of Defense.

The Board President, Commander Rene Campos, and eventual signer of my "honorable discharge certificate," ruled that I had failed to provide her the witnesses list in a timely manner. Out of the kindness of her heart, however, she would allow me thirty minutes to obtain three witnesses to testify on my behalf.

I had a witness list of over 75 people who could have presented testimony and evidence supporting genuine issues that I presented to Broyles. I guess being allowed three people was a considerate gesture from Campos!

I could not believe that in America, one's guaranteed constitutional right to "due process of law" from the arbitrary acts of those in power, could be so easily obstructed. But I was in the Armed Forces, and it only got worse.

One of the Board members, hand picked by Lekberg and Powell with apparent orders to obstruct my right to question the government witnesses, was Lieutenant Commander Gumpright, a drinking and golfing buddy of both Lekberg and Powell. Photos in the base newspaper show the two enjoying a good time together on the golf course. I believe that Gumpright's placement on the Board was designed to prevent me from obtaining a fair hearing. His mission was carried out.

Gumpright was Keller's department head, and because of my assistance in the Keller matter, his appointment would never

91

have taken place in any legitimate court of law. It would have been seen as a "couple in bed."

I wanted to challenge Gumpright's presence on the Board, but my defense attorney felt it was not a good idea to challenge him and "piss off" the Board too early on in the proceeding. I followed his advice.

Gumpright's placement on the administrative Board clearly was intended to deprive me of due process and to counter any questions posed or evidence in support of my claim that the mental health system was used to cover up corruption at the Grove.

I was doomed before the Board convened. The government did not finish presenting their case before they ordered me to defend myself against claims that were not established by fact or evidence. My defense attorney and I both knew that the Board was fraudulent, but we were helpless in doing anything to prevent the blatant violations against my rights as protected under the U.S. Constitution!

The Government's Case Does Not Add Up

The government's brief presentation contained no evidence to support my placement into the alcohol rehabilitation system or to justify my alleged failure to participate in the program.

It was countered with a most compelling document.

As a matter of fact, one month prior on October 16, 1993, DAPA Cassidy submitted a six-month treatment assessment follow-up report which reflected the command's perception of my personal and professional conduct. In this report, it reflects that I was recommended for *advancement and retention*, and that no detrimental behaviors or examples of alcohol abuse were observed by my command since my release from ARS.

Cassidy also stated that, "Although Petty Officer Trueman stated he would not follow his aftercare regimen, he is "now participating."

As I stated earlier, the CAAC aftercare contract states that two unauthorized absences will result in termination from the program. Cassidy's report and the command's approval of that

92

report proves that I did not fail the aftercare program! Then why an administrative separation board?

In addition to my command's favorable outlook of my person and to further prove the Board was a sham, Administrative Board questionnaires were provided by my leading petty officer, division chief and department head. They all stated that I was a 4.0 sailor; that I was an asset to their department, that I got along well with others and that they considered me to be an asset to the Navy.

Unfortunately, this evidence was never considered by the Board. Instead they further obstructed my due process rights to defend false claims of the government. At the time of the administrative discharge board, my department head forwarded my annual performance evaluation to Powell and Lekberg. The evaluation includes recommendations for advancement and retention along with many favorable comments about my performance in the Environmental Department.

However, as I stated previously, when Lekberg and Powell got their hands on it they "rewrote" the evaluation to support their position that I was detrimental to good order and discipline.

To support the government's position that I had engaged in an alcohol-related incident and then failed to participate in the in the aftercare program, McGugin called two witnesses to support their case. They were the officials primarily responsible for placing false information of mental illness into my records, Master Chief Donald Feener and DAPA Cassidy.

McGugin started questioning Feener about my alleged alcohol abuse and reasons for my placement in the program. Feener stated that there was an alleged alcohol incident dating back to December 1991. His testimony was contradicted by his own written statement that "no incident ever occurred" in his letter of June 10, 1992 which states:

> "This is to clarify an apparent misunderstanding resulting from my report and referral on YN1 Trueman. I stated in my report that YN1 Trueman had been late to work on several occasions. That was a true statement, however, I did not

mean to imply, nor is there **any evidence** that his lateness was due in any way to the use of alcohol. I liken his occasional lateness to the occasional lateness of the typical sailor who comes in 10-15 minutes late for a variety of domestic reasons.

I feel it is necessary to make this clarification due to the fact that my original statement apparently attracted an inordinate amount of attention in his case."

I obtained the above memorandum from Feener after I confronted him in May 1992 and told him I was going to obtain an attorney to go after him and all others who have slandered my reputation by placing false information in my medical records, a criminal violation of Article 107 of the UCMJ ("falsification of an official document"). These events took place after the Jones fiasco.

Even with Feener's admission that no alcohol related incident was documented, the discharge process continued. As Feener provided more false testimony about the alleged incident, he was opening the door to every witness from my department who could attack his credibility and contradict his testimony. I was not the problem in the department, he was!

Feener was opening the door to a cross-examination that would have led to the true reasons for the reprisals I had faced. Gumpright knew this and also knew that the testimony being given by Feener would be detrimental to the government's case when the cross examination began. Out of the blue he objected to the testimony of the government's number one witness and requested a recess!

To my astonishment, President Campos called a recess. At that point, I told my attorney that the administrative board was bullshit. Since I knew my career was over anyway, I wanted to assume my own defense because I knew every question that needed to be asked, and I already knew the answers!

In about fifteen minutes, the Board reconvened and much of Feener's testimony was stricken from the record, although it would be used later to obstruct justice at the BCNR (Board for

Corrections of Naval Records)[2]. The testimony that was stricken would have allowed witnesses on my behalf from impeaching his testimony. However, Feener's comment that I was a 4.0 sailor was kept in the record.

The President of the Board then dismissed Feener, thus, failing to allow me any cross-examination of the author of the "false and fantasy" theory whereby the Navy Department gave me the boot for allegedly being unfit to serve my country.

The ruling of the Board President to dismiss Feener was set forth in the following legal conclusion: "The issue is not how he got into the program, but why he failed to complete the program." In other words, Feener's testimony was irrelevant.

How can one be tried for a crime which did not take place? How can one be considered detrimental to the military when one's military record is meritorious? How can one not be afforded the opportunity to present evidence and witnesses on one's behalf in a legal proceeding that is supposed to be supported by the U.S. Constitution?

The Next Obstruction of Due Process at the Board

DAPA Cassidy was not present at the Board so that I could properly cross examination the person who accused me of failing the aftercare program by failing to attend meetings. Furthermore, no records of "meeting attendance" were ever kept by Cassidy. His testimony was based upon his memory.

Although Cassidy was not physically present at the Board, the government was gracious enough to set up an telephone conference call to lay the foundation that Cassidy participated in the proceedings. This action gave the appearance that due process had been granted and that I had an opportunity to question my accuser.

Cassidy was shielded from my questions regarding his testimony by Gumpright, who objected to every line of questioning I

2.The BCNR is the administrative remedy process set by Public Law Title 10, U.S.C. Sec. 1552. Before a discharged military member can petition a federal court on "due process" issues, this remedy must be engaged. It allows two or three years to pass before an injustice or material error will be reviewed. A delaying tactic is thus built into the system.

posed to Cassidy. Each of his objections was sustained by the Board President.

When I asked the Board President why Cassidy was not going to be physically present at the administrative Board, Gumpright—not the President of the Board—responded by saying "Cassidy could not be present due to a injury."

Since all my questioning of Cassidy was challenged by Gumpright, I was never able to establish the fact that Cassidy was covering for his buddy Feener's misconduct and incompetence. At one point in Cassidy's telephone testimony, I challenged his claims that I had failed to keep up with my weekly meetings and questioned him about his attendance logs. Gumpright interrupted by saying words to this effect: "How could he testify to the specific facts of alleged alcohol abuse and attendance issues when he doesn't have your file in his possession?"

He was testifying by telephone but didn't have my file in front of him. You would think that the DAPA file would be the most important piece of evidence to support the government's case that I failed to participate in aftercare.

Although I was deprived of this opportunity to discredit Cassidy's testimony, after my discharge I filed a lawsuit to obtain the DAPA record. More on that in the next chapter. I did receive a sworn declaration by Cassidy's replacement stating that he (Cassidy) "did not keep attendance records." That was a very damaging admission, considering that my discharge was undertaken because of attendance issues.

After the Feener and Cassidy performance at the Board, I knew my fate in the Navy was sealed. I requested to made a statement to the Board, and my request was granted.

I proceeded to tell them that it was obvious what was taking place and that my career was over. I assured them that once I left the confines of NAS Willow Grove, I would see to it that justice was served and that they would all be held accountable.

This statement was greeted with looks of amusement and disbelief, especially by Gumpright. The Keller $200,000 settlement and the fact that my fight made its way to national television, is victory in my eyes.

After about six hours of "babble and bullshit" on the part of McGugin and Gumpright, the Board recessed to make their determination as to whether or not my eleven and one half years of meritorious military service would be spared.

While waiting for the Board to reconvene, I was standing outside the hearing room with my attorney and McGugin.

McGugin said to my attorney, "So how do you think I did in my first administrative Board?"

As reflected in his letter to the Chief of Naval Personnel, my attorney knew that a grave injustice within the military's administrative discharge process had just taken place. He shook his head and with a look of disgust walked away.

The Board was still in recess when my attorney returned to the building. McGugin informed both of us that the Navy IG would be on Board the following morning to investigate my Inspector General Complaint against Powell of September 13, 1993!

According to the Whistleblower Protection Act, the investigation of claims of reprisals under the law are to be "expeditiously initiated." Here we were, one day after the administrative Board sham, and the IG was coming to investigate whether my administrative Board was legal or not.

It is obvious from the "modus operandi" of Lekberg and Powell that the Navy IG intentionally delayed their investigation until the administrative Board was finished and had ruled against me.

When the Board reconvened, it was stated that in a vote of 3 to 0, I was found to have failed the aftercare program and was recommended for a general discharge. My attorney objected to the general discharge recommendation. He said, "No matter what, the man's record is meritorious and the only discharge he is entitled to is an honorable!"

97

After a moment of silence, the Board agreed that a certificate of honorable discharge would be recommended to the brass in Washington, D.C. at Navy Headquarters.

The Board's findings were only a recommendation. The ultimate decision to forward a discharge recommendation was solely in the hands of the convening authority, Defendant Lekberg. Even if Lekberg agreed with the recommendation of the Board, the final determination agency as to whether a member will be discharged rested with the Bureau of Naval Personnel. At that time this agency was headed by Admiral McKinney. His involvement in cover up and abuses of human and constitutional rights in the system comes into play later in the book.

After the Board concluded, I left the base and did not return until the next morning. No incidents of misconduct were reported.

Would Due Process Be Granted in The IG's Investigation?

On the morning of November 19, 1993, Commander Williams, an investigator assigned by the Navy IG, arrived to investigate the Powell Complaint of abuse of power. Standing by and willing to testify to abuse of power and other improprieties were all those subordinates that I once led, the witnesses who were never questioned during the Smedberg inquiry in March 1993.

Commander Williams's questioning of me lasted only about forty-five minutes. As he went down the Powell Complaint point by point, he had no pertinent questions that a good investigator might ask such as what evidence do you have to support your claims?

I could have provided statements, documents, and the most important piece of evidence all together—Feener's admission that no incident took place. This was not to be. Williams' investigation was just a simply formality to reject any future claim by me that I was not afforded due process under §1034.

At the conclusion of the interview, Williams said, "Return to your work center to await further questioning." I thanked him and

98

told him that there were others on the base who wanted to speak on my behalf. I said that I assumed Williams would question these key witnesses.

As the day went on I heard nothing from Williams. During my lunch hour, I passed Ski. He said, "We were told that our testimony was not required by the IG."

The long train of abuses that originated on February 7, 1993 continued right up to the very day of the IG investigation! Ski's notification that my witnesses would not be questioned sealed my fate, and career-ending reprisals were about to take place.

At approximately 1330, I was in the CO's building performing job related functions when I was approached by McGugin. He told me that I was to report to the administrative officer at 1530. I had no idea what this meeting was all about. I thought maybe something positive was going to happen.

When I arrived at the administrative officer's office at 1530, I was immediately surrounded by six or seven personnel, including security officers with sidearms. I did not know what to expect or what Lekberg and Powell had up their sleeves.

I soon learned that the very day of the IG inquiry, unfavorable personnel action against me continued to take place before any determination had been made concerning the merits of my complaint. I was informed that I had been found to be "detrimental to the good order and discipline" at NAS Willow Grove and because of that, I was being "barred and transferred" from the command.

To be considered detrimental to good order and discipline is a death wish in the military. I was shocked about how arbitrary these personnel actions were, especially since Williams did not even return to his base to fill out his report for approval of his recommendations.

Therefore, on November 19, 1993, not only had Navy grievance procedures, federal law (i.e. §1034) and the administrative discharge process been severely abused in my case, but the IG, the agency mandated to investigate fraud, waste and abuse, was now openly participating in covering up the corruption at the

99

Grove. (Remember the Navy Inspector General's report on fraud, waste, abuse and reprisals at the Grove?)

After I received notification that I was being barred and transferred, I was escorted to my automobile by a base security officer who said he was going to scrape my base decal off my vehicle. After he did this, the security officer wished me good luck. I can only imagine that the word around the security department was that I was being reprised against, especially in light of the fact that most of my football team worked in that department.

Conflicts of Interest Will Not Be Tolerated

The Pentagon stands by its claim that "even the appearance of conflict will not be tolerated." Nevertheless, from the moment I was barred and transferred I cried foul to Senator Specter and Congressman Weldon of Pennsylvania, pointing out to them that Investigator Williams was in my direct chain of command and that was a conflict-of-interest.

Although I did not know it at the time I spoke with Williams, I later found out that he worked at our headquarters for Captain Brazell, my former department head, executive officer, and subject in the Article 138 complaint! Obviously, from the moment I filed the Article 138, the boys coordinated the effort to continue to discredit my claims of abuse and colluded to obstruct the administration of justice within the military's grievance procedures and the Inspector General program.

I filed a follow-on complaint of reprisal with the Navy IG, Specter and Weldon, claiming that the investigator was biased, that the administrative Board was unlawful and that the process had been abused.

Although a separate investigation under §1034 is required by statute to investigate reprisals, that would never happen. The Navy IG, Specter nor Weldon were not going to pursue the case any longer as it was turning into a political bombshell! What started out between Feener and myself was now snowballing into something larger than life. The military's legal and medical systems were being placed on trial.

I provided my congressional representatives and the Navy IG with evidence that supported my claims that Williams was biased. I did this by explaining that he was a direct subordinate of Captain Brazell at our headquarters. In addition, his position as the "Director of Aviation Training" combined with my former position as the Leading Petty Officer, Aviation Training Department at the Grove, made Williams a direct superior in my chain of command. This was a clear conflict of interest and a violation of the "independence rule" for IG investigations. This point was clearly established but never acted upon by any lawyer within the government.

The Final Months of a Once Promising Career

At the conclusion of the capricious administrative discharge board, and the sham IG investigation of Williams, I was barred and transferred from the Grove to Naval Base Philadelphia, to await a decision from Bureau of Naval Personnel in Washington D.C., as to the fate of my career.

After I reported for duty in Philadelphia and met with the Command Master Chief, I was assigned to the Naval Legal Services Office (NLSO), to perform administrative functions within the Navy's legal system. I found it ironic to be assigned to the very program that was condoning human right abuses in the military's mental health system.

I determined to make the best of it. I was inspired by the assignment and it did help me to keep the faith to continue to fight the war even if I was unlawfully discharged. I was surprised when I was assigned to NLSO. I figured I would be assigned to supervise a clean-up crew or some other menial job so that I would not have access to anyone or anything that could help me build a strong case against abuses of our rank and file members in the Armed Forces by corrupted leaders.

During my assignment at NLSO, I provided administrative assistance to the NLSO Officer and his staff. Except for one civilian employee, I respected and got along with all of them.

My primary duty was to review Court Martial proceedings to assure that all required documents were in order prior to submission to higher authority, along with other legal assistance work. In light of the tremendous abuses in the military medical and legal systems that were taking place in my case at that time, and my determination to fight those abuses, one would think that the Navy would keep me as far away from anything pertaining to legal issues and procedures, or cases that could help prove that when the "Pentagon" wants to destroy someone who criticizes the system for its improprieties, it can with ease due to Feres.

Another Example of How the Administrative Discharge Process Can Be Easily Abused

I am going to share a story of a young sailor I met when I was a recorder at his administrative Board to provide you with another example as to how the administrative process can be abused by commanders who are out to get you.

A young sailor was being processed for sexual harassment. He had already faced a court marital on that charge, was found guilty and reduced in rank but not discharged. Obviously, the court for whatever reasons felt that the evidence did not justify discharging the sailor, so they gave him the opportunity to continue to serve his country.

At the conclusion of the Board, I had an opportunity to speak with the young sailor and I asked him about what he felt about being tried for the same alleged crime twice. He said, "I think it is really messed up." He went on to tell me that his CO did not like him and because the court martial did not recommend his discharge, he had it in for him and used the administrative separation process to achieve his desires.

At the conclusion of the Board, the three panel members recommended that the sailor be allowed to continue his career because a court martial did not discharge him. I asked the man if he had sexually harassed the female sailor in question. He said he only tried to "console" her because they were friends and gave her a hug.

Because his command needed a scapegoat to put the issue at rest, he was chosen.

After talking to him for about a half hour, I believed him and felt sorry for him. If anyone knew how the system could be abused to benefit a corrupt CO, I did. What caught my attention is that the young sailor stated that the female he was alleged to have sexually harassed stood up on his behalf and said that he did not sexually harass her! However, once the process was underway, facts were ignored and evidence was obviously manipulated because his CO was out to get him. When all was said and done, the Board recommended him for retention and wished him well in his remaining months in the Navy.

Working Closely with Those Who Deal with the Nut Cases and Problem Children

With my assignment at NLSO, I worked closely with personnel assigned to the Transient Personnel Unit (TPU). This unit is for Navy personnel who are awaiting transfer to another command or awaiting discharge for either honorable or dishonorable reasons. TPU is the Navy's "holding tank" until the paperwork from Washington D.C. arrives on the scene for those awaiting orders to move on.

Due to my daily contact with TPU, many personnel thought I was part of the staff. When I made it know that I was awaiting discharge myself, they were surprised. I wore my uniform with pride, achieved many personal and unit awards and was a young looking First Class Petty Officer. Because of this, many of the people in TPU did not understand why I would be getting out of the Navy. When they asked me about this, I would tell them, "I am being reprised against for standing up for the rights of my subordinates."

On further questioning I would explain the facts. Many wished me well and said things such as, "Beat those ass holes from your former command for initiating a retaliatory discharge against you." One young petty officer said, "You should write a book because you know what you're talking about. Maybe you can help others in the future to bring about a change in this system."

Knowing the end was near, I found the final weeks at my aftercare meetings were kind of fun in that I had a chance to speak my mind with the counselors who controlled my destiny in that program. Each Thursday when the group met, I would get them involved after repeatedly stating that the program is being abused for retaliatory reasons. (Remember, I was accused of not attending these meeting.)

When asked the "weekly question," "Jeff, how are you doing with your recovery?" I would make comments such as, "It is hard to recover from a disease that you don't even have!"

This would outrage some of the counselors, and they would respond, "Jeff you're in denial." In all fairness, there were some pretty cool dudes who administered the program, but none powerful enough to prevent abuses within it.

In any case, my comments set the tone for others to speak their minds, and I learned that most of them were also in the program for reasons other than alcohol abuse. My strong stance and claims that I was in the program due to reprisals and my speaking my mind about it seemed to open the door for others to tell their stories of retaliation resulting in their placement in the alcohol abuse program. Some claimed that they experienced the same abuses in the system that I had.

I drove those counselor nuts by engaging my fellow groupies in pointing out their feelings as to abuses in the system and the lack of accountability of those who administer the system and abuse their professional ethics, if not the law!

For one meeting the Regional Director was in attendance and listened to our stories. At the end of the session, he said to me, "Maybe we will use your situation as a case study" and I responded "That's fine, but, how about correcting the injustices in my case now!"

"Jeff," he said, "you know the system is the system and there is not much I can do."

His answer was total bunk, and I said, "You're in charge of the program. Fix it!" I never heard from him again.

At the time of my assignment at the Philadelphia Naval Base, I believed that I was falling deeper and deeper into depression. Each morning it was getting more and more difficult to get up and motivated to go to work. Each day, the ten-minute drive from my hometown to the base seemed longer as I awaited the word from Washington D.C. as to my destiny in the Navy. In some ways the waiting to find out what my life had in store for me was almost as difficult as dealing with the many reprisals I had faced the prior year.

The Decision is Finally Handed Down From Washington

On the morning of January 10, 1994, I was informed by the NLSO Officer that the Navy Department had authorized my discharge and that I had to report back to NAS Willow Grove for out-processing. I was told to report to the main gate on the morning of January 11, 1994 and await an escort from the security department. Although I was saddened that my career could be terminated without ever being convicted or charged with any crime that actually took place, I was ready to move on!

When I arrived at the base on the morning of January 11, 1994, I was met by two armed security officials at the main gate. They had been appointed by Powell to escort me through both my medical and administrative out-processing. Here I was, a Veteran with eleven and a half years of honorable service to my country, being escorted by armed guards!

I knew one of those guards because he'd played third base for me when I coached the Navy's softball team.

After I reported to the base medical department, there was a problem finding a doctor who would clear me for discharge. Since I was friends with many medical personnel who also played on my football and softball teams, those in the medical department knew that I had been retaliated against for attempting to get a congressional investigation of the base. After several attempts by one of the Navy corpsman to find "anyone" who would perform my discharge physical, finally, after the first two doctors he asked said "no", a new doctor on station agreed to do my physical.

Before the physical started, I informed this doctor that I was in physical therapy for an previous neck injury. I asked to be put on medical hold and granted a medical board prior to my discharge. My request was ignored. However, after my discharge, the Veterans Administration rated me with a 10 percent disability due to the injury.

After some probing and the usual "bend over and cough" routine and about an hour's time, I was physically cleared for discharge. As many hundreds of thousands of military people have experienced, medical holds sometimes last for months and even longer in some cases. The fact is that you cannot be enlisted into the military with an existing medical injury, nor can you be discharged with one! For most people who have been placed on medical hold, I can guarantee if they could get an "hour" release from active duty, they would take it without any questions asked!

When I joined the Navy at eighteen, I had no pre-existing medical conditions. I should have never been cleared for discharge with an existing neck injury. I would be willing to bet that I achieved one of the fastest discharges in the history of the Navy because my claims were legitimate.

At the conclusion of the medical process I was escorted to the Personnel Support Detachment (PSD), to begin my administrative out-processing. I had worked closely with many of those folks at PSD when I was assigned to the Reserve Programs Department. They knew that I was being retaliated against but could not do anything about it except wish me well.

During the out-processing phase, the discharge clerk assigned to my case stopped what she was doing and look me square in the eyes and said, "Can I ask you a question, Petty Officer Trueman?"

I smiled and said, "You can call me Jeff, I am no longer in the Navy."

"I have done many discharges for alcohol abuse in my career," she said, "but I have never seen one like yours."

"Why is that?" I asked.

"I have gone through your record, and I cannot find anything to justify this discharge."

"You know what happens to people who challenge the good
ole boys," I replied.

She just shook her head in disbelief. She was probably
thinking that if I could be railroaded out of the Navy with a perfect record, so could she! Her unbiased opinion made it possible
for her to look at the facts and know that an injustice was taking
place. Her words were compelling words and reflect the devasta-
tion the Feres Doctrine places on innocent victims of abusive or
incompetent military personnel.

On the morning of January 12, while PSD was continuing to
prepare my paperwork for discharge, I was given my Department
of Labor, Transition Assistance (TAMP) seminar. For most honorably discharged veterans the seminar is five days in duration.
Once again, I was cheated out of benefits rightfully due me. **I was
given my transition benefits brief in one hour!**

Lekberg and Powell wanted to continue to slap me in the
face until my final moments on the Grove.

The Foundation of My Fight at The
United States Supreme Court

I arrived to be briefed as to my involuntary-honorable discharge
benefits. The one-hour meeting with Brian Hontz, the TAMP
Coordinator, would eventually lead to a false arrest and malicious
prosecution against my person as a private citizen of the United
States.

I had known Hontz in my position as the Training Department Leading Petty Officer. We provided classroom and other
support for the TAMP seminar he provided at the Grove. Hontz
was a pretty decent guy and a former Marine.

He explained to me that I could continue to utilize base
facilities such as the base's employment computer system and
exchange on any military installation in the world for a period of
two years from the date of my discharge. I told him that Lekberg
had barred me from the base as a military member. He responded,

107

"You are an honorably discharge veteran now, and you have the right to utilize our employment system."

His words, added to the failure of the Navy Department to release any evidence to support their allegations that I suffered from mental illness or engaged in any conduct of a detrimental nature and its failure to comply with the Freedom of Information/ Privacy Act (FOIA/PA) and release the documents it claims justified my discharge, would lead to the malicious prosecution.

The Final Hours in the Service of My Country

On the morning of January 12 Captain Hargis, an investigator from the CNARF IG, was at the air station to investigate my claims that the Williams' investigation of November 19, 1993 was biased and that the barring and transfer orders issued that same day violated federal law.

The Williams' inquiry which went down on the day I was unlawfully barred and transferred in violation of §1034. Not surprisingly, the follow-up inquiry to determine whether Williams was biased in his investigation was conducted on the next to last day of my military career! Since my career was down to its final hours, at the advice of my civilian attorney I denied to be interviewed by Hargis. I knew it would be futile.

I told Hargis, who was sent from New Orleans that I had nothing further to say. Hargis made a quick phone call to Olson and Brazell to find out what he should do. After the call Hargis said to me, "This is your last chance to tell your side of the story."

I told Hargis that on the advice of my attorney I would not answer any further questions.

Finally, after all the paperwork was signed on January 12, 1994, I was escorted off the base by Chief Koslak from the Manpower Department. In our short ride from PSD to my car which I was ordered to park outside the main gate, the chief wished me good luck. Although I did not know him well, I had seen him around the base. As we pulled up to my car, the chief said, "If I can be of any help please let me know."

"Thank you," I said, wondering why he had said this.

"My career is essentially over also," he said, "and I plan on retiring later in the year because Feener destroyed my chances for future advancement."

He told me that when he worked at PSD, the leading chief there was facing charges of fraternization. Koslac said Feener had approached him and tried to convince him to protect his buddy who was on trial by testifying on his behalf as a character witness. Because Chief Koslac refused to do so, Feener's ability to use his rank to destroy anyone he thinks has crossed him again prevailed. Koslac told me that after he refused to lie on behalf of Feener's buddy, he was transferred from his department and sent to the manpower department, essentially a demotion that would reflect negatively on his next performance evaluation.

Chief Koslac's department head was no other than Commander Campos, the president of my administrative board. The circle of good ole boys and gals in charge at the Grove, although small in numbers, held tremendous powers, which they all used to cover up the substantial amount of corruption that I have so far documented in this book.

Another Insult to Injury

Even as my career was coming to an end and I was facing a serious dilemma as to how I was going to support my family, Feener's career continued to flourish. Just before my discharge, the Navy promoted Feener to Master Chief Petty Officer, the top rank in the enlisted rank structure. Feener was also granted the right by Lekberg to reenlist and chose Gary Powell as the officer to administer the "oath" to defend and protect the Constitution.

This troubled me, considering the fact that Feener reenlisted in downtown Philadelphia, the home of the Declaration of Independence, United States Constitution and birthplace of our freedom and that I had given eleven and one-half years of my life representing that part of our country and its people.

Life is strange, especially in the U.S. Navy!

109

A Moment Of Reflection

I said good-bye to Chief Koslac and sat in my car for a few minutes trying to regain my composure. Reality set in like a ton of bricks dropping on my head as I slowly realized that the only life I had known as an adult had ended.

During the past year while faced with repeated abuses of my human and constitutional rights, I kept the hope alive that someone in the system would intervene and stop the retaliation and abuses. That would not be the case. Feener, Rumery, Powell, Broyles, Lekberg, and the others made a complete mockery of their constitutional oaths and the systems of justice and medicine within the United States Armed Forces.

As difficult as that day was, I technically had one more day left in my career due to the fact that my honorable discharge certificate, DD-214, and severance pay would not be issued until January 13. Once again I had to return to base to meet with my former co-worker Nancy Presley, who was now in charge of the discharge section at PSD, to retrieve all relevant documents for my transition into civilian life.

When I awoke on the morning of January 13, 1994, I was in a state of severe depression. As I drove the forty miles from my hometown to the Grove, I kept thinking what was I going to do with no job and a family with two young children to support. On top of losing my military career, the only life I had known since the age of eighteen, I knew that the strain of it all and my placing "duty, honor, country" over my own family's well-being, was finally taking its toll on my marriage.

Mental health professionals agree that the three most difficult periods in a person's life are (1) losing a loved one; (2) losing a job; and (3) relocating to a new home. I was hit with all three events almost simultaneously.

I knew I had to pull myself together and lose any self-pity that I may have been experiencing. I set out to vindicate myself and expose to the nation the U.S. Military's practice of destroying people who, for the good of the American people, report corruption.

110

Chapter 5

Beginning Anew

Finding the positives out of the negatives

At approximately 10 a.m. on January 13, 1994 I was handed my discharge papers. Nancy handed me my papers and gave me a hug. We both wished each other well. My journey into a new life was beginning, and I knew I had to pull myself together and focus on many things. My biggest concern was how I was going to support a wife and two children. Although I was honorably discharged from the military, the reasons stated by the military for my discharge were detrimental. Who was going to hire a guy who was thrown out of the military with an alleged mental disorder after eleven and a half years in the service. My prospects for employment were not positive.

In 1994 my total income was only $1,773.51 according to the Social Security Administration. Imagine trying to feed and house a family of four on that small amount of income! I felt worthless and almost broke mentally as a result.

The Moment I Vowed to Fight Corruption in the System

As I approached the exit to my hometown, I decided that I had to go see my mentor Steve to let him know what had happened after I proceeded up the chain of command. I had not seen Steve since I spoke to him about the problems at the base prior to my February 1993 meeting with Broyles. I knew something positive would come from talking with him about my future and how I should proceed with continuing my own fight for justice.

By the time I arrived at the Italian restaurant where Steve bartended, I was falling apart emotionally. I truly needed to talk with him. I always knew that no matter how bad things seemed to be for me, Steve was would always be there to get me through it no matter what it took! I looked up to him so much as a "big brother." He was always there to listen when I needed a true friend. Only God knows that on the afternoon of January 13, 1994 I needed more than ever, any advice my "brother" could offer. As I walked into the restaurant and sat down at the far end of the bar, I looked around to see where he was. I did not see him.

I waited for someone to approach me. All of Steve's coworkers were at the end of the bar talking. Suddenly I heard the most distressful yell from one of the waitresses who was on the phone. She said the following words that changed me forever: "Oh my God, they just found Steve dead in his apartment!"

My heart dropped, and the faces of all of Steve's co-workers turned towards me with a look of disbelief and sorrow. They knew that we were like brothers, and Steve always spoke highly of me as a person to many of his family and friends. I left the restaurant and drove to Steve's apartment praying to God that what I heard was not true. When I arrived at Steve's apartment I asked a police officer on the scene if Steve had passed away, and he said, "Yes."

The abuse of power, reprisals, lies, intimidation, etc., that I had just experienced over the past eleven months no longer seemed important. No amount of money or professional accomplishments compared to the loss of one of the dearest friends I could have ever have.

At that moment in time, nothing seemed to matter to me. With all the scum that walks among us in life, why did a truly decent person like Steve have to leave this life before his time? I felt sorrow, anger and rage inside me that January evening.

Steve's passing changed me forever. To deal with his loss, I walked out of his apartment and for the next two hours until my dear friend was taken away, I stood in a cold January rain and sobbed like a child. As Steve's family members and friends departed, I felt sorrow for all those who loved him dearly, especially for his mother, Mrs. Condi, who had lost her husband of 51 years one year earlier and now had lost her only son.

Not only did I lose a military career that day, a career in which Steve had been a major influence, but I also had to face the pain of knowing my buddy of only 52 years was gone due to a heart attack.

I wasn't sure if I could overcome so much heartbreak all in one day. We were living with my buddy Huzz at that time. As day became night I started on my way home to inform my wife and Huzz that the end of my career had just taken place. I walked in the apartment and saw Huzz and my wife and children sitting there talking. I looked at them and said, "Well, my career is finally over, and I just found out my buddy Steve has passed away." I went straight to bed and cried myself to sleep.

For the next couple of days, I tried to focus on what I was going to do in life. I was twelve years behind my fellow graduates of 1981. With so many issues to deal with at one time, it would take me about a year and a half before I could cope with the aftermath of the events of January 13, 1994, and finally put my life into some form of normalcy.

Good-bye My Friend

Four days later I awoke to a day I was not sure I could deal with. My buddy Steve would be laid to rest that day. It was also my thirtieth birthday. There I was, turning thirty years old with two children and no job and a marriage that was all but over, going to the funeral of a man who meant so much to me.

On the drive to South Philadelphia where the mass for Steve was held, I felt sorrow. When I walked into the Roman Catholic Church were the service was being held, I began to shake. I could not face the reality that Steve was no longer with us.

After the mass was completed, the procession left South Philadelphia for our final journey to lay to rest my good buddy in Darby, Pennsylvania at the same cemetery where my Italian relatives were buried. As Steve was laid to rest, I waited for all his family and friends to pay their last respects so that I could deal with my loss in my own way. To ensure that forever I would be with him, I lay on top of my buddy's casket my dress blue Navy

113

jumper top with all the medals that I had received for service to my country.

As I explained previously, I had given Steve a shadow box a year earlier when he received his medals twenty-seven years after he left Vietnam. In exchange, he gave me the lighter the members of his unit received when they departed Vietnam. I also asked him if I could have one of his dog tags. Steve thought that request was a bit strange, but after I was persistent with him, he gave it to me. From that day on I've worn his dog tag to give me strength to make it through each day.

My thirtieth birthday was a somber day, and the events of that day helped me realize that I had to fight with everything I had inside me. I had no choice but to wage battle against a civilian and military government that has continued for decades to screw "rank and file" military members and their families because of political agendas.

After the mass and burial for Steve, a couple of his buddies asked me if I wanted to join them for dinner. I accepted. That evening we joked about our experiences with Steve, and I found out how special this man was to many people. When the night ended, there was still a tremendous void inside me. I felt isolated from the world, even with many family and friends on my side.

I Picked up a Pen Rather than a Rifle

The next day after Steve's funeral and five days after my wrongful discharge, I started writing this book to deal with my thoughts of revenge. My fight for whatever I had to do to bring about reforms to protect the rights of our "rank and file" military members started in earnest that day. With no money to defend the cause, I set out armed only with determination and the mindset that no matter the difficulties and hardship I knew I would face, I was going to prevail in one way or another.

I began my fight for vindication to clear my military records of false information by putting my mind in a quarterback mode and taking on the challenge of the constitutionality of the Feres

114

Doctrine. I would do this the same way I still move my football team down the field: planning execution and luck.

The drive began from our one-foot line, and we had 99.9 yards to go to victory, a successful challenge against Feres at the U.S. Supreme Court.

The Drive Begins

I began the drive for self-vindication and justice for all rank and file members by preparing my first request to obtain all the detrimental information which the Navy claims they used to justify their discharging me for alleged mental shortcomings.

I began by putting together a plan of action to attack the government's legal position that my mind evaporated from the period of December 23, 1992 through March 27, 1993. At the same time I was struggling with the heartache resulting from the fact that my wife and I had lost touch. On January 18, 1994, we decided that separation and moving her and the kids back to her hometown in Duluth, Minnesota was the best thing to do.

My intentions were to continue to pressure Senator Specter and Congressman Weldon to investigate Broyles, Lekberg and Powell for abuse of power and misuse of the military's mental health system. I knew it would be best to remove my family from my presence to ensure they were in no danger of retaliation. We all know that sometimes those who run our government will set up people who are perceived as a threat to their power. I have been asked hundreds of times over the years if I was afraid that the government would take me out. I always reply: "Many have sacrificed for this country long before me. I am not afraid to die for my family and friends' freedom.

My wife and I decided it would be best for me to remain in the Philadelphia area and attempt to find myself and continue the fight against the boys at the Grove. As stated previously, I was working at that time with Tony Keller and others from the base to provide aides of Senator Arlen Specter and Harris Wolford with enough evidence to initiate a congressional investigation of Lekberg and Powell.

Standing in Line for a Handout

A few days after Steve's funeral and just prior to moving my family, I proceeded to the unemployment line to wait for the government to provide me with money so that I could survive. I felt beaten and battered. Standing in line waiting to register for unemployment made me feel like a complete nobody. The reality that I might not be able to feed or shelter my family started to set in.

My self-esteem may have been at an all-time low, but I was not going to quit fighting. I continued to seek the "positives" out of all the "negatives" that had consumed my life. I had to rely on unemployment to get by for six months, but I was home and surrounded by my family and friends who were supportive of my dilemma with the U.S. Government.

I was also lucky to have a true friend in my buddy Huzz who housed my family during the final months of my career and allowed me to stay with him until my eventual return to Minnesota. Without Huzz's help, I don't think I could have made it to where I am today!

Good People Make All the Difference

The next positive happened while I was at the unemployment office talking with the Veterans Representative in Chester, Pennsylvania, a Vietnam veteran.

He told me about a businessman in the community named Carl who helped veterans prepare resumes for civilian life. Besides preparing a resume for me, Carl also help me prepare a rebuttal to my final evaluation, which the Navy Department refused to allow into the official record.

Remember, my final performance evaluation submitted by my department head recommended me for advancement and retention and called me an "asset" to the Navy. Once in the hands of Powell and Lekberg, the evaluation was rewritten to state that I was detrimental to order and discipline. The issue of the rewritten evaluation should never have been brushed under the carpet as it was by the bigwigs in Washington.

116

The rebuttal to this mangled evaluation was never submitted into the official record. Lekberg's falsification of that official document was therefore approved by the highest ranks of the United States Navy Department.

Carl reassured me that the fight was worth fighting and told me a story about his brother who was once a bigwig in the Navy Department suffered an injustice similar to mine. He was fired unlawfully and maliciously, but later he won his battle with the government. This gave me reassurance that I if I kept fighting I'd prevail in the end.

Carl's story about his brother was the first story in a long train of stories[3] that I heard about an American who was destroyed by a government official.

I deeply appreciated Carl's kind words and assistance in helping me achieve employment.

Saying Good-bye to my Family

The day arrived when I had to relocate my family back to Minnesota for the second time in less than a year.

After my discharge finally arrived, the loss of Steve and my decision to fight the Clinton military establishment caused tremendous stress between Tina and myself. For a long time, we did not see eye to eye on the issue of my seeking vindication for our family—nor may we ever. Tina took the logical approach that most reasonable people would: to "move on in life" after one experiences an injustice. My approach to life is quite the opposite. I truly believe that if government officials can maliciously violate the constitutional rights of any one person, and one does not challenge that abuse, it could happen to all of us! Because I love my country and its people for the most part, my convictions as an American and a veteran, prevent me from simply moving on in life.

With totally different belief systems, we were unable to communicate effectively with each other. This cost us dearly with

---

3. Stories that VERPA intends to publish in the future.

respect to our marital bond, and it was a painful experience to go through.

When we decided to separate, my emotional state of mind was challenged with the knowledge that I would not be seeing my children for a long time.

The presence of my kids in my life has helped me control my anger and thoughts of retaliation. The drive to Minnesota was long and difficult. Neither my wife Tina nor I really knew what to say to each other. Here were two people who had shared each other's lives for the past ten years who felt like complete strangers because I had placed duty to country over my own self-interests.

I sometimes wonder if it was worth all the hardships, but there was no turning back from the road I chose to take. When we finally arrived in Minnesota, I started looking for a place for my family live as I knew I would be returning immediately to Philadelphia to pursue a congressional investigation against the leadership officials at the Grove. I knew I could not continue to fight on if I were worried about my family's well-being. After looking at various places, I took a chance and moved into a home on the hillside area of Duluth. Our next-door neighbor was Paul Chesney, a man who became one my most special friends.

Paul is another average American who gave me a helping hand when I needed one. He has been there for my family and I from the first day we met. When Paul and I first met, I told him that I was an honorably discharged veteran but that I had to go back to Philadelphia to deal with ongoing legal issues against the Navy. I told him that I would probably not be returning to Duluth for six months or more.

Paul told me he had grown up in the house he occupied. He was a musician and a music teacher. Paul assured me that he would look out for my family when I was away.

When it was time to leave Duluth for Philadelphia, I felt guilty saying good-bye to my children but placed my complete trust in Paul. He came through for me, making my stay in Philadelphia a lot less worry free and stressful than it would have been otherwise.

Paul and his wonderful wife Rhonda are still close friends.

The War Between This Civilian and the U.S. Military Begins

When I returned to Ridley Park after relocating my family, I began the arduous task of figuring out how I was going to gather enough evidence to support my claim of wrongful discharge as well as proving that the Navy IG obstructed justice by falsifying its investigative reports to support Lekberg's unlawful acts.

I knew I needed a sharp focus on the facts to win the war. I also knew my quest would be obstructed all the way by the government because my vindication would open the floodgates, and hundreds if not thousands of people would surface with stories of similar injustices during their military career. Unfortunately for government officials, the playing field these days is much more level thanks to the Internet.

For the first several weeks after my return to my hometown, the fact that I could not see my children weighed heavily on my mind. Huzz, my crazy ex-sailor buddy, helped me get through the difficult times without my kids.

Huzz was a genuine one-of-a-kind person. I met him the summer of 1986 on the day of "Live Aid," when I was stationed at the Philadelphia naval shipyard while my ship, the U.S.S. Independence, was in dry dock for a four-year major overhaul. "Live Aid" was a big event involving two concerts simultaneously conducted in Philadelphia and London to raise money for famine victims in Africa.

There was electricity in the air that day. Everyone in the entire Philadelphia area was "partying it up." I was sitting outside my neighbor's apartment cooking out and having some brew while we watch the concert on TV. About 4:30 p.m. I saw "Huzz" walking towards his apartment from work.

I had seen Huzz many times before and always said hello, but that day I yelled, "Hey do you want a beer?"

119

He responded "Be right down!" I must say that it was the best beer I ever offered in my life!

From that day Huzz and I became great friends. If one of us is "off his rocker" I would have to say it is Huzz. He once said to me, "The Navy Department was corrupt when I was in there (1951-1955). There is no doubt about it. You are correct in your claims." To this day, we still communicate and see each other every couple of years.

Once I settled in, I began to build a case against the U.S. Navy Department to prove that my discharge was unlawful and that military investigators obstructed justice to cover up human right abuses in the military's mental health system. To begin the discovery phase, I filed requests under the provisions of the Freedom of Information/Privacy Act (FOIA/PA) to obtain any information that remotely reflected that I was detrimental to good order and discipline and/or suffered from mental illness.

By law, the government has ten business days to respond to a FOIA/PA act request and if they do not, it must be appealed to the next level of command known as the Initial Denial Authority (IDA). If the IDA refuses to act on the appeal, then a citizen can file a lawsuit in federal district court to compel release of the documents requested.

I knew there were no documents of a detrimental nature in my record to support any misconduct or mental shortcomings as the military has claimed because I obtained my official microfiche record from Washington D.C. and a hard copy of my military records prior to discharge.

My first FOIA/PA request was sent to NAS Willow Grove, requesting all documents from my military records reflecting; fit-for-duty counselings, alcohol incident reports, and any other documents reflecting I was detrimental to good order and discipline and suffered from mental illness. My request received a response from Lekberg that stated: *"Fishing expeditions are not authorized under the Act."* Fishing expedition? All I asked for was the documents to justify the negative statements that were placed in my files. Was I so wrong to seek this information?

Not only was the response months late in violation of the law, Lekberg felt that he did not have to comply with the law, so he did not. In the wake of Lekberg's deliberate attempt to cover up the fact that no detrimental information ever existed in my military records, I proceeded to file additional requests with the Navy IG.

I took this route because the Inspector General's office ultimately ruled against me regarding the merit of my claims of fraud, waste and abuse and reprisals. They must have had evidence reflecting that Lekberg and Powell were justified in taking unfavorable personnel actions in the wake of protected communications made in accordance with federal law. Or at least that's what I thought.

At this point I didn't care so much about losing my career. Honor and my family's name, however, were definitely worth fighting for.

The Drive to the Goal Line (The U.S. Supreme Court) Gets Underway

In addition to my request to the Navy IG for the information they relied on to justify my discharge, the next tactical move was to for me to obtain my G.I. Bill benefits, which were not offered me at my discharge out-processing. I figured at a minimum, while I waited the long drawn-out process of attempting to gain reinstatement, I could attend college. I also assumed that if I could get the government to admit that I had not been afforded my transition benefits, it would be a small victory in supporting the fact that my one-hour transition seminar was outrageous since I received an honorable discharge.

The first play I called was on February 8, 1994, when I wrote the Assistant Secretary of Defense Force Management and Personnel and expressed my concerns that my discharge had been rushed, and that I had not been afforded my full college education benefits as required under the law. I provided them with the names of three individuals who handled my discharge processing and could corroborate the deprivation of my benefits. In response to my initial request, I was notified by some bureaucrat at the DOD that *"I was afforded all my benefits"* and it was further stated that I acknowledged that fact due to my signing an administrative remarks statement of January 12, 1994.

This response from the DOD, needless to say, made me angry, and I became more determined than before to fight the issue and gain an admission that I had not been not afforded the opportunity to enroll in college.

I figured that this "play" would result in an incomplete pass and was surprised when I received a letter dated November 22, 1994 (nine months after my initial inquiry), from a Linda Thomas in the DOD. She had spoken to Carol Reiss about my request and follow-up rebuttal to the DOD's initial denial of my benefits. Her letter reads in part:

> "In response to your recent inquiry concerning your Montgomery G.I. Bill (MGIB) enrollment status, we have verified that **you were eligible**, but it appears that you were **never** counseled and afforded the opportunity to enroll."

This verification that I had been denied my honorable discharge benefits due through the G.I. Bill was one of the first big yardage plays in proving the lack of concern or sheer incompetence of people we call public servants. Finally, the offensive attack was on the move!

Abuse of Power and Reprisals Are Condoned at the top of the Navy Department

One month after my discharge in February 1994 and nine months after I began the Article 138 complaint process, my hopes were high that the civilians running the Clinton Navy Department would intervene and address my claim of abuse of its mental health system and corruption at the Grove. However, the Assistant Secretary of the Navy, Manpower and Reserve Affairs (ASN M&RA) who at that time was Frederick Paug, ruled that none of the issues claiming abuse of the military's mental health system and corruption at the Grove had any merit.

Therefore, no investigation was ever initiated. The cover-up to protect Broyles and his buddy Olson had reached the highest levels of the Clinton Navy Department.

In May, 1994, after the ASN (M&RA) condoned intentional and deliberate violation of §1034's prohibition of sending military members for mental health examinations in the wake of protected communications, I filed my "Application for Reinstatement" with the Board for Correction of Naval Records (BCNR) as required by law.

I must take a moment to explain the BCMRs (Board for Corrections of Military Records) their functions, and connection with the MWBP Act. Each military branch has a BCMR, which are mandated under Public Law, Title 10 U.S.C. §1552 to correct an "error or injustice" placed in a service member's military records.

The boards consist of civilian employees assigned under each branch of the military, but are supervised by federally appointed officials. Independence and justice are not always rendered when a case points out severe abuses within the medical and legal systems in the Armed Forces. Instead, politics come into play. The buck stops nowhere, especially in a government that is anti-military.

Holding the Navy's Top Dog to His Word

During the time I was preparing to seek reinstatement and after I had exhausted the Navy Department's Article 138 process, I happened to be watching the News Hour and listened to the Secretary of the Navy, Mr. Dalton emphasizing "the importance of people and Core Values in the United States Navy."

As I listened to Secretary Dalton speak of the importance of "people" in the Navy, I knew I had to challenge his words as to "core values" and the importance of "people" in the military service, especially considering the fact that human right abuses were taking place on his watch. I wrote him a letter explaining that I had been unlawfully discharged from the Navy after engaging in protected communications under federal law. I further explained that the Navy IG was obstructing the administration of justice under the whistleblower statute and explained how this was revealed with the assignment of Williams. Additionally, I requested that Article 138 be re-investigated and that all evidence be considered. Most importantly, I requested that individuals who had been willing to testify on my behalf and corroborate the facts of corruption at the Grove, be interviewed.

On May 25, 1994, I received a letter from Rear Admiral H. C. McKinney which stated:

Dear Mr. Trueman,

Thank you for your letter of May 1, 1994, to the Secretary of the Navy requesting a reinvestigation of your Article 138. I am responding for Secretary Dalton. I recognize that you are dissatisfied with the results of the investigation. Your allegations were taken very seriously and were properly investigated by the Navy Inspector General, who found the allegations to be not substantiated. Consequently, your request for reinvestigation cannot be approved.

The Board for the Correction of Naval Records received your petition on May 20, 1994. Because your case is currently under review, it would be inappropriate for me to comment further.

I appreciate your bringing this matter to my attention."

At the time he wrote this letter, Admiral McKinney was Deputy Chief of Naval Personnel, the same agency that had approved the Lekberg discharge recommendation. That document was filled with false and misleading information that fit his strategy to discharge me with false claims of mental illness and detrimental behaviors. It was accepted by McKinney's agency even though my attorney had filed a letter stating that "a grave injustice" had taken place at my admin board.

McKinney's agency is also the one that refused to place into the official record the rebuttal to my final performance evaluation.

For Mr. McKinney to assert that the Article 138 process was "taken very seriously and properly investigated" by the Navy Inspector General" is disingenuous.

Does the Rule of Man Govern the Rule of Law in America?

One day after the McKinney response, I received a letter from Captain Turner, Legal Assistant to the Navy IG. He stated that my request under the FOIA/PA seeking any "official" document that reflected I had been involved in any way with wrongdoing, should be obtained directly from NAS Willow Grove. This notification changed the landscape of the legality involved in my quest to expose human right abuses in the military's mental health system.

At that time I was in the planning stages to rejoin my family in Minnesota because nothing was being done by my Congressional Representatives, and remaining in the Philadelphia area working with others from the base seemed futile.

Therefore, when I received the letter from Turner telling me to submit my request directly to NAS Willow Grove I realized I could take care of two birds with one stone. At approximately 5:30 a.m. on the morning of May 27, 1994, I was sitting in my kitchen pondering over a cup of coffee as to whether or not I should hand deliver my FOIA/PA Act request to the Grove. I thought maybe that would not be a good move in light of the hostilities that had taken place there during my active duty assignment.

However, I had been told by Captain Turner to deal directly with the base, and the Transition Coordinator had given me official notification that I was allowed access to any base in the world, including NAS Willow Grove, for two years following my discharge. I proceeded to take care of my "official business" and to retrieve benefits rightfully due me under law.

When I arrived at the main gate of the base, I was stopped by the base sentry and asked to produce identification. Once my DOD vehicle decal was checked for its validity, I was granted access to the base by police at the base where Lekberg held command. **I was granted access by Lekberg's base police once I produced valid U. S. government identification.** As you probably know, you cannot just walk onto a military installation if you are not escorted by a sponsor or in possession of valid government identification.

Federal law further grants a military commander the legal authority to bar civilians from installations if they feel they are detrimental to the safety of people or facilities on the base. A commander can lawfully issue a barring order under federal criminal statute Title 16 U.S.C. §1382, which prohibits civilians from enter a military reservation on pain of federal criminal prosecution for trespassing.

None of these restrictions were applied in my case. At approximately 6:30 a.m. I was legally granted access to the Grove. I had arrived early, before administrative personnel or transition assistance personnel were on the base. I proceeded to my last place of duty at the Public Works Department where I had a few laughs with several of my former shipmates and civilian friends. As I waited for time to pass, I asked several people about how things were on the base and their response was simply "no change!" I then asked how Powell was doing and one guy responded that, *"He is as crazy as ever!"* I just had to laugh!

At approximately 7:30 a.m. I was about to proceed to see Mr. Hontz, the Transition Coordinator at the base, to obtain my G.I. Bill benefits. The court record states that Feener saw me on the base and called Powell. In return, Powell and Lekberg ordered the security shift leader to arrest me for *criminal trespass*!

The stage was set for military officials to blatantly violate their constitutional law enforcement powers by arresting a private citizen predicated on military law. Simply speaking, such an act outside a condition of martial law ordered by the President of the United States is unconstitutional.

As I was standing in the hallway out front of the Environmental Department administrative offices, I was approached by Jim DeLong, my former friend and fellow teammate who had played third base for me. He happened to be the security shift leader that morning. Jim said, "Jeff, what are you doing on the base?"

I responded: "Jim, I am attempting to submit a FOIA/PA request and to obtain benefits from the TAMP coordinator."

"Jeff, I hate to do this," Jim said, "but Powell wants me to arrest you!"

Because I had broken no laws, created no disruptive situations, provided no "probable cause" to be arrested as a private citizen predicated on military law, and was protected for the entire landscape and legal issues resulting from my First Amendment protected communications on active duty, I assumed events were about to shift to my favor.

I am positive that at that time Jim was ordered to arrest me, he knew that I was being railroaded and that I was being arrested unlawfully and without probable cause. Jim had been my armed escort during my out-processing from the military. Knowing that the orders to arrest me were unlawful, he had a duty to refuse to obey such orders. Unfortunately, if he did so, his fate would have also been sealed and his military career placed in serious jeopardy.

Our walk to the security department gave me a moment to ask Jim about how he and his family was doing, and we caught up a bit on our news. Then he read me my Miranda rights and stated I was being charged with criminal trespass for violation of Lekberg's barring order.

I said nothing. Moments later, an officer from the Horsham police department (the local police department adjacent to the base), cited me for criminal trespass. It was totally unlawful for the military base to use the local police department to enforce a military order, but that's what Lekberg and Powell did. I was escorted back to my vehicle in handcuffs and released.

My constitutional rights had been infringed upon, but I soon saw that my attempts in continuing to prove corruption at the Grove had not been forgotten. Jim removed the handcuffs, and we said our good-byes. About six Seabees I knew from playing ball were standing in the smoking area across the street from my car. As I turned and made eye contact with them, each one of them gave me a smart hand salute!

This show of support eased my mind that day, and it was once again, another stepping stone to continue fighting. Thanks, guys!

Looking back, I found the events of that day to be astonishing. On the day of my discharge Lekberg had the power to issue a barring order against me, prohibiting me from accessing the Grove as a civilian under federal law. Lekberg knew that if he did bar me in the wake of my honorable discharge, I would have immediately sought a federal injunction blocking his action. Lekberg would then have had to defend his action by "evidence" in a federal court. He could not have done this. Any barring order issued on the day the Navy IG was on board, was unjustified until an official determination had been established that I was detrimental.

I was ordered to stand trial in Pennsylvania State criminal court on July 6, 1994. Ten minutes after the trial started, the case was *dismissed!* The Court's logic in throwing the case out was that (1) no "probable cause" existed to support a charge of criminal trespass as I had a valid transition ID card issued by the U.S. Government and had been granted permission to enter the base, and (2) the arrest was predicated on a military barring order, and I was a civilian no longer under the jurisdiction of the U. S. Military! In this case, Lekberg and Powell's attempt to further besmirch my reputation failed, and the Court rendered its opinion of the events as follows:

> "This is an issue between Mr. Trueman and the Commanding Officer of Willow Grove. This case is dismissed!"

The dismissal of the case was a major victory for me. The government had been unsuccessful in arguing that the "barring order" was valid and the arrest legal. Finally, I thought, I had a legal cause of action. The Feres Doctrine was a non-issue as far as my false arrest was concerned. At least I thought this to be the case, since a "barring order" issued in the wake of speech protected under the First Amendment has been rendered invalid by the U.S. Supreme Court. Now I could fight Lekberg and Powell to expose their abuse of power and misuse of the mental health system in a court of law.

After the criminal charges against me were dismissed, I attempted in good faith to resolve the issue by filing a complaint of constitutional right violations with the DODIG. I did this with the hope of preventing a lawsuit and further waste of taxpayer money due to the continued unlawful actions of both Lekberg and Powell.

In response, the DODIG forwarded my complaint to the Navy IG. The next issue would be whether or not the Navy IG would investigate the complaint. I did not hold my breath as I wondered what obstructions of justice and intentional violations of official government powers were on the horizon!

The Time to Rejoin My Family Arrived

After six months in Philadelphia, I faced the reality that no one in the Military Establishment or my Members of Congress were going to help me. It was time to rejoin my family in Minnesota.

It was a bittersweet time in my life in July 1994. I knew I had to move on, and relocating to Minnesota meant that I was now leaving those I truly loved such as my many friends and especially my father, mother, sister Marion, her husband "Big Ed," my nephew Jimmy, my buddy Huzz. On the flip side, I knew my children were awaiting my return and that fact restored a glimpse of hope, faith, and determination. Even through all the bad experiences I had endured in the Philadelphia area, I knew things were going to get better once I rejoined my kids!

Rejoining My Children

After a six-month separation from my kids, it was a great feeling to see them, hear them and hold them! The moment I saw my children and hugged them was the beginning of a most wonderful time. Seeing them gave me a long-awaited positive feeling that I truly needed after all that had transpired over the previous six months.

Although I was back with my kids, my relationship with my wife no longer existed. We agreed to work together to look out for the best interests of our kids, but we felt like strangers.

I sought positive experiences in my life, but I was not sleeping well and could not focus on what, if anything, I would accomplish by continuing to fight the Clinton Administration. Besides fighting with my own emotions and the struggle against the government, I knew that my dignity would be challenged once again by government bureaucrats who administered the welfare system in the county where we lived when we had to apply for assistance. My experience in the welfare system is a book in of itself, and I can only say it was not a pleasant time for either my wife or myself.

Resuming The Discovery Process

As I have explained, the first small victory I achieved was the admission by the DOD that I had not been afforded my G.I. Bill benefits. I thought that just maybe, a critical play to gain even more yardage would be to seek financial reimbursement through the BCNR for moving my family from Pennsylvania to Minnesota during my final months of active duty.

I knew it was a long shot. My BCNR file was probably flagged due to the ASN (M&RA's) knowledge that I was taking on abuses in the military's mental health and legal systems. I could only hope for a bureaucratic blunder to see me through this one. On August 28, 1994, I filed an application for financial reimbursement for moving my family without transfer orders under the provisions of the MWBP Act. Chances of success weren't great, but it was a tactical move—like a quick kick in football, designed to catch the opponents off guard.

In the section of the Application entitled *"I believe the record to be in error or unjust in the following particulars,"* I provided the following claim:

"Under the provisions of the Military Whistleblower Protection Act of 1989, reprisals were initiated against me, and, to protect my family, I moved them out of state."

The reasons for my filing the Application are self-explanatory, but I thought there was no way in hell that the BCNR was going to approve the Application, which essentially would have overridden the ASN (M&RA) findings of no merit to my claims of mental health reprisals under the provisions of §1034.

After submitting my request for financial reimbursement to the BCNR, I applied for a waiter job at an Italian Restaurant to bring in some sort of income to feed my family. After only about a month's time at the restaurant and diminished hours for work, I left the restaurant and started sending out resumes to obtain productive employment.

I received a couple of phone calls for interviews but nothing worked out. Now I was starting to worry for the well-being of my family and falling into a state of severe depression, essentially holding on by an emotional thread. However, I had Paul and Rhonda on my side to ease the stress.

The Hardships on the Home Front Continue

By the end of October 1944, things were getting worse. In addition to the welfare predicament and my failure to find productive employment, we could not keep up with our rental payments and were being evicted from our home. My wife and I decided that it was best to sell all our furniture and move the family back to Pennsylvania.

We started to make signs for an "everything must go sale" because we needed the money to relocate our family back to the Philadelphia area.

On the morning of October 27 I was reading the paper with the hopes that maybe a place in town was for rent that we could afford. I was giving one last effort to see if we could somehow stay in Minnesota. I glanced through the classified section of the paper. I noticed an advertisement for a small home and called the number to inquire about the property. A very nice women by the name of Lynn answered the phone.

I explained to Lynn that I had a family of four and gave her a description of the household goods we had. She said she was sorry, but the house advertised was too small. I said I would put whatever belongings I had to into storage so we could fit in the home, but she said that the home was really too small for a family of four.

I was just about to hang up when for some reason I mentioned my VA loan eligibility. She said she had a house in the East side of Duluth that she could get us into with the VA eligibility. I thought, "Finally, after eleven and a half years of my life serving my country, it's paying off."

I knew the neighborhood Lynn was telling me the home was in, was way out of our price range. We were still on partial welfare at that time. I tried to explain to her our financial situation and my difficulties in finding employment, but Lynn assured me that we could move into this house, so we set up an appointment and met that afternoon.

When we pulled up to the house, I kept thinking that there is no way that we would be able to afford this home. I walked in, and the place was simply beautiful! Things were taking their toll emotionally on both my wife and myself at that time. We looked at each other and just grinned, insinuating that there was no way we could afford the home.

After Lynn took us on a tour of the home, we sat down in the kitchen. She started filling out paperwork for us to assume the Contract for Deed that the owner was offering us until we could assume the mortgage on our own. Lynn said that if we could come up with $3,000 down payment, the home was ours. I knew that the only way I would be able to come up with that kind of money was to suck up my pride and ask my father for the money. My father came through for us as he has always does when his family needs help!

Buying a home in less than forty-five minutes was a big gamble, but we figured we had nothing to lose. I completely trusted Lynn even though I had known her only for about an hour! The next kind act that Lynn did for us was that she told us she would accept $2,000 for the down payment rather than $3,000 she originally stated. I believe her actions were truly considerate.

We signed the initial paperwork, and after the money from my father arrived, we met again. We signed the paperwork, turned over the money, and Lynn handed us the keys to the home! We were amazed that we had found a home that was everything that my wife and I had dreamed of. The entire situation was a gift from above!

In October 1994, although we were finally secure in a home, my difficulties with obtaining employment continued. I kept the faith believing that good things were to come, considering I'd moved into a hundred thousand dollar home with only 46 cents in my checking account!

Finally, the Big Break was About to Arrive

In spite of many negative things in my life such as failing to find productive employment and being controlled by the welfare system, I was finally about to receive a positive development in my pursuit for reinstatement.

On December 12, 1994, I received a letter dated November 1, 1994 from the BCNR. In the letter the following "official" statement by the BCNR was made with respect to my application for financial reimbursement incurred in my unauthorized move:

> "Upon review and considering of all evidence of record, and especially, in light of the contents of enclosure (2), the Board finds the existence of an injustice warranting the following corrective action..."

Needless to say, I was pumped up. It was the longest gain in the drive. We had finally crossed the fifty yard line! The BCNR's Executive Director, W. Dean Pfeiffer, had approved my application on behalf of Secretary of the Navy Dalton. I was confident that since my pending application for reinstatement was due for review in December 1994, according to the 180-day review provision of §1034, that December 1994 would finally be the end of my struggle. Once my BCNR case for reinstatement was reviewed, I was certain that I would be back on active duty.

The Big Game Was Approaching

After we were settled in our new home, I had to prepare for the showdown at the BCNR with respect to my reinstatement application. The 180-day review period was quickly approaching, so on December 2, 1994, I wrote the BCNR and requested the status of my application with respect to the 180-day provision of §1034.

In response the BCNR contacted the relevant agencies and the Navy IG to obtain confirmation as to whether or not my case was to be processed under the provisions of §1034. I thought I had finally pitted the BCNR against the Navy IG. After all, just one month earlier, the BCNR had granted me financial reimbursement under §1034!

I was not holding my breath because I knew that anything is possible in the government. I was confident that the BCNR would review the case in December 1994. However, I was in for a major blow to my rights to "due process of law."

The Conspiracy to Obstruct the BCNR Review Process is Undertaken

The facts I am about to present reflect intentional violations of laws including §1034 and §1552 by the BCNR and Navy IG to cover up corruption at the Grove and the long train of abuses within the mental health and administrative discharge systems.

On December 7, 1994, Captain George Kraus from the Office of the Navy IG responded to the BCNR's inquiry as to whether or not my case fell within the provisions of §1034. I found this to be somewhat hypocritical since the BCNR had already reviewed and approved my previous application for financial reimbursement under the law. The letter from Captain Kraus includes the following assertion:

> "Review of your case indicates that your 1993 complaint to this office was of alleged reprisals as a result of *your com-*

plaining to your Commanding Officer (Lekberg) *about your Executive Officer* (Powell). That initial complaint did not qualify as a protected disclosure under the terms of the Act..."

(Emphasis and explanation in parentheses added).

Government officials are good at manipulating facts, and Kraus was as good as any. His assertion that my September 13, 1993 complaint against Powell for "abuse of power" and addressed to his agency under the provisions of §1034 was a complaint filed with Lekberg is simply outrageous! I finally obtained evidence to prove that the Navy IG engaged in intentional violations of the Inspectors General Act of 1978 and MWBP Act.

When the watchdogs of fraud, waste and abuse engage in illegal activity, it is a public trust issue. The law provides for such issues to be addressed by the U.S. Attorney General if notification of such corruption is brought to the attention of the Justice Department.

The Beginning of the Obstruction of Justice by the BCNR

On December 12, 1994, the BCNR initiated an attempt to cover up violations of human and constitutional rights in the Navy's mental health system and administrative discharge processes. Pfeiffer, the Executive Director of the BCNR, forwarded the BCNR's official findings to me stating that my application for reinstatement would not be considered under the provisions of §1034. I immediately responded by challenging Kraus's statement in his December 7, 1994 letter, pointing out that the Powell complaint in question was clearly addressed to the Navy IG and *not* to Lekberg. There was no way that protected status did not exist. Again, Pfeiffer informed me that he was sticking with the Navy IG's position and that he was not going to consider my case under §1034.

In this way Pfeiffer bought Clinton's Navy Department two years of delays because my application would be proceeded routinely.

When I informed Pfeiffer that the Navy IG's conclusions were incorrect and he failed to act, he willingly violated his fiduciary responsibilities to the U.S. Congress under federal law and compromised the integrity of the BCMR system of justice. The abuse of power and obstruction of justice Pfeiffer engaged is a very serious public trust issue, especially considering he had been the Executive Director of the BCNR for twenty years. The United States Congress must ask the question: "How many more Navy and Marine Corps personnel are claiming injustice at the BCNR?"

Pfeiffer is now 73 years old and knows he will not be held accountable whether or not he abused his powers in dealing with others in the past.

Seeking Help Through the Clinton Justice Department

Kraus and Pfeirrer has successfully obstructed my rights to a fair hearing at the BCNR under federal law. With this fiasco I had just about had enough of the stonewalling and obstruction by military officials within the administrative realm of the Clinton Military Establishment. On December 14, 1994, I filed a criminal complaint of conspiracy to obstruct justice with the Clinton Justice Department (DOJ) claiming violations of the Inspectors General Act 1978. According to law, this type of claim must be reported to the Attorney General of the United States, Janet Reno. Her agency is mandated to investigate government corruption and those who violate federal law within our government.

Fifteen months later, in March 1996, (15 months after I notified the DOJ), I received an official response from the Civil Rights Division of the Clinton Justice Department. The letter stated that my complaint did not reflect any illegal conduct by the Navy IG in violation of the IG Act and that there had been no vio-

136

lations of my civil rights resulting from the malicious prosecution that went down on May 27, 1994.

Although there is much more to this issue, the best way to sum up it up is that Robert Gaudett, a paralegal with no constitutionally appointed authority to make legal findings within our government, closed the books on the issue. In this way the issue of human right abuses and obstruction of justice within the Clinton Navy Department was brushed under the carpet!

On October 23, 1996, in the wake of Paralegal Gaudett's findings, I filed another complaint directly to Deval Patrick, who was then the director of the Civil Rights Division. In that complaint I pointed out conflicts of interest with the DOJ's free representation of Lekberg and Powell in the lawsuit I had filed in the wake of the malicious prosecution of May 27, 1994. (Chapter Six covers in full detail the malicious prosecution that steered me to the United States Supreme Court.)

I did not receive any reply from the Clinton DOJ to my second complaint. As a matter of fact, the DOJ claims they don't have any "correspondence" reflecting I ever made any complaints of violations of the IG Act.

To keep the offensive drive going, on January 31, 1995, I filed my first reprisal complaint with the DODIG. In this document I claimed that both the Navy IG and BCNR were falsifying official documents and obstructing justice with respect to my application for reinstatement. What would follow, as I will explain, is simply astonishing!

Going to the Final Official in My Chain of Command— William Jefferson Clinton

Corruption was taking place under the Clinton White House with respect to fraud, waste and abuse within the military's mental health, administrative discharge, and Inspectors General and BCMR processes. I knew it was time to bring to the attention of Commander-in-Chief William Jefferson Clinton the serious misdeeds of military officials under his direction. On February 2, 1995, I sent Clinton a letter explaining that my Navy career had been meritorious until I had filed a request to speak with my commanding officer, and that this had resulted in my military career being destroyed. I requested the President's help so that my family and I could have the opportunity to move on with our lives.

A letter dated March 20, 1995 arrived from the Special Assistant to the President, Director of Correspondence and Presidential Messages, responding as follows on behalf of President Clinton.

Dear Mr. Trueman:

Thank you so much for your letter. President Clinton greatly appreciates the trust and confidence you have shown in him by writing.

To ensure that your concerns are addressed, I am forwarding your letter to the Department of Defense for review and any appropriate action. Please bear in mind that it may take some time to look thoroughly into the issues you have raised.

Many thanks for your patience.

Hence, after proceeding through every possible avenue within my chain of command, my letter to the Commander-in-Chief was forwarded right back to the Department of Defense, which would send it to the Navy. This ticked me off, and the vicious cycle began all over again.

On March 28, 1995, I received a letter from Lieutenant Commander Gregory R. Nowak, Director, White House Liaison Office, Office of the Secretary of the Navy. He was writing on behalf of the President of the United States. The only thing Mr. Nowak had to say was that—

"The BCNR will give your case full and fair consideration and make its decision after a review of the evidence submitted on your behalf."

When I received Mr. Nowak's letter, I immediately placed a call to him and was able to speak directly with him. I told Mr. Nowak that the abuses that had taken place in the legal and medical systems pertaining to my case were serious public trust issues. Although polite, he made the following comment that simply blew me away:

"Mr. Trueman, there are thousands in the military claiming injustices."

If any one conversation throughout this entire ordeal put things into perspective, it was that one. Thousands of present and former military members have been wronged and have suffered because of immunity defenses and the Feres Doctrine! At least I now had an admission that "thousands" are claiming injustice. This comment reaffirmed my claims that abuses of military members are widespread and that the system of checks and balances is flawed.

On April 18, 1995, I wrote Dorskind once again and attempted to point out all conflicts of interest and my concern that the Navy IG and BCNR were engaging in unlawful activity. This time the White House simply did not respond.

At that time the corruption and scandals at the White House were in full swing. Misuse of psychological evaluations, obstruction of justice by the Navy IG and BCNR, and the Justice Department's failure to act to correct injustices were obviously low priority issues in the eyes of the Clinton Administration.

Getting Back Into Sports Saved Me

As summer approached, I read an article in my local paper about tryouts for the Duluth-Superior Dukes, a semi-pro baseball team in the Northern League. I loved baseball, so went to the tryouts. I caught a ball off the wall and hit two doubles, a pretty good tryout. However, I realized that I was too slow and at 32 years old, my chances were slim to none to make it as a pro. Still, there were opportunities for me to participate in something truly loved to do—play ball! It turned out that softball and all those who played it in Duluth would be my mental therapy. I became surrounded by hundreds of new friends who made me finally realize that I was not crazy—"they" are!

139

For five years I met thousands of wonderful people who participated with me in softball and football in the Duluth/Superior area. This book is possible because of my friends.

Finally Breaking Into The Working World

By June of 1995 I had exhausted all of my attempts to find full-time employment on my own. I felt that leaving the military after eleven and a half years service and being labeled mentally unstable were probably a contributing factors in my not finding employment. I believe this is true because when one is discharged for negative reasons as set forth on the DD-214, any potential employer can pull that document up from Department of Labor and determine why a military person was discharged. In my case, during job interviews I was asked on several occasions why I got out with only nine and a half years to go for what would amount to a million-dollar pension. More than once I told the truth about being discharged with alleged mental illness and guess what? I did not receive any job offers!

One day in a moment of desperation I walked into Manpower Temporary Services in Duluth to seek temporary employment. That was the right choice! Because of my administrative background and understanding of the legal system, I was assigned many challenging jobs in private law firms, government agencies and private businesses in both Minnesota and Wisconsin.

I enjoyed being back in a professional atmosphere and working with government officials and lawyers. Since I knew I would be taking my case to the United States Supreme Court one way or another, I needed to learn the civil legal system. This work gave me an opportunity to feed and house my family. Besides that, I considered it apprenticeship training that would help me learn how to fight injustice within our government, using lawful means within the legal system. For the most part, all those for whom I met through temporary employment were supportive of my determination to expose the chilling effects of Feres within

140

the military's medical and legal systems. Additionally, I became certified as a legal assistant/paralegal.

As time moved on through the summer of 1995, I continued to await a determination from the DODIG as to whether or not they were going to investigate the Navy IG and BCNR for obstruction of justice. By year's end, the DODIG had not made any determination on the merits of my complaint, nor did the Clinton Justice Department respond regarding their inquiry into my claims of violation of the Inspectors General Act of 1978.

As 1995 came to a close, many positive things had taken place, and they overrode the negatives, but it was the great people I met and associated with that really made 1995 a good year over-all!

Year Three Of The Quest Begins

On February 13, 1996, I finally received the letter I had anticipated for over a year from the DODIG. Of course, I was hopeful that a massive investigation into corruption within the military's mental health system and inspectors general program was under way or would soon be initiated. My heart pounded as I opened the letter. I was confident that the evidence the DODIG possessed would be enough for them to compel Clinton's Navy Department to attempt to justify their actions not only in discharging me but also to provide a legal explanation of how a 4.0 sailor on December 23, 1992 could become mentally unstable on March 27, 1993, when the evidence states the contrary.

In the letter of February 13, 1996, Ms. Marcia Campbell, Chief, Special Inquires Division, Office of the DODIG, stated her findings which read:

> "A review of your records disclosed that your contacts with Navy IG offices and Members of Congress occurred *after your discharge* from the Navy for alcohol abuse rehabilitation failure. Therefore, we do not find a personnel action that occurred after your contacts with the IG and Members of Congress."

141

I read the letter a second time to make sure I hadn't missed something. I was amazed at the DODIG's conclusion and surprised that this agency, which is mandated to investigation corruption in the Armed Forces under federal law, had insinuated that I had never made a protected communication under public law while on active duty!

I knew then that the government was not going to conduct an investigation to correct the abuses in the legal, medical and investigative systems in the Department of the Navy. A million-dollar investigation of the Navy's entire internal workings would be a political nightmare. Once again my constitutional rights as an American to be free from unlawful government intrusion and abuse were ignored and I was further betrayed by government officials whose duty it is to clean up corruption in the Armed Forces.

My Big Break Would Finally Come

After that outrageous response from Ms. Campbell, I immediately consolidated more than thirty pages of evidence that would counter her findings. I submitted the evidence via facsimile. In response to my fax, on April 29, 1996, after a year of being stonewalled by the Clinton DOD, I finally crossed paths with a government official who clearly saw the injustices taking place in my case. That individual was Mr. William Shea.

For two years and four months, my legal right for protection under §1034 had been manipulated and withheld from me. Now Mr. Shea stepped up to the plate and attempted to address and correct the obvious injustices that were in my military records.

As a result, I received notification from the DODIG that they were going to initiate another "preliminary investigation" of my claims of reprisals under §1034. This action kept the hope alive that my situation would be concluded and that Broyles, Lekberg, and Powell, would be investigated for violations of the whistleblower statute. Although I am grateful that Shea was able to obtain my protection under the law, the "spin lawyers" in Washington took over. They knew that if I prevailed with my case, many military personnel in leadership positions would be placed under the microscope. The cost of a full-scale investigation would have been substantial both in financial and political terms.

"A reprisal is a reprisal." These words reassured me that the evidence he was looking at clearly established the fact that if I had not proceed with a grievance or if I had accepted Rumery's ultimatum, I would still be in the military. If not for Mr. Shea, all my constitutional rights would have been obstructed. Because of his integrity, he is a true hero in my eyes, the kind of person we need in positions of leadership within our government!

Taking The Fight To The Federal Judiciary

On May 24, 1996, after two years of facing stonewalling and obstructions by the Navy Inspector General, Department of Defense Inspector General, and the Clinton Justice Department, I filed a claim of false arrest, false imprisonment, and malicious prosecution regarding the retaliatory false arrest, a violation of my Fourth Amendment rights, that was ordered by Lekberg and carried out by Powell on May 27, 1994.

My attorney filed the lawsuit under the provisions of the Federal Torts Claim Act (FTCA) of 1946. On July 6, 1996 he filed a second lawsuit known as "the Bivens action for Constitutional right violations" against Lekberg and Powell in their individual capacities for violating my constitutional rights with the malicious prosecution of May 27, 1994. Eventually, I combined these two claims into one lawsuit for the benefit of judicial economy. I wanted to prevent two separate trials to avoid wasting further tax dollars defending Lekberg and Powell.The premises and facts were the same as on the FTCA claim.

At the time my attorney filed my claim under the FTCA and the lawsuit under Bivens, I was confident that once these cases were joined and presented to a jury for the Bivens claim, and to the court for a verdict regarding the FTCA action, the evidence against the government would be so overwhelming that investigation of human right abuses in violation of §1034 could not be ignored.

Additionally, due to the fact that I was repeatedly denied access to alleged documents I requested under the provisions of the FOIA/PA Act, my attorney also filed a lawsuit under the provisions of the Privacy Act to obtain documents the Clinton Navy Department claims existed to justify my orders into the mental health system and eventual discharge such as "fit-for-duty counseling, incident reports, etc." As I explained earlier, the documents I obtained from this lawsuit produced only favorable documents on my behalf, and the government could not release even one detrimental document to justify its official actions when they claimed I was detrimental to good order and discipline.

The Showdown at the BCNR

On July 31, 1996, after two and one-half years of unlawful delays, my Application for Reinstatement was reviewed by the three-panel civilian board assigned under the supervision of the ASN (M&RA). The board refused to allow into evidence the following: (1) three sworn affidavits on my behalf which stated the improprieties I discussed with Broyles and the affiants' belief that I was retaliated against for initiating a grievance; (2) the Feener admission that no alcohol-related lateness had occurred; (3) the DODIG §1034 protection status determination, and (4) other evidence reflecting that I was a 4.0 sailor only one month prior to being ordered to appear before an administrative separation board!

The refusal to introduce material evidence into the proceeding reflected arbitrary and capricious conduct on behalf of Pfeiffer. The entire BCNR process can be summed up as follows: "absolute power corrupts absolutely"! If my due process rights and the BCNR process could be obstructed so easily, I have to wonder how many Navy personnel and Marines and their families have suffered injustice at the BCNR since Pfeiffer's tenure began.

144

At national conferences VERPA intends to hold in Duluth, I hope one day to speak with all those who have been betrayed within this administrative remedy process.

1996 Comes To A Close

The year 1996 came to a close, and the stonewalling and obstruction of the U.S. Constitution and my rights to due process under the Fifth Amendment continued. I was starting to put things back into perspective. Although my career was over, I saw that I could still improve things in the future for rank and file members. Just as I had the previous year, I felt that 1997 would be a better year since I was gaining the support of people in my community who now realized that my fight for justice was not only for me but also for the many hundreds of thousands of other average Americans serving in the Armed Forces.

The First Legal Showdown Finally Arrived

The *first legal showdown* in my lawsuit against the Navy and Lekberg, Powell *et al*, took place on January 17, 1997, when I appeared in front of the Honorable Judge Rosenbaum, in Minneapolis, Minnesota. Ironically, that was the day that President Clinton was lying under oath in the Paula Jones lawsuit, another case of an average citizen being abused by a government official. The hearing was called to consider a motion by the government to dismiss both the Bivens and FTCA lawsuits arising from the malicious prosecution of May 27, 1994.

I was arguing that the false arrest resulted from the unlawful barring order of Lekberg and that his action was invalid because it was issued in the wake of protected communications under the whistleblower law. Hence, the attack against "qualified immunity" was also on the table. It was my thirty-third birthday and the third anniversary of my buddy Steve's burial. I felt it was going to be a good day and a major completion in the trek towards the goal line.

When I arrived at the Federal Courthouse in Minneapolis, I was excited because finally the government had to defend the merits of both the Bivens and the FTCA actions. If I prevailed, the cases might be set for trial before the end of the year.

At the conclusion of the hearing, Judge Rosenbaum ruled that he was moving the case back to the jurisdiction of the Federal Court in Philadelphia, but he did dismiss the Privacy Act lawsuit due to failure to exhaust administrative remedies. Although I appealed that decision with the Eighth Circuit Court of Appeals, the Court's Order for Dismissal was upheld.

As the hearing was coming to a close, unexpectedly, Judge Rosenbaum and I had the following exchange of words which are documented in the Court transcripts. The Judge opened by saying:

"Mr. Trueman, are those your children?"

"Yes, sir. They are."

"They are, ah, handsome children and well behaved."

"Well, thank you very much."

"No. Thank *you*!"

This exchange between the Court and myself further motivated me to continue to seek justice.

In addition to the Judge's comments, another *positive* that took place after the hearing was when the U.S. Attorney, Mr. Bryan, who was handling the government's defense, stated to me in front of my wife, a friend, and my attorney the following:

"Mr. Trueman, I wish you a lot of luck in this matter, and if you need a good attorney in Philadelphia I recommend the following individual..."

Mr. Bryan's comment shocked me because he had fought to dismiss the case (and I realize he was only doing his job). I was unsure why he had given me that reference. I can only guess that after Mr. Bryan reviewed all the facts, circumstances and evidence, he knew his clients were guilty but were going to walk!

I would like to say to Mr. Bryan, "Your words of encouragement are truly appreciated, sir, and I'm sure it must be really hard to have to defend individuals which we all know make a mockery of our system of justice."[4]

The case was sent back to Philadelphia, the proper venue since the false arrest and malicious prosecution took place at the Grove, which is within the federal district for Eastern Pennsylvania.

Newly Discovered Evidence

On January 19, 1997, I provided "newly discovered evidence" to the DODIG and the BCNR. These documents established the fact that one month before my discharge I was recommended for advancement and retention and was considered a 4.0 sailor, as I had previously pointed out. This evidence was too explosive, and the DODIG and Pfeiffer, denied to consider it. Once again, the DODIG and BCNR had violated their fiduciary responsibilities to the People of the United States (i.e. the Congress). Simply stated, justice would not be rendered in the Clinton Department of Defense.

It was clear to me at that time that the war between myself and the Clinton military establishment would have to be taken to a new level. My case at the BCNR had been obstructed by Pfeiffer, and the position of trust which he had violated seemed to be of no concern to anyone in a position of power above him. Accordingly, I filed an ethics complaint with the Office of Bar Counsel of The Board on Professional Responsibility (BPR) at the District of Columbia Court of Appeals. This agency is in place to investigate lawyers in its jurisdiction who violate their court-appointed ethical requirements. I pointed out to the BPR all of the obstruction of justice issues initiated by the government attorney.

On March 4, 1997, the BPR informed me that they were not going to investigate the issues because my complaints with the Navy and Department of Justice were still pending. The BPR took the position that if either the Navy or Justice Department

---

4. And are defended at taxpayer's expense

should find misconduct, then I could write them again and enclose the decisions of these agencies. Of course, the government will *never* investigate the massive amount of corruption at the BCNR until the public and veterans deprived of justice demand that this action be taken.

Seeking Assistance From Independent Governmental Watchdogs

After the hearing in Minneapolis the lawsuit was still alive. Mainly due to the comments of the Judge Rosenbaum and U.S. Attorney Bryan, I felt I had enough evidence to send a request for review of my case to the Government Accountability Project (GAP) in Washington D.C. This nonprofit organization is a "watchdog" group in place to that ensure government officials are kept in line. Their role in my case was to obtain an "outside independent opinion" as to the merits of my claims of abuse of power, human right abuses in the military's mental health system and to determine if my claims were supported by evidence in the court record.

I took this avenue because I felt that if the GAP believed my claims were meritorious, I might be able to bring national exposure to my claims of the military's misuse of the psychological evaluation and the chilling effects of the Feres Doctrine.

On January 27, 1997, I received a letter from the GAP. They requested documents I had discussed in my telephone conversation with Ken Blosser of the GAP. I provided a summary of events and evidence to support my position that corruption festered throughout the judicial processes in the Department of Defense. To my surprise, I received a phone call in late May 1997 from Mr. Blosser. He asked me if I wanted to take my story to the media.

I said, "I really do not want to go to the media, because I was hoping for the "system" to fix the problems, but now it appears the media is the only way to address the issues." Yes, I was interested in taking my story to the media.

The fact that my story was offered up to the national media was a major victory. To gain national exposure, the issue must be of public concern and supported by substantial evidence. I was gaining yardage!

The National Media is Interested in My Story

Several days after I told Mr. Blosser that I was willing to go to the media, he called to tell me that ABC News' *Prime*TIME Live was looking for former military members who have claimed that the psychological evaluation was unlawfully used against them as reprisal! Finally, it was apparent that others had suffered the same fate and that now my claims of human right abuses in the Clinton military's mental health system were about to make national news. Finally, my big break had come, and I was going to be able to tell my story.

ABC News would be able to expose to the nation the awesome power military officials can use to silence people such as myself who uphold duty to country above personal agendas.

In anticipation of telling my story to ABC News, I arrived home from work to see on my caller ID, a call from ABC News and I played the message left by Mr. John Siceloff, a Producer at ABC News left a message for me to call him the following day. I was overwhelmingly excited knowing that here was a national news organization interested in my case! The feeling truly felt like the days of childhood when one anticipates the opening of gifts on Christmas morning, is the only way I can describe how I felt.

The following afternoon during my lunch break, I spoke for the first time to John Siceloff at ABC News and told him the basis of my story. I explained going from a 4.0 sailor to being mentally unbalanced, according to the Navy Department, in an eight-week period, and explained briefly why I believed I had been attacked in that fashion. Mr. Sliceloff told me that the issues I discussed with him sounded very compelling and that he wanted me to attend an interview with Mr. Sam Donaldson!

I had to pinch myself to ensure that the telephone call and the fact that I was taking my fight to the national media was truly taking place!

The Moment of Truth

On the evening of June 23, 1997, I found myself on a flight from Duluth to Washington D.C., to attend an interview with Mr. Donaldson. I was booked a room at the Renaissance Hotel in downtown Washington D.C. The following morning I was preparing documents and getting into a mindset I hoped would help me make it through the interview.

The morning passed, and a few minutes before my appointment at 1 p.m., I walked across the street from the hotel and entered ABC News Headquarters in Washington D.C.

After a short wait, I was met by Robin Brown, another producer. She escorted me to a studio and told that I would be participating in an interview with Mr. Donaldson that would last about an hour and a half. As I was being prepared for the on-camera interview, the folks at ABC News were very nice and made me feel at home.

As I sat awaiting the arrival of Mr. Donaldson, I could not believe I was about to be questioned by this prestigious individual and an American icon, a man who has access to world leaders, who was going to interview this average American.

Mr. Donaldson arrived and introduced himself to me. He told me that at any time during the interview, if I felt I needed a break we would stop. However, he said he preferred if we proceeded without delays. I told him that I had been silenced for such a long time that I was ready to answer any questions he may wish to pose to me.

In the interview, we discussed many issues concerning how and why the psychological evaluation was ordered against me. I spoke from the heart and was honest with my answers. At the conclusion, the entire staff who were present during the interview wished me well and good luck in my fight. It was a very moving time in my life. I felt a tremendous burden being lifted from my shoulders. Somehow I believed that the struggle and hardships I had put my family through were worth it.

If I could not receive justice and expose the chilling effects of Feres in the legal system to a jury, then getting the issue in the public's eye was the next best thing.

I thought that ABC News was going to "attack" the issue of abuse within the military's mental health system. With this in mind, I felt somewhat at ease. When I departed ABC News, I was informed that the program was scheduled to air in September 1997, at the onset of the fall television season so that broadcast would be seen by the largest possible audience.

Unfortunately, in September 1997, all major American news outlets were entrenched with the unfortunate and untimely death of Princes Diana and virtually all coverage was dedicated to that story. Scheduled programs such as "Abuse of Power" were put on the back burner. As the end of 1997 approached, I called ABC News to find out the status of the program and was told that all efforts were being made to air the program.

Although I am grateful to ABC News for taking the initiative to expose human right abuses in the military's mental health system, once again, I found that the reality in America, is that all media sources (the fourth branch of government), unfortunately "go with the big story" and the "bottom line" comes into play.

I adored Princes Diana as I think most decent people did. However, I could argue that although the death of the Princes was tragic and the world had lost another wonderful and caring icon, the simply fact of the matter is that Princes Diana was British and the program that I participated in to expose human right abuses in the Clinton Armed Forces was an American public trust issue.

Once again I had to face the reality that in our society, the bottom line dictates that the injustices placed upon average Americans will always take a back seat to what goes on in the lives of the rich and famous.

151

Attempting to Move On in Life

After three years of working through Manpower, I was offered a full-time job in a law firm handling performance administrative functions and I gladly accepted. During the hiring process, I discussed with the President of the firm my situation with the military. He asked me if the matter would affect my performance of duties. I said it would not, that I was positive that everything would work out and was looking forward to putting all issues behind me.

The timing was perfect. Not only was I fortunate to work with wonderful people, but I also learned a great deal about the litigation process. The lawyers I worked for were outstanding. My job made it possible for me to work towards certification as a legal assistant/paralegal, which I received.

I figured that once my attorney joindered my unlawful discharge cause of action with my pending lawsuit resulting from the events of May 27, 1994, I would be reinstated into the Navy by the end of 1998. I was also confident that the testimony and evidence presented at trial would force the federal court to refer the case to the United States DOJ for investigation of intentional violations of federal laws with respect to the Inspectors General Act and Military Whistleblower Protection Act.

A Major Setback Was on the Horizon

Things were going well with my job as 1998 began, and I felt pretty good mentally, although I was still eager to go to trial. However, I was about to face another major setback and this one really blew my confidence in the legal system.

On January 12, 1998, I received a phone call from my attorney. He told me he had bad news! I immediately said, "Don't tell me my case was dismissed due to expiration of statutes of limitations."

My attorney replied, "All claims were dismissed due to time bars except the malicious prosecution claim." I almost hit the roof. Once again I was faced with another major setback. I was getting sick of the legal system and was losing faith in it. I was starting to realize that just as with the media, the legal business is also predicated on the "bottom line" issue of money rather than justice!

I asked my attorney, "When did you get the notification from the Court as to its decision?"

When he told me December 24, 1997, nineteen days earlier, I lost it! I said, "Why did it take you so long to communicate with me?"

"I did not want to ruin your New Years." Although I knew that getting upset would achieve nothing, I told my attorney to send me a copy of the Court's Memorandum decision so that we could at least focus on the "First Amendment" retaliation claim leading to the issuance of the Lekberg "barring order" and malicious prosecution claim.

I also asked my attorney to look at filing an appeal. On April 16, 1998, the memorandum was finally released by the Court. My claims for false arrest and false imprisonment as well as my constitutional claims under the First, Fourth, and Fifth Amendments were all dismissed. Essentially, because of my attorney's failure to file my claims in a timely fashion, all issue of abuse as I have described in this book were essentially dead issues.

On May 20, 1998, my attorney filed an appeal on my behalf regarding what I still believed were viable claims for First Amendment free protected speech retaliation and malicious prosecution. On June 22, 1998, the United States Attorney in Philadelphia filed its brief countering our legal position. I called my attorney to obtain a copy of the government's brief, so that we could counter it. He left it outside his office door for me to pick up, which I did.

After reviewing the brief, on July 1, 1998 I hand-delivered rebuttal information that would be necessary in order to file a Reply Brief challenging the government's position. I was confident that we could get the Appellate Court to reverse and remand the First Amendment and malicious prosecution claims to the trial court. In response, my attorney looked me square in the eyes and stated: "I don't have the time to file a Reply Brief!" Again, I almost lost it and was furious to say the least.

Because of my attorney's outrageous professional conduct as well as to protect my interests, I filed a ethics complaint with the Office of Professional Responsibility, the watchdogs mandated to ensure ABA Rules are complied with. Then I attempted to search for another attorney somewhere in the country who would help me with my appeal. However, time was not on my side. In complete frustration, and knowing I had to reply to the government's brief, I terminated the attorney-client relationship on August 20, 1998 and proceeded *pro se* (self-representation).

On May 19, 1999, the Office of Lawyers' Professional Responsibility issued an "admonition" against my former attorney. For purposes of a potential legal malpractice suit that decision was helpful. As for fighting to incorporate equal protection of the laws of this nation to the people who defend them, my attorney's incompetence destroyed a case that should have been sent to trial to challenge Feres and its unconstitutionality due to its obstruction of the enforcement of §1034. Although this was a major setback, I pressed on.

As I faced difficulties within the legal system because of an attorney who failed me, I still kept the hope alive that the ABC News broadcast would bring some sort of closure and initiation of reforms within the Department of Defense without having to proceed any further within the legal system.

On Friday evening, October 28, 1998, ABC News finally aired the long-awaited program of human right abuses in the Clinton military's mental health system. About the same time, in a "good faith" effort, I attempted one last time to bring about an amicable closure to all issues in my lawsuit by once again communicating with Members of Congress and the Clinton Justice Department.

My primary goal is to defuse claims by government officials that my complaints are due to a litigious mentality or that I am looking to make a quick buck. The lawyer who mangled my case cost me a million-dollar pension. He tried to help me, but his procrastination lost the case. I've been advised to launch a malpractice suit, but I think enough is enough. Instead, I settled the potential litigation in exchange for two house payments and am signing a release forever forgiving my attorney's mistakes.

On October 30, 1998, I forwarded a letter via certified mail, return receipt requested, to Attorney General Janet Reno, providing a fourth request for investigation of violations of the Inspectors General Act of 1978. Once again I requested verification of a potential conflict of interest. The Justice Department was providing "free" representation paid for by tax dollars to defend Lekberg, Powell, et. al. Instead of defending them, they should have been prosecuting them for intentional violations of federal law. Of course, no response was ever received.

In December 1998, I communicated with both Senator Wellstone (D-MN) and Congressman Oberstar (D-MN), referring to questions raised in ABC's 20/20 broadcast. For the first time I was receiving positive vibes from the military liaisons with both of these Congressional Representative's military liaisons. However, as the months passed by, my communications and requests for the status of their inquires went unanswered. I was once again faced with the reality of politics and never heard from either Congressman again!

The government has played dirty pool from day one. I believe they figured I would just go away in time. That is what so many others have done due to the enormous amount of red tape involved in seeking justice if one is injured in the United States Armed Forces.

I am totally disappointed in our elected officials who condoned the abuses in the military's mental health system. Thus, I have decided to take the fight to the United States Supreme Court as you will see in the next Chapter.

Chapter 6

Turning the Blind Eye

"A Justice System Which Condones Injustice"

I n this chapter I am including a lot of legal and technical information that you can skip over if you want to. The purpose of these documents is to lay out carefully exactly what is involved in taking a legal case to the Supreme Court and to describe how my case has to be presented in order to make it to the highest court in the land.

How Does a Legal Case Make it to the Supreme Court?

Our nation was founded on the precept that government should be of the people, that the will of the majority shall always prevail, and that the "rule of law" must always take precedent over the "rule of man." However, when the "rule of law" clearly infringes on the constitutional protections of a specific class of people, the law must be rendered unconstitutional by the United States Supreme Court. Hence, in this Chapter, I will show the reader specifically how for forty-nine years the United States Supreme Court's decision in the Feres case has had a chilling effect on the equal protection of laws of our men and women who serve in the United States Armed Forces.

Getting one's case reviewed by the Supreme Court is a tremendous challenge. A rule the Supreme Court follows in determining what cases they will hear known as the *"Rule of Four."* Under this rule the Court will not issue a *Writ of Certiorari* (an order to a lower court to forward the case record), unless at least four justices approve of the decision to issue the writ. In the United States, the U.S. Supreme Court is the final appellate authority within the judicial branch of our government. Each year, thousands of cases are filed with the high court, but it only hears fewer than 150 cases on average per year. If the Court denies Writ of Certiorari, the case is a dead deal. However, even if a case is not selected for review, it does not mean the Petition filed does not have merit!

In my lawsuit, *Trueman v. United States, et al*, the "facts and circumstances," as you will see, should have rendered a "case of first impression" consisting of facts, circumstances and requested relief that have never before been adjudicated by a federal court of law in this country. The Navy Department's initiation of the May 27, 1994 false arrest and malicious prosecution against me as a private citizen and predicated on military law is unconstitutional and should never have been condoned by the United States Supreme Court.

Therefore, to begin, I must provide a "Concise Statement of Claim" as reflected in my Petition of Writ of Certiorari which states:

"On May 27, 1994, Respondents were officials of the United States Armed Forces and arrested Petitioner, a private citizen for alleged criminal trespass onto NAS Willow Grove, Pennsylvania. The uniqueness of this case is that the arrest of Petitioner was predicated upon a barring order issued under military law; however, Petitioner was a private citizen of the State of Pennsylvania. With this fact alone, Petitioner believes Respondents' actions were unconstitutional and the lower courts should have never allowed this act to go unremedied under law. Petitioner believes the lower courts' misapplication of case laws and failure to allow him any period of discovery, are due process issues that merit review by this Court. Furthermore, Petitioner believes the facts, circumstance and requested relief in this case are distinguishable from any other previously tried in the federal circuit and therefore, merits consideration as a "case of first impression." Finally, Petitioner believes that the direct evidence in the court record reflects official misconduct and failure to enforce federal laws by military and civilian officials in the Executive and Legislative branches of the Government."

My ultimate goal in taking my case to the high court was to fight for repeal or at a minimum reform of the "incident to service" bar of relief from intentional torts and medical malpractice under Feres. After experiencing obstruction of justice within the military's BCMR process, I also felt it necessary to incorporate a "private cause of action" provision within the Military Whistle-blower Protection Act. My objective with this action was to meet the needs of military members and their families who are wrongfully discharged for engaging in protected communications claiming fraud, waste and abuse. I wanted to give these people the opportunity to seek financial compensation by jury trial. These legal objectives would open the door for the public to see just how corrupt military officials who abuse their powers are.

On April 20, 1999 (six years and two months from the first retaliatory act), I filed the first petition at the United States Supreme Court pointing out human right abuses in the military mental health system, along with many other public trust issues amounting to betrayal of the American people by civilian and military officials. The brief as filed follows:

**IN THE SUPREME
COURT
OF THE UNITED STATES
APPLICATION NO. A-675**

JEFFREY A. TRUEMAN,
Appellant-Petitioner,
AGAINST-

**ERIC LEKBERG, GARY POWELL,
JAMES DeLONG; AND THE
UNITED STATES OF AMERICA,**

Appellees-Respondents.

ON WRIT OF CERTIORARI
TO THE
UNITED STATES COURT OF APPEALS
FOR THE THIRD CIRCUIT
CASE NO. 98-1075

PETITION

ADDITIONAL PARTIES

Commander-in-Chief
United States Armed Forces
The White House
Washington, DC 20006

Department of Defense

Inspector General
400 Army Navy Drive
Arlington, VA 22202-2884
Department of the Navy
Office of the Inspector General
M Street SE
Washington, D.C. 20370-5006

Department of the Navy

Board for Correction of Naval Records
Washington, D.C. 20370-5100

Department of the Navy

Office of the Judge Advocate General
200 Stovall Street
Alexandria, VA 22332-2400

Commander, Naval Air Reserve Force

Office of the Inspector General
New Orleans, LA 70146-5000
United States Attorney General

Department of Justice

5011 Main Justice Building
10th Street & Constitution Avenue
Washington, D.C. 20330

JURISDICTION

Petitioner believes the United States Supreme Court maintains jurisdiction over this appeal under; (1), Article III, U. S. Constitution, § 2, (U.S. a party); (2), 28 U.S.C. § 1254(1) (on Final Order and denial of Petition for Rehearing dated November 30, 1998 of the Third Circuit Court of Appeals), and (3), misapplication by the District and Appellate Courts of relevant prior decisions by the U. S. Supreme Court.

Jurisdiction is further appropriate under 29 U.S.C. § 2403(a) as Petitioner believes the Feres Doctrine's "incident to service bar" on intentional torts and medical malpractice deprives constitutional protections for free speech and due process from arbitrary and retaliatory acts prohibited under The Military Whistleblower Protection Act, Title 10 U.S.C. § 1034. Hence, Petitioner requests the Court to declare the "intentional tort and medical malpractice bar" unconstitutional.

Finally, a determination by the Court is requested as to whether the direct evidence reflects Government officials of the Executive and Legislative branches have abused their powers and/or failed to perform duties imposed by statutes (Inspectors General Act of 1978 and Whistleblower Protection Act (1992) and whether the facts, circumstances and requested relief in this case, render it a "case of first impression".

Extension of Time to File Petition was granted by Order of this Court on February 16, 1999, extending the time to file until April 28, 1999.

QUESTIONS PRESENTED

1.   Whether Petitioner established a prima facie case reflecting a genuine issue of factual dispute overlooked by the lower courts, which supports his position that the "Lekberg barring order" at the heart of this lawsuit was issued in violation of federal law. Hence, did the lower courts' err when they granted Respondents qualified immunity wherein a violation of the Military Whistleblower Protection Act ("Act"), is a punishable offense under the Uniform Code of Military Justice (UCMJ)? Should this Court not reverse the lower courts' grant of immunity to Respondents and remand Petitioner's malicious prosecution claim to trial in light of these facts?

2.   Whether the United States Military has the Constitutional and/ or other legal authority to arrest a private citizen of the United States for an alleged crime in peacetime, predicated upon military law?

3.   Whether a former military member is obligated by law to comply with a military order, once the member leaves the jurisdiction of the U. S. Armed Forces?

4.   Whether the lower courts erred in failing to order an evidentiary hearing to determine whether the military barring order used as

probable cause for Petitioner's arrest was valid under the <u>Albertini</u> standard, to ensure its issuance did not violate the "Act".

5.   Did the lower courts deny Petitioner's constitutional "due process of law" when they failed to afford Petitioner any period of discovery in this case?

6.   Did the lower courts prejudice Petitioner's case when they failed to address Petitioner's First Amendment whistleblower reprisal claim, the foundation for Petitioner to prevail in a legal claim of malicious prosecution?

7.   Whether the Appellate Court's ruling affirming the District Court's Judgment by asserting Petitioner "ignored" the barring order, thus wiping from this litigation an entire legal claim of malicious prosecution is prejudicial error; especially in light of the fact that Petitioner was acquitted of criminal trespass by the Commonwealth of Pennsylvania?

8.   Whether the lower courts erred in failing to afford Petitioner an evidentiary hearing to challenge the "Certification of Scope of Employment" in keeping with this Court's ruling in <u>Martinez v. Lamagno</u>. Does the direct evidence in the court record reflect the "Certification" is fraudulent and a conflict of interest?

9.   Whether the <u>Feres Doctrine's</u> "incident to service bar" on intentional torts and medical malpractice impedes enforcement and denies constitutional due process protections of servicemembers who engage in First Amendment protected activity under the "Act". Hence, should the "intentional tort and medical malpractice" bars be rendered unconstitutional as it allows for Governmental misfeasance and malfeasance to go unchecked if Military Inspectors Generals and Congress fail to enforce the statute?

10. Whether the <u>"Act's"</u> failure to provide a "private cause of action", impedes First Amendment free speech protection under the statute, thus violates the military member's right to "due process" under the Fifth Amendment of the U. S. Constitution? Does the preponderance of the evidence in favor of Petitioner, establish the fact that the "internal system" of justice within the Armed Forces has been severely abused and its integrity compromised, demanding judicial intervention by this Court?

11. Whether the lower courts erred in dismissing Petitioner's claim of malicious prosecution by deciding this case based upon precedent set in <u>United States v. Albertini</u>. Do the facts, circum-

stances and requested relief in this case distinguish this case as a "case of first impression"? Should this case not be tried as a "matter of fact" rather than a "matter of law" in light of this fact?

12.   Should legal claims arising from abuse of power in the U. S. Government that are of constitutional and public trust importance, be dismissed by <u>any</u> federal court based upon legal technicalities? Is protecting the U. S. Constitution from the willful and deliberate abuses of those who betray their "Military Oath" and fail to uphold its mandate, a compelling question of national importance demanding review within the Federal Judiciary?

13.   Does Petitioner's direct evidence and Respondents' lack thereof, establish a prima facie case of Governmental malfeasance, misfeasance and negligent failure to perform duties imposed by statute by officials within the Executive and Legislative branches of the U. S. Government in this case? Does this fact demand the United States Supreme Court to invoke its supervisory powers to determine possible misconduct within these two branches?

14.   For a determination if prejudicial error occurred when the Appellate Court failed to accept and consider the newly discovered evidence (as provided hereto as Exhibit "A"), prior to its denying Petitioner's Request for Rehearing with the Third Circuit Court of Appeals. Does the investigation of ABC News, its compelling issues and Petitioner's participation in it, not provide the "motive" and a "genuine issue" for Petitioner to prevail on his claim of malicious prosecution?

15.   Can human rights abuses in the U.S. Military's mental health system be ignored by the United States Supreme Court? Must this Court not act to address this compelling issue in the name of justice?

STATEMENT OF THE CLAIM

Appellant-Petitioner Trueman ("Trueman") served on active duty in the United States Navy from the period of July 12, 1982 through January 13, 1994. In order for the privilege to serve his Country, Trueman was required to take the following oath:

"I do solemnly swear that I will support and defend the Constitution of the United States against all enemies foreign and domestic; that I will bear true faith and allegiance to the same; that I take this obligation freely, without any mental reservation or purpose of evasion; that I will well and faithfully discharge the duties of the office on which I am about to enter; so help me God."

Hence, Trueman's absolute devotion and belief in the above sacred oath and his refusal to betray the oath, is the primary circumstance that ultimately led to this cause of action.

From the period of July 12, 1982 through the morning of February 7, 1993, Trueman's military records were exemplary and he was consistently recognized as a top notch military member. However, on the afternoon of February 7, 1993, Trueman came face-to-face with either upholding his oath and/or turning his back on issues amounting to fraud, waste and abuse at NAS Willow Grove. (Evidence of this abuse is at App. Brief Exh. Q. p. 191).[5] When Trueman placed loyalty to the Navy and his Country over the wants, wishes and personal agendas of former superiors in his chain of command at NAS Willow Grove, his mental stability was maliciously attacked to discredit his claims of improprieties as confirmed in Exhibit Q. To further discredit Trueman's credibility and prevent his access to other base personnel also claiming fraud, waste and abuse, Respondent Lekberg wrongfully barred[6] and transferred Trueman from the command alleging he was detrimental to good order and discipline. As a result of the unsubstantiated and false claims of Respondent Lekberg, Trueman was involuntarily discharged from the Navy due to alleged mental illness on January 13, 1994.[7]

In light of the Navy Department's breaching Trueman's enlistment contract with the American People and his honorable discharge status, Trueman received "transitional benefits" provided by the U. S. Government. These benefits allowed Trueman continued access to any military installation in the world for a period of two years following the date of discharge. Hence, on January 14, 1994 Trueman could no longer be prosecuted under military law. However, he was still allowed access to Willow Grove, since Respondent Lekberg never barred Trueman from entering NAS Willow Grove as a private citizen.

---

5. What the Navy IG's report confirms is that 1 out of 10 military personnel at NAS Willow Grove reported claims of fraud, waste, abuse, while Respondents Lekberg and Powell held command authority. Obviously, the first indicator of governmental misfeasance in this case is the fact that the Navy Department knew problems existed at NAS Willow Grove prior to Trueman's engagement in First Amendment protected speech.

6. The underlying issue in dispute in this lawsuit is whether the Lekberg military barring order was issued as reprisal for Trueman's First Amendment protected speech and whether its use, as probable cause to arrest Trueman as a civilian is constitutional.

7. Trueman's "Application for Reinstatement" under §§ 1034 & 1552 was denied by the BCNR on July 31, 1996. Since that time, Trueman has repeatedly attempted to provide the BCNR with "newly discovered evidence" which undercuts the Navy's justification for his discharge. However, the BCNR has repeatedly "failed to correct" clearly evident false statements placed in the record by Respondent Lekberg. Therefore, under Yee, the BCNR has violated "its mandate, and such a violation, contrary to the evidence, is arbitrary and capricious." Yee v. U. S. 1975, 512 F.2d 1383, 206 Ct. Cl. 388. Essentially, the BCNR is attempting to place a direct estoppel on Trueman's wrongful discharge claim by alleging that claim was dismissed in this lawsuit. However, in a telephone conversation on Friday, February 19, 1999, Trueman confirmed with Mr. Richard Mentzinger, the U. S. Attorney in Philadelphia who defended Respondents in this case that a claim of wrongful discharge is not at issue in this litigation. Therefore, the seriousness of Congress' failure to uphold its own statute and allow this obstruction to take place under §§ 1034 & 1552 is clearly provided for at Argument VIII of this Petition, and supports Trueman's argument for a "private cause of action" under § 1034.

In preparation for filing his "Application for Reinstatement" under Title 10 U.S.C. §§ 1034 and 1552 claiming wrongful discharge for engaging in protected activity, Trueman submitted numerous Freedom of Information/Privacy Act (FOIA/PA) requests to the Navy Department.[8] On May 26, 1994, Trueman received notification by U. S. Mail from the Navy Inspector General (Navy IG) that the documents he was seeking should be obtained from NAS Willow Grove. (App. Brief Exh. P. p. 72.1)[9]. Due to the repeated failure of the Navy to release the documents Trueman requested, on the morning of May 27, 1994 Trueman proceeded to hand deliver a FOIA/PA Act request directly to NAS Willow Grove as directed by the Navy IG to head off any further delays in obtaining alleged documents Respondent Lekberg claims support his reasoning for Trueman's discharge. (App. Brief Exh. Q. p. 73). Additionally, due to the expediency of his discharge, Trueman, attempted to obtain G.I. Bill educational benefits owed him by the Government, but not provided him at the time of his discharge. (App. Brief Exh. R. p. 74). When Trueman approached the main gate of the base he was stopped by Respondent Lekberg's base police, and asked to produce valid identification to enter the based. Trueman complied and was then granted permission to enter the base. **He did not trespass** nor was he notified by base police that his presence as a civilian on NAS Willow Grove was prohibited. Within approximately one hour of his arrival Respondent DeLong approached Trueman and asked him, "Jeff, what are you doing on the base?" Trueman explained to DeLong his reasons for being on base and DeLong responded; "I hate to do this to you, but Commander Powell wants me to arrest you." Obviously, without want of probable cause, actuated by malice, DeLong acting on illegal orders from Respondents Lekberg and Powell instituted a criminal prosecution against Trueman.[10]

On July 6, 1996, Trueman challenged the Respondents' want of probable cause for his arrest and criminal trespass charge in Montgomery County, Pennsylvania, criminal court. In sum, Respondent DeLong stated that Trueman caused no disturbance and engaged in no unlawful behavior. Hence, the Court discharged the case.[11] On August 29, 1994, Trueman filed a Complaint with the Department of Defense Inspector General (DODIG) to address Respondents' unlawful conduct in an attempt to address and correct the injustice within the Department of Defense. This Complaint was forwarded to the Navy Inspector General (Navy IG) who on

---

8. As of the date of filing this Petition, the Navy Department has not released any direct evidence to support its claim that Trueman was detrimental to good order and discipline and/or suffered from mental illness.

9. At (Exhibit O-1 p. 71), Trueman establishes the fact that he attempted to retrieve the requested documents through the Navy IG, specifically to prevent any potential "conflict" at NAS Willow Grove, prior to his malicious prosecution of May 27, 1994.

10. The lower courts' finding that Trueman "ignored" a barring order and cannot state a claim against DeLong would be disproved if discovery was allowed in this case. Not only were Trueman and DeLong once friends until this lawsuit, more importantly, DeLong was assigned by Respondents Lekberg and Powell to arm escort Trueman during his discharge outprocessing. Hence, DeLong was fully aware of all reprisals Lekberg and Powell took against Trueman - to include the retaliatory barring and transfer orders. Simply stated, if DeLong disobeyed the unlawful orders of Lekberg and DeLong, he too would have been targeted for retaliation.

11. The Court predicated its decision to discharge the case due to jurisdictional reasons; (the arrest was based upon military law and Trueman was a private citizen of the State of Pennsylvania), in addition to the fact that Trueman was granted permission to enter the installation by Lekberg's own military police.

December 7, 1994, ruled that the Lekberg barring order of November 19, 1993 was still valid.[12]

On May 24, 1996 and July 5, 1996, Trueman filed claims under the Constitution of the United States, Bivens v. Six Unknown Named Agents of Fed. Bureau of Narcotics, 403 U.S. 388 (1971); and the Federal Tort Claims Act (Title 28 U.S.C. § 2671 et seq.), respectively, after the DODIG refused to act on Trueman's complaint of constitutional right violations. On December 24, 1997, the District Court granted Respondents Summary Judgment dismissing all Trueman's legal claims due to "time bars", noting an exception to the claim of malicious prosecution. However, the District Court ruled that Trueman "cannot state a viable claim for malicious prosecution against any defendant" and that "the individual defendants are shielded by the doctrine of qualified immunity". Thus, the malicious prosecution claim was also dismissed by the District Court.[13] On January 21, 1998, Trueman appealed the District Court's Judgment essentially arguing that the direct evidence in the case supports a claim of First Amendment retaliation in violation of § 1034 which lead to his malicious prosecution. On October 27, 1998, the Appellate Court affirmed the District Court's Judgment (basing its decision solely on the assumption that Trueman "ignored" the Lekberg barring order). On November 6, 1998, Trueman filed a Petition for Rehearing In Banc, arguing the facts and circumstances should render this case a "case of first impression" and that it should be remanded to trial based on "matter of fact" as opposed to "matter of law". On November 30, 1998 the Petition for Rehearing was denied by the Appellate Court.[14] On January 29, 1999, Trueman filed a Request for Sixty Day Time Extension to File Writ of Certiorari. On February 16, 1999, the Honorable Justice Souter approved Trueman's request and extended the time of filing from February 27, 1999 to April 28, 1999. This Petition for Writ of Certiorari follows.

SUMMARY OF ARGUMENT

When the District Court ruled that Trueman could not state a viable claim for malicious prosecution and granted Respondents qualified immunity, these decisions were wholly inconsistent with the facts and circumstances before the Court. Furthermore, the Court's failure to consider Trueman's First Amendment whistleblower reprisal claim, failure to allow him any period of discovery to prove the Lekberg bar-

---

12. Considering the Navy IG is a third party to this lawsuit, its determination that the barring order remained valid is improper. Furthermore, in this letter, the Navy IG <u>willfully</u> provided the BCNR with false information to deprive Trueman his protection under § 1034, giving rise to Trueman's argument that <u>Feres</u> obstructs the enforcement of § 1034.

13. Trueman concedes that due to his former legal counsel's breach of the duty of competence, all legal claims with the exception of the malicious prosecution claim are time barred. However, Trueman strongly contests the dismissal of the malicious prosecution claim based on the fact that the lower courts failed to consider the nexus between his First Amendment whistleblower reprisal claim, the barring order and the May 27, 1994 arrest.

14. On January 11, 1998, Trueman verified with Ms. Melton, Informational Officer, Office of Staff Attorneys, United States Court of Appeals that the Petition for Rehearing In Banc was treated as a Petition for Rehearing under Rule 13.4. Ms. Melton confirmed that the Petition was considered as both a Petition for Rehearing and Rehearing In Banc.

ring order unlawful, and its misapplication of the Doctrine of Stares Decisis, amounts to a gross abuse of judicial discretion and a rush to judgment without considering all the facts. Essentially, Trueman believes that because the facts, circumstances and requested relief in this matter places the Feres Doctrine and the U. S. Military's medical and judicial systems on trial, he did not receive a fair opportunity to litigate this case and was denied due process of law by the District Court.

After Trueman appealed the District Court's Judgment and the Appellate Court affirmed the District Court's ruling by "asserting" Trueman "ignored" the Lekberg barring order in light of the fact that Trueman was acquitted of criminal trespass, a grave injustice took place. So much so that now, a precedent has been set that allows the U. S. Military the legal right to arrest private citizens based upon military law if this decision stands.

Contrary to the lower courts' ruling that Trueman could not state a viable claim for malicious prosecution, provided at Exhibit "A" is newly discovered evidence that provides a genuine issue of material fact in dispute, which supports Trueman's claim that he was maliciously prosecuted on May 27, 1994.[15] To lay the foundation as to the true reason why Respondents maliciously violated Trueman's constitutional rights on May 27, 1994, and the underlying reason for the false arrest, the following introductory statement sums up all the malfeasance and misfeasance overlooked by the federal courts in this matter:

> "You will find this story we are about to show you very hard to believe I think, indeed we consider it explosive! It's about the U. S. Military and the awesome power it can use to strike back at personnel who are in any way critical, even when their criticism may be in the best interest of the country." (*Ms. Barbara Walters ABC News' 20/20, October 23, 1998*).

Although Respondents' abuses of power and the condoning of that behavior by Members of Congress, Military Inspectors Generals, Navy Judge Advocate General (JAG) and the Department of Justice (DOJ), is without any doubt an outrage and betrayal of the public's trust, the true villain in all of this rests solely upon the chilling effects of the Feres Doctrine's "incident to service bar" on intentional torts and medical malpractice. If not for this law, Respondent Lekberg could not have falsified Trueman's military records to reflect he was detrimental to good order and discipline, when in fact, the direct evidence reflects Trueman was a 4.0 sailor.[16] To allow "false leaders" in the U. S. Armed Forces "unbridled power" to abuse "rank and file"

---

15. Exhibit "A" is an approximately fifteen month ABC News 20/20 investigation of the U.S. Military's practice of sending its members who report fraud, waste and abuse against command authorities into its mental health system to discredit and cover-up such allegations. Trueman requested leave of the Appellate Court to submit this Exhibit into evidence in his Petition for Rehearing, however, this request was denied.

16. As Trueman pointed out in his Reply Brief, if a subordinate military member even made a "finger gesture" at a superior in rank, that individual would face disciplinary action under the UCMJ. Therefore, if Trueman was truly detrimental to good order and discipline (the reason for the barring order), then why was he never written up and/or ever disciplined? In short, Trueman was a 4.0 sailor and only because Respondents were superior in rank, the "system" that is on trial in this case refused to stop the blatant abuses of Respondents.

members of the military due to <u>Feres</u>, is simply not in the best interests of this Nation.

As Trueman pointed out in his Petition for Rehearing, our Armed Forces are in serious trouble due to manpower shortages. Although the present military leaders believe a 4% pay raise and spending hundreds of millions of dollars in recruitment advertisements is the solution to the manpower shortages, the true solution is treating our men and women in uniform with respect, dignity and holding accountable those who intentionally and deliberately abuse their official powers. To achieve this goal, the <u>Feres Doctrine's</u> "incident to service bar" on intentional torts and medical malpractice must be repealed, and a precedent must be established under § 1034 to ensure protection of our servicemembers who report fraud, waste and abuse is <u>absolute,</u> and accountability held against military officials such as the Lekberg and Powells who intentionally and deliberately abuse their powers. To justify these needed reforms, one only needs to look at the inactions of Congress' in this case.

ARGUMENT

The critical constitutional question Trueman has been attempting to litigate in this cause of action, is whether the U. S. Military had the legal authority to arrest a private citizen predicated upon military law. If the Supreme Court rules that Trueman's arrest was unconstitutional, then the legal issues arising from intentional and deliberate violations of federal law (i.e. Title 10 U.S.C. § 1034) are many, and the facts, circumstances and requested relief in this case distinguish it as a "case of first impression".

Although Respondents cite 67 prior court cases to support their legal position in this matter, the only relevant case that was cited is <u>Feres v. United States</u>, 340 U. S. 135, 71 S.Ct. 153, 95 L.Ed 152 (1950). The relevance of <u>Feres</u> in this matter is that this law has allowed for unthinkable abuses of power and medical malpractice by Respondents to take place against Trueman, for his engaging in protected speech as a military member under § 1034. The evidence in the court record reflects serious public trust concerns are present such as the failure of Members of Congress, Military Inspectors Generals, the BCNR, the Department of Justice and the Commander-in-Chief[17], to either act to prevent and/or enforce, the <u>Inspector General Act of 1978</u> and the <u>Military Whistleblower Protection Act</u> (1992). Hence, Trueman makes the following arguments to convince the United States Supreme Court to invoke its supervisory powers to; (1) address misapplication of case laws by the lower courts, (2) address substantially documented facts of governmental malfeasance, misfeasance and abuse of taxpayers' monies to defend Respondents' illegal conduct, (3), to determine whether a private cause of action under § 1034 should be incorporated into the statute, to protect the liberty and property interests of career military members

---

17.On February 2, 1995, Trueman initiated his first communication to the President of the United States pointing out the abuses in the military's mental health system. This communication was answered by the Office of the Secretary of the Navy, stating "The BCNR will give your case full and fair consideration..." Trueman then followed up with a letter dated April 18, 1995 pointing out his concerns of conflicts of interest and other obstructions as pointed out in Argument V. No response was received by the White House and/or any official thereunder. Thus, a question of national importance is whether the DOJ, the enforcers of federal law have condoned violations of those laws to protect their boss, the President of the United States.

who report fraud, waste and abuse for the good of the American public, and (4), to repeal the Feres Doctrine's intentional tort and medical malpractice immunity clause to prevent a repeat of the unthinkable abuses of governmental powers that has taken place in this case, from happening in the future.

I. Can a private citizen of the United States be prosecuted under military law?

The underlying critical unanswered question in this case is whether Trueman's arrest as a private citizen predicated on military law is constitutional. On May 27, 1994, Respondents arrested Trueman for alleged criminal trespass predicated upon military law, however, Trueman was a private citizen. As stated above, on January 13, 1994 the U. S. Navy cut all legal ties with Trueman when it ordered his involuntary-honorable discharge at the recommendation of Respondent Lekberg. Due to this fact, Trueman was provided with U. S. Government transitional benefits which granted him access to any military installation in the world for a period of two years.[18] The question of ignorance is this; If Respondent Lekberg felt that Trueman was a potential threat to the command as a civilian, and knew he could legally return to the base due to his transitional benefits, then why did he fail to bar Trueman as a civilian prohibiting his reentry to the base under Federal Criminal Code, Title 18 U.S.C. § 1382? Respondent Lekberg's own testimony at the Keller MSBP hearing (App. Brief Exhibit Z. p. 274), states the following about his fear of Trueman: "He was admined (sic) out of the Navy, and he, too, we were concerned he still had it out for a lot of people..." Hence, if Trueman truly posed a threat to "a lot of people" at NAS Willow Grove, then common sense would dictate that Lekberg had a "duty" to bar him as a civilian to protect his command. Obviously, this preventive measure was not undertaken for one simple reason; Trueman was a 4.0 sailor and for Lekberg to issue a retaliatory barring order under § 1382, would have been defeated by injunctive relief. Again, for the Respondents to base an arrest and prosecution of Trueman on an invalid barring order predicated upon the force of military law is simply outrageous and most definitely unconstitutional.[19] At the very minimum, the lower courts should have conducted an evidentiary hearing to ensure Trueman due process of law to challenge the validity of the Lekberg barring order and to comply with this Court's holding that; ("[A] bar order issued in response to activity protected by the First Amendment is invalid.")[20] Albertini, 472 U.S. at 701 n. 10. An evidentiary hearing is further justified especially in light of the evidence which reflects Trueman was considered a 4.0 sailor and recommended for advancement and retention, just one month prior to creation of the barring order. (App. Brief Exh. H., p. 122). In light of

---

18. Although the U. S. Attorney argues that it would make no sense for Trueman to have greater access to NAS Willow Grove after his discharge, Trueman's transition benefits provided for this reality. Once again, if Trueman was truly detrimental as alleged by Respondent Lekberg, then where are the disciplinary reports and why was he issued an "honorable discharge"?

19. In Footnote 1 of the District Court's findings it states in part: "No underlying explanation accompanied the order, and none has been given by defendants Lekberg or the United States." Essentially, Trueman believes the failure of the District Court to make a showing that the barring order was justified is an abuse of his due process rights and a rush to judgment in granting Respondents qualified immunity.

20. Another reason "qualified immunity" in this case is inappropriate is that a violation of § 1034 by military personnel is a punishable offense under the UCMJ.

the direct evidence provided by Trueman which establishes the barring order was issued as reprisal in the wake of his First Amendment protected activity, combined with the failure of Respondent Lekberg to defend the bar order with any evidence to support its legality, the barring order <u>must</u> be rendered invalid and Trueman's malicious prosecution claim remanded to trial.

II. Does a military barring order remain valid indefinitely against a discharged military Veteran?

In an attempt to cover-up for its malfeasance and misfeasance to prevent Respondents Lekberg and Powell's corruption from reaching higher authority, the Navy IG made a legal determination that Lekberg's barring order remains in effect indefinitely. This determination by the Navy IG demands judicial review. Even if the Court holds that civilians can be arrested under military law, it still does not means the Lekberg barring order is valid. To date, the only official authority who has decided the validity of the barring order has been the Navy IG. As pointed out in Argument VIII below, this agency has engaged in illegal conduct under the <u>Inspectors General Act of 1978</u>, thus, any determination in the court record by this agency is highly subjective and carries no credibility. Hence, Trueman requests this Court to rule whether a military barring order issued against an active duty member of the Armed Forces, remains in effect against the "former member" as a private citizen. If not, then clearly, a viable claim of malicious prosecution exists. The claim must be remanded to trial.

III. Did the lower courts' failure to afford Trueman discovery violate his right to "due process" under the Fifth Amendment to the U.S. Constitution?

As Trueman argued in his Reply Brief, "due process" is the essence of our freedom from unlawful Government intrusion; an inalienable right due all Americans. However, an obvious injustice has taken place in this case due to the lower courts' failure to allow Trueman any period of discovery to obtain sworn testimony and/or documents that support Respondents' claims, that Trueman was detrimental to good order and discipline. Essentially, what the federal lower courts have done is to overturn the Commonwealth of Pennsylvania's findings that Trueman did not engage in criminal activity. In essence, the federal lower courts have convicted Trueman of criminal trespass on the "word" alone of Respondent Lekberg. (Clearly, the District Court did not base its decision on evidence as stated in Footnote 1 of its decision). As a matter of fairness and justice, and to afford Trueman due process of law, if Respondent Lekberg's claims that Trueman was detrimental to good order and discipline are truly meritorious, then he must be held to prove his allegation under oath.

169

IV. Did the lower courts err when they failed to consider Trueman's First Amendment whistleblower reprisal claim, the foundation to support his claim of malicious prosecution?

The legal position of the Respondents in this case has been that Trueman was allegedly "detrimental to the good order and discipline" at NAS Willow Grove, and was therefore barred from the command on November 19, 1993. However, contrary to this <u>unsupported</u> and <u>unsworn testimony</u> of Respondent Lekberg, the evidence in this case reflects Trueman was a continued asset to the Navy.[21] In addition to Trueman being denied discovery, for the lower courts to ignore Trueman's First Amendment retaliation claim removes the essential element to establish a viable claim of malicious prosecution. Therefore, to prove the arrest of May 27, 1994 was unconstitutional and undertaken with malicious intent to silence Trueman's claims of human right abuses in the military's mental health system, the following critical factors to support a viable claim of malicious prosecution are as follows:

(1) On February 25, 1993, Trueman's "structured discharge" was set into motion. After being informed that his request to speak with his Commanding Officer (CO) was approved by Respondent Powell and the CO, Trueman was then formally counseled by his immediate supervisor for alleged insubordination. (This counseling is the first and only written counseling of Trueman's entire career). Hence, the conspiracy to destroy Trueman's mental stability was callously employed that day. From that moment forward, Trueman's fate in the military was sealed.

(2) On February, 28, 1993 Trueman discussed with his CO what he reasonably believed were issues reflecting fraud, waste and abuse in his department. Ironically, Trueman proceeded with these issues out of loyalty to his CO, knowing the improprieties could have reflected negatively on his CO during the triennial inspection scheduled for early March 1993.[22] At the conclusion of the meeting, Trueman was notified by his CO that corrective action would be taken against anyone under his authority if they were abusing their power.

21.(The hypocrisy of this case is that two (2) days after Respondent Lekberg claimed Trueman was detrimental to good order and discipline, he awarded Trueman with a "Letter of Appreciation." (App. Brief Exh. I. p. 123). In combining this evidence with the evidence reflecting Trueman's favorable recommendations for advancement and retention one (1) month prior to his career ending classification, (App. Brief pp. 122-138), clearly establishes a prima facie case of whistleblower retaliation. The "word" of Lekberg should be given <u>no</u> credibility by this Court until he "testifies under oath" to his official actions.

22.Some of the issues Trueman raised in his meeting with his CO, are corroborated by the sworn affidavits of Chief Petty Officer Sund and former-Petty Officer Second Class Donald Serkleski. (See App. Brief Exh. N. p. 139 and Exh. O. p. 145). Additionally, both Affiants affirmatively state that they believe that Trueman was retaliated in the fashion he was (abuse of the mental health system), to remove him from the command prior to the triennial inspectors' arrival.

(3) On March 3, 1993, an internal investigation was ordered and initiated by order of the CO. The first conflict in the investigative process occurred when the CO appointed a "department head" under his authority as investigating officer. Hence, the integrity and independence of the investigation was compromised from the onset and would lead to a long train of abuses within the § 1034 investigative process. Throughout the internal investigation, no personnel with first-hand knowledge of the improprieties (such as Affiants Sund and Serkleski), were ever questioned and/or their statements recorded to corroborate Trueman's claims of improprieties.

(4) On March 26, 1993, (one day prior to the official release of the investigative findings), Trueman was fired from his position as Leading Petty Officer, Aviation Training Department. On the following morning, March 27, 1993, Trueman was officially notified by his CO that his grievance issues had no merit. In the wake of this notification he was then ordered to undergo mental health examinations to address both his alleged paranoid thought process and alleged alcohol abuse to cover-up the corruption he exposed at NAS Willow Grove.[23] Hence, the nexus between "Exhibit 'A'", Trueman's involvement in it, and this case has now been established.

Obviously, because Trueman upheld his "solemn oath" rather than bowing down to the threats of Respondents, he became a liability. Once this perception was taken by Trueman's superiors, the awesome power granted by the Feres Doctrine to abuse Trueman's constitutional and human rights became their offensive weapon and legal defense. In sum, what Trueman did and the Respondents failed to do, was to live up to the "Military Oath" and United States Navy "Core Values" (i.e. HONOR, COMMITMENT and COURAGE) which states in part:

> "I will bear true faith and allegiance... Accordingly, we will conduct ourselves in the highest ethical manner in all relationships with peers, superiors and subordinates;... be loyal to our nation, ensuring the resources entrusted to us are used in an honest, careful and efficient way; Abide by an uncompromising code of integrity,... Illegal or improper behavior or even the appearance of such behavior will not be tolerated... We will be mindful of the privilege to serve our fellow Americans... Care for the professional, personal and spiritual well-being of our people; Show respect towards all people... Treat each individual with human dignity; Exhibit the highest degree of moral character, technical excellence, quality and com-

---

23. In 1992, the United States Congress passed legislation which made it illegal for military officials in positions of authority, to refer a military member for mental health examinations in the wake of protected activity. The law states in part: "Mental Health Examination/Evaluation... no person may refer a member of the Armed Forces for a mental health examination as a reprisal for making or preparing to make a lawful communication to a Member of Congress; an Inspector General; a member of DOD audit, inspection, investigation, or law enforcement organization; or to any appropriate authority in the chain of command. Military Whistleblower Protection Act, Title 10 U.S.C. § 1034 and the National Defense Authorization Act for Fiscal Year 1993, Pub. L. No. 102-484, sec. 546, 106 Stat. 2315, 2416-19 (1992). (emphasis added).

petence in what we have been trained to do... make decisions in the best interest of the Navy and the nation, without regard to personal consequence;... Courage is the value that gives us the moral and mental strength to do what is right, even in the face of personal or professional adversity." (1994 Navy Leader Planning Guide).

Ironically, as a result of Trueman upholding these Values and Respondents' complete disregard for them, Trueman was placed into a five week inpatient treatment facility to discredit his mental stability for his absolute belief in these Values and his military oath.[24]

Upon Trueman's return to his command, he proceeded with additional complaints of reprisals under the provisions of § 1034. Once again, Trueman was threatened; this time by Respondent Powell not to proceed with continued claims of abuse of power against the command. Trueman proceeded however, this time under § 1034 despite the threat and the following additional reprisals occurred:

> (1) On August 30, 1993, Trueman filed his first claim of retaliation under and request for assistance under § 1034 with Senator Arlen Specter of Pennsylvania. Trueman then followed up with continued claims of § 1034 reprisals to the Navy Inspector General dated September 14, 1993, alleging abuse of the Navy's mental health system and obstruction of his transfer orders (App. Brief Exh. A3' p. 277) against Respondent Powell.[25] Finally, Trueman headed a contingent of base personnel in a mid-October 1993, whistleblower meeting in the office of then-Senator Harris Wolford.[26] In all, Respondents knew Trueman was engaging in § 1034 protected activity and took unfavorable personnel actions in direct violation of federal law despite this fact.

> (2) On November 18, 1993, Lekberg initiated a "kangaroo court" and Trueman was recommended for discharge. At the conclusion of this abuse

---

24. Essentially, what Feres allowed Respondents to achieve without any evidence is; (1), to classify Trueman allegedly psychologically dependent on alcohol in a fifteen minute interview with a non-mental health expert, (even though he committed no alcohol related incident as required by Navy regulations), and (2), that the diagnosis was so arbitrary that Trueman was found **"fit for full duty"**, (although Level III is reserved for bona fide alcohol dependency cases). However, no one to include the Navy IG and Members of Congress cared to consider this blunder. What has taken place here is fraud and abuse of the mental health system to remove Trueman from access to the triennial inspectors at substantial costs to the American taxpayer.

25. If Trueman was afforded discovery, he could have proven that his transfer orders were unlawfully interfered with by Respondent Powell to prevent his contact with the FBI. In sum, Trueman's pending "top secret" transfer orders, would have opened the door to Respondents having to answer to the FBI, as to why Trueman allegedly suffered from a paranoid thought process. This fact alone, would have exposed Respondents to potential liability under § 1034.

26. As reflected in the court record (App. Brief Exh. P. pp. 149-265), at that meeting was one-Tony Keller. In Keller v. Lekberg, Powell, DeLong, et al., Keller defeated the Defendants' Motion for Summary Judgment on his "reprisal" claim. Hence, the very same U. S. Attorney's Office fighting this case, settled the Keller case. Another indicator of Feres' depriving due process is that another Defendant in Keller, one-Commander Gumpright, was hand picked by Respondent Powell and approved by Lekberg as a sitting member at Trueman's administrative discharge board. This individual objected to all Trueman's questions posed at the Government. In all, Respondent Lekberg and Powell have cost the American taxpayer somewhere in the ballpark of $300,000.00 and counting, for their abuses of power and the failure of Members of Congress and the DOJ to enforce the Inspectors General Act and § 1034.

of the administrative discharge process, Trueman was then notified that his § 1034 complaint to the Navy IG alleging Respondent Powell abused his power would be investigated, ironically, the following morning.

(3) On November 19, 1993, after a forty-five minute meeting with the Navy IG, Trueman was told to return to his workcenter to await further questioning. During this time frame, Respondent Powell (the subject of the inquiry) informed Trueman's former Department Head that the testimony of his former subordinates was not required by the Navy IG. Trueman was then barred and transferred from NAS Willow Grove at approximately 3:45 p.m. the day of the inquiry.[27] Clearly, Respondent Powell's involvement in deciding whose testimony was relevant in an investigation initiated against him, would surely lead a "reasonable person" to conclude the investigation was a sham, and potential criminal liability under § 1034 was initiated that very day.

Therefore, for the lower courts to ignore Trueman's First Amendment reprisal claim (the most essential legal claim in this case), Trueman was deprived "due process of law". This issue must be addressed if a just decision can be determined in this case.

V. Did the lower courts err when they failed to afford Trueman an evidentiary hearing to challenge the Department of Justice's Certification of Respondents as "acting within their scope of their employment"?

The District Court ruled and the Appellate Court affirmed that Trueman "offered no evidence warranting an evidentiary hearing on the issue of certification." To the contrary, and if afforded an opportunity to challenge the Certification, Trueman could have proven that the DOJ's Certification was improper and self-serving due to the following conflict of interests:

(1) On December 14, 1994, (two weeks after the Navy IG and BCNR obstructed Trueman's right to § 1034 protected status), Trueman initiated a Complaint to the U. S. Attorney General claiming that Respondents Lekberg, Powell and the Navy IG had engaged in intentional and deliberate violations of the Inspectors General Act of 1978 ("Act") (A mandatory notification required under the statute). On March 23, 1995, (15 months later), Paralegal Specialist Robert Gaudet, Jr., Criminal Section responded on behalf of the Attorney General. It was found that there was no prose-

---

27. In addition to the barring order, Lekberg also issued a transfer order on November 19, 1993. To further establish a prima facie case of § 1034 retaliation, the transfer orders were "pre-dated" November 17, 1993. (See App. Brief Exh. X p. 271. See also the Affidavit of Chief Sund). Obviously, a reasonable person would conclude that the "fix was in" to silence Trueman's claims of abuse of power and human right abuses in the mental health system and the IG investigation was concluded even before the Investigator Williams left his command.

cutable violation of federal criminal statutes with respect to Trueman's Complaint.

(2) On October 23, 1996, Trueman sent a letter to the DOJ requesting clarification as to whether a potential conflict of interest existed with its representation of Respondents, in this matter. Trueman further pointed out the nexus between his case and that of <u>Keller v. Lekberg, Powell, et al</u>, for which the DOJ's did not defend in court. This letter was <u>never</u> answered by the DOJ.

(3) On February 7, 1997, Trueman followed up his October 23, 1996 letter and again, requested clarification as to a potential conflict of interest. Trueman also pointed out verifiable false statements made by the Navy IG to further support criminal obstruction in violation of the <u>Inspectors General Act</u>, requiring the DOJ to investigate. Essentially, Trueman asserted the very facts as documented in Argument IV above. Once again, no response was received by the DOJ.

(4) Finally, on October 30, 1998, (one week after the airing of the ABC 20/20 broadcast), Trueman once again requested verification as to a conflict of interest with the Certification. Once again, the DOJ refused to inquire as to a potential conflict of interest in this regard prior to the filing of this Petition.[28] In <u>Martinez</u>, this Court held that; (certification of "scope of employment" is subject to judicial review in an evidentiary hearing). <u>Martinez v. Lamagno</u>, 515 U. S. 417, 115 S.Ct. 2227, 2236 (1995)(Ginsberg J.) See <u>Melo</u> (question of substantive federal law, "as that term is used in Art. III," reviewable by federal court), <u>Melo v. Hafer</u>, 13 F.3d 736, 747 (3d Cir. 1994) (Stapleton, J.)(evidentiary hearing required).

As evident by the facts in Argument IV above and the nexus between Respondents' "pattern of abuse" in both <u>Keller</u> and this case, and the fact the <u>very same</u> U.S. Attorney's Office who failed to defend Respondents in <u>Keller</u>, invoked the Certification in this case, would make a reasonable person suspect the Certification is highly suspect. Furthermore, since the Commander-in-Chief is a third party to this lawsuit and has refused to address human right abuses in "his" military mental health system and "appoints" U. S. Attorneys to their positions, are all credible factors and public trust issues which merit an evidentiary hearing in this case. The Federal Judiciary must ensure the DOJ is not abusing tax dollars to cover-up corruption in the U. S. Armed Forces as Trueman brings to the bar in this matter.

Therefore, due to the many "conflicts of interest" in the record and the failure of the DOJ to investigate Respondents and the Navy IG for violations of the <u>Inspec-</u>

28.On February 5, 1999, Ms. Marcia W. Johnson, Legal Counsel, Executive Office for the United States Attorneys failed to address Trueman's assertion that a conflict of interest exists in this case. Obviously, the "top" officials in the DOJ are aware of this issue but just as the BCNR, they too, are citing the dismissal of this action by the lower courts makes the issue moot. However, on April 16, 1999, the DOJ released documents in Trueman file that reflect <u>no</u> preliminary inquiry with regard to any of Trueman's claims was ever initiated.

tors General Act, a "reasonable person" would conclude that the May 12, 1997 Certification by Mr. Michael R. Stiles is self-serving, improper and was not made in good faith.[29]

As a matter of public trust, Government officials who willfully and deliberate abuse their official powers and act beyond their scope of employment cannot and must not be defended with public monies; they must be held accountable with those monies. For all these reasons, review of the Certification must be afforded under the Martinez and Melo standards.

VI. Should the lower courts' Judgments be vacated as the facts, circumstances, and requested relief in this action, qualify this case as a "Case of First Impression"?

As the court record in this case reflects, throughout Trueman's assignment at NAS Willow Grove and leading up to his claims of improprieties, Trueman was considered an asset to his command and the U. S. Navy. However, once Trueman engaged in First Amendment protected speech on the afternoon of February 7, 1993, all previous praise to include the 4.0 performance evaluation issued on December 23, 1992 (only eight weeks prior to his protected activity), was overshadowed by unsupported allegations that he suffered from a paranoid thought process due to alleged alcohol abuse.[30] Clearly, if not for Feres' "incident to service bar" on intentional torts and medical malpractice, Respondents could not have falsified Trueman's military records and violated his constitutional and human rights within its mental health system by a simple stroke of a pen. Although Respondents had a field day with obstructing Trueman's constitutional "due process" rights under both military grievance and §1034 due to Feres, on May 27, 1994 Respondents' conduct opened the door for a long awaited legal precedent to be established to address intentional torts and medical malpractice in the U. S. Armed Forces.

When Respondents arrested Trueman for criminal trespass as a private citizen and based probable cause on an invalid barring order predicated upon military law, although Trueman was; (1) allowed access to NAS Willow Grove by the U. S. Government, and (2), was granted permission to enter the base by military police, the circumstances clearly distinguished this case as a "case of first impression" arising under § 1034 retaliation. Although, the District Court likened this case to that of Albertini, 472 U.S. 675, 105 S.Ct. 2897, 86 L.Ed.2d 536 (1986), and the Appellate

29.Mr. Stiles is the U. S. Attorney who failed to prove that Respondents acted legally in Keller, thus, at (App. Brief Exh. T. pp. 262-263), the effect of their abuses of power at NAS Willow Grove is clearly evident by the substantial amount of monies paid for their retaliation.
30.As Trueman pointed out in his Reply Brief, to allow 4.0 sailors to be thrown out of the Navy due to alleged alcohol abuse, without engaging in any alcohol incident and/or misconduct will backfire on the Armed Forces, if the federal courts do not intervene to stop this form of retaliatory discharge. Essentially, individuals who want to breach their contracts now only have to allege alcohol abuse problems and refuse to comply with the rehab program must be discharged. Abuse of this system must be prevented or the investment of the American public's monies to train and maintain a strong Armed Forces, can and will easily be exploited as it has been in this case if Trueman's wrongful discharge for alleged alcohol rehab failure stands.

Court affirmed that Judgment, the facts, circumstances and requested relief are distinctly different in nature. To compare the two cases is not only an injustice to Trueman, but, an injustice to all military men and women who engage in protected activity under § 1034 for the good of the Nation. Therefore, to defuse the two cases and to set the foundation for a determination by this Court as to whether this case demands status as a "case of first impression", the following differences in fact and circumstances are as follows:

> **In Re: Albertini:** In 1972 Albertini accessed Hickam Air Force Base with unlawful intent wherein he destroyed government documents. As a result of his conduct, Albertini was convicted of conspiracy to injure Government property and was then issued a bar order from the commanding officer. The bar order directed Albertini to Title 18 U.S.C. § 1382 and based a violation of this statute on pain of fine or imprisonment. In total defiance, Albertini entered Hickam on May 16, 1981 during the base's annual open house for Armed Forces Day. Subsequently, Albertini was charged with violating § 1382 because he "unlawfully and knowingly" reentered Hickam after being notified his presence on base was illegal.

> The Albertini case is pretty cut and dry. That individual willingly engaged in criminal activity on a military installation and was then barred as a civilian under § 1382. When he reentered the base knowing he was barred under § 1382 the government took appropriate action when they arrested and tried him under federal law.

> **In Re: Trueman:** In 1993, Trueman was assigned to NAS Willow Grove as an active duty member of the U. S. Navy. After just receiving recognition as one of the best sailors on that command (App. Brief Exh. A, pp. 111-112), Trueman felt it was his duty to inform his commanding officer of improprieties that could affect the integrity of his command. In the wake of this protected activity, Trueman was ordered for mental health examinations in direct violation of federal law. In an attempt to redress this unlawful act, Trueman communicated to Members of Congress and the Navy Inspector General the reprisals he was facing in addition to exposing human right abuses in the military mental health system. As a result, Trueman was classified "detrimental to good order and discipline" (the "death wish" of any servicemember) and was then transferred and barred from Willow Grove. These acts further violated federal law and were done on the very day of the § 1034 inquiry. Hence, due to the Respondents obstructing Trueman's right to "due process", Trueman was involuntarily-honorably discharged from the Navy.

> In light of his involuntary-honorable discharge Trueman was issued transitional identification from the U. S. Government. This privilege allowed Trueman to access any base in the world for a period of two years following his discharge. Knowing this fact and having initiated Trueman's discharge, Respondent Lekberg should have taken immediate action to

protect his command, knowing Trueman could gain access. He did not and unlike Albertini, Trueman never received any notice that he was barred as a civilian under § 1382. Furthermore, unlike Albertini, Trueman was notified by a Navy Department official that he could utilize base facilities granted him by his transitional benefits. (App. Affidavit pp. 105-106, para. G-h) (draft affidavit omitted by Trueman's former legal counsel).

On May 27, 1994, Trueman attempted to conduct lawful business and was granted permission to enter the base by military police. Without probable cause (as evident by his acquittal), he was then arrested and charged for criminal trespass based upon a military barring order which its law enforcement power was predicated upon military law. Unlike, Albertini, the U. S. Government provided Trueman the legal right to enter NAS Willow Grove by issuing him transitional identification. Finally, Trueman faced a criminal charge of trespass and the charge was discharged. To the contrary, Albertini was found guilty of trespass.

Therefore, for the lower courts to rule Albertini as a precedent in this matter, is simply an error in law that must be reversed. From the above facts, there is a clear legal distinction between the Albertini and this case. Obviously, Trueman was pro-government while Albertini was apparently anti-government and the application of Albertini is clearly erroneous.

On May 27, 1994, Respondents' official actions were not undertaken in good faith to protect the base and its personnel, their acts were simply unconstitutional and intended to further besmirch Trueman's character and to prevent him from gaining access to the FOIA/PA Coordinator and an admission, that no evidence whatsoever exits in his military records to support any fact other than Trueman was retaliated against for engaging in First Amendment protected communications. Although Congress did not intend for a private cause of action under § 1034, it is this branch of Government whose own inactions and failure to enforce the statute in this case, is the primary justification for such a case law precedent within our judicial system. "Blatant violations of § 1034 cannot and must not be tolerated."

Trueman has clearly established by a preponderance of the evidence in the court record, that his arrest was not only initiated with malice, but was clearly unconstitutional as civilians cannot be prosecuted predicated upon military law. Due to the unique facts and circumstances in this case, Trueman requests the Court to vacate the lower courts' grant of Summary Judgment on the malicious prosecution claim and remand the issue to trial. Additionally, due to the Navy Department's failure to allow Trueman to submit "newly discovered evidence" at the BCNR under §§ 1034 & 1552, and Congress' "turning the blind eye" to this obstruction of justice, Trueman requests the Court to grant joinder of his pending "wrongful discharge" claim. Joinder is appropriate not only in the wake of the BCNR's obstruction of Trueman's due process rights under §§ 1034 & 1552, but, for consolidation of this closely related issue as a matter of judicial economy.

To the best of Trueman's research and knowledge, never before has a malicious prosecution claim arising from an unlawful barring order issued in violation of § 1034 been litigated in the federal circuit. Hence, this case must be adjudicated based upon fairness by "matter of fact" rather than "matter of law" due to its "unique" facts and circumstances.

VII. Do the facts, circumstances and documented abuses of governmental powers in this case call for the Feres Doctrine's "incident to service bar" on intentional torts and medical malpractice to be rendered unconstitutional for the good of the Nation?

On February 7, 1993, when Trueman thought that upholding his military oath was the right thing to do, rather then becoming a party to Respondents' abuses, unbeknownst to Trueman was a 49-year-old court decision named the Feres Doctrine. Simply stated, if Trueman knew of this law and its chilling effects that it would have on both his constitutional rights as a military member and a private citizen, his claims of improprieties leading to this lawsuit would not be at issue. Essentially, instead of facing relentless retaliation from his own Government, Trueman would have just "played the game", became a "slacker" and collected a paycheck every two weeks for the remainder of his military career. Trueman would have betrayed his oath to protect his military career and family's liberty and property interests. Hence, the question of national importance is whether; "Turning the blind eye to abuse of power in the U. S. Military to protect one's liberty and property interests is in the best interests of this Nation?" As this Court is well aware, under Feres v. United States (1950), it has long been held that the government has no Federal Tort Claims Act liability for injuries to members of the military service. Hence, for the past 49 years, intentional torts, medical malpractice and negligence claims arising from the military have been brushed under the carpet within the Judicial Branch of Government. Because of Feres, instead of holding accountable incompetent and/or abusive leaders, doctors, lawyers and investigators who engage in legal and medical malpractice, and intentional misconduct in office while acting under the "color of law", not only destroys the lives of honorable people who are above corruption, but poses a potential serious threat to the national security of the United States of America. What the Feres Doctrine's "incident to service bar" has allowed in this case is intentional torts, medical malpractice and intentional violations of federal statutes to go "unchecked". More importantly, Feres prevents enforcement of the Military Whistleblower Protection Act and deprives a military member his/her "due process" rights under the U. S. Constitution. If there is any law that is unjustified and simply bad law in the United States of America - it is Feres; the "silent third party" most responsible for allowing unthinkable abuses of American citizens in the Armed Forces to go unremedied. Although Trueman does concede that Feres and its "incident to service bar" on injuries suffered during combat is not at issue, the bar on intentional torts and medical malpractice must be repealed if true reforms in the system are to be achieved. We must not forget that the U. S. Military is a military of the People and is manned by millions of ordinary everyday citizens (i.e. the "rank and file"). To allow unthinkable abuses of rank and file members to go "unchecked" by a bogus assertion that holding accountable abusive leaders will be a "disruption to military discipline and effectiveness", is simply a legal rationale that can no longer be justified.[31]

Therefore, incorporating a private cause of action under § 1034 to wholly compensate victims of reprisals will be a "deterrent" to those who feel they can use their rank and power for self-gain and/or personal agendas. If we are to rebuild our Armed Forces and regain the trust of the American Public, this Court must take an active role to help achieve this goal.[32]

Essentially, when blatant abuses of power and intentional and deliberate violations of federal law <u>as clearly documented in this case</u> are condoned by Congress, IGs, the BCMR and DOJ, the federal courts must intervene to protect the constitutional and human rights of this Nation's military members. Essentially, *"Feres was wrongly decided and heartily deserves the widespread, almost universal criticism it has received."* <u>In re: "Agent Orange"</u> 481 U.S. 681, 701. In light of the substantially documented instances of Governmental malfeasance and misfeasance in the court record and explained in precise detail in this Petition, Trueman requests the Court to declare the "intentional torts and medical malpractice bar" under <u>Feres</u> unconstitutional. This law deprives military members' their right to "due process" and allows for government corruption to go covered up at the expense of the public's trust and monies.

VIII. Does the failure of § 1034 to provide a private cause of action violate the "due process" clause of Fifth Amendment? Does the law's failure to provide a legal mechanism to address arbitrary and capricious conduct of the BCMRs violate the due process clause?

If the United States Congress condones intentional and deliberate violations of its own statutes, does this not give the American People the "God given right" to declare any law passed by Congress as "meaningless?"[33] To support this fact and as provided for in the Declaration of Independence which reads in part:

---

31. When Congress passed the <u>Military Whistleblower Protection Act</u>, it gave the military member the absolute right to circumvent the military chain of command. Because of this fact, the "decisions" of military officials in command positions are subject to "outside" review under the law by Military Inspectors General and Members of Congress. Hence, if these public officials condone intentional and deliberate abuses under the law, then, the federal judiciary and the American public (i.e. juries) <u>must</u> intervene to enforce the law and ensure accountability.
32. Cases of this nature could be consolidated within the U. S. Court of Claims to ensure "uniformity" of decisions arising from claims under § 1034.

179

> "... When in the Course of human events... That whenever any Form of Government becomes destructive of these ends, it is the Right of the People to alter or to abolish it, and to institute new Government, laying its foundation on such principles and organizing its powers in such form, as to them shall seem most likely to effect their safety and Happiness..." (The Declaration of Independence, July 4, 1776).

It is quite obvious as the evidence confirms in this case, that the Clinton Administration to include the Department of Defense, Justice Department and most shocking of all, the United States Congress have all betrayed their oaths to protect and defend the United States Constitution. To think, that the leadership of this Country would allow for human right abuses within the military mental health system to go "unchecked", even after this <u>fact</u> was broadcast to the Nation and the World, <u>demands</u> a private cause of action under § 1034 to ensure "abusive leaders" are removed from military service either by a Federal Judge and/or the American People.

Although the Government will argue that <u>Acquisto v. United States</u>, 70 F3d. 1010 (8th Cir. 1995) set the precedent whereby no private cause of action under § 1034 was intended by Congress, again, where does a servicemember seek justice if Congress fails to uphold its own laws? Assuming the Government will further argue that the BCMRs are the proper legal administrative remedy to correct an "error or injustice" the following conflicts of interest and obstruction of justice issues are supported by direct evidence in this matter, which Trueman believes have been ignored due to the <u>Feres Doctrine's</u> "incident to service" bar:

Conflicts of Interest & Obstruction

(1)   On September 14, 1993, Trueman filed an abuse of power complaint against Respondent Powell to the Navy IG. The complaint alleged abuse of power and abuse of the Navy's mental health system. This § 1034 complaint was ironically investigated by the Navy IG on November 19, 1993 (one day after Respondent Lekberg recommend Trueman's discharge) and (the <u>very</u> day of the Lekberg issued barring and transfer orders to Trueman). The first conflict in this matter arises from the investigator assigned to Trueman's complaint, one-Commander Williams. Investigator Williams was in the <u>direct</u> chain of command of Respondents Lekberg and Powell. Hence, the "independence" of the investigation was compromised from the onset. In addition to the unfavorable personnel actions (i.e. bar and transfer orders), Trueman's witnesses who would have corroborate his claims of improprieties were informed by Respondent Powell that their testimony was <u>not</u> required by Investigator Williams.[34]

---

33. As the court record shows, Trueman's reports of reprisals under § 1034 were made to three U. S. Senators (a Republican and two Democrats) and two U. S. Congressman (one Republican and one Democrat). All legal issues arising from § 1034 in this Petition were presented to these lawmakers, but, <u>all</u> completely failed to uphold their own laws in this matter.

(2)   Again, on or about mid-October 1993, Trueman along with <u>Keller</u> and six
        other members of NAS Willow Grove participated in a whistleblower
        meeting with then-Senator Wolford (See Keller Affidavit, App. Brief Exh.
        R. p. 195). All participants claimed various abuses of power and retalia-
        tion directed at Respondents Lekberg and Powell. No issues were
        addressed by either Senator Wolford and/or Specter of Pennsylvania. This
        failure to act to insure the law was not being violated by Respondents,
        resulted in the demise of both Trueman and Keller's service to this Coun-
        try. (A chronology of the "abuse" is at App. Brief Exh. Q' pp. 187-190).

Obstruction of Due Process Under § 1034 & 1552

(1)   In November 1994, the BCNR approved "financial reimbursement" to True-
        man for an unauthorized move of his family during his active duty period.
        This official notification was provided Trueman in a letter dated Novem-
        ber 1, 1994, wherein W. Dean Pfeiffer, Executive Director of the BCNR,
        acting on behalf of the Secretary of the Navy, pursuant to §§ 1034 & 1552
        concluded: "Upon review and consideration of all the evidence of record,
        and especially in light of the contents of enclosure (2)[35], the Board finds
        the existence of an injustice warranting the following corrective action..."
        (App. Brief Exh J. pp. 58-59). The importance of this event is that <u>only</u>
        one month later, Trueman's protection under § 1034 with respect to his
        "Application for Reinstatement" under §§ 1034 & 1552 was then denied
        by Mr. Pfeiffer. The denial of Trueman to receive § 1034 review status
        resulted from the Navy IG's December 7, 1994 letter alleging Trueman's
        complaint against Respondent Powell was not a protected communication
        § 1034.[36] Obviously, the BCNR made a tremendous mistake by granting
        Trueman § 1034 status in November, thus, arbitrarily and capriciously
        denied Trueman his protection one month later. This about-face by the
        BCNR, deprived Trueman his "due process" rights under § 1034 for an

---

34. In sum, before Investigator Williams even left the base and prepared his report to higher authority,
    further reprisals in direct violation of § 1034 continued. Although the Navy IG and BCNR col-
    luded to obstruct Trueman's § 1034 "expedient review" right under the statute, and unlawfully
    denied him protected status under the law, on April 29, 1996, the DODIG recognized this com-
    plaint as a protected communication under the law. (In October 1998, the law changed whereby a
    communication to departmental IG's render a member protected under the whistleblower statute)
    (Re: DODIG E-Mail Bulletin Board). Furthermore, from the letter of William Shea, Investigator
    at the DODIG, (App. Brief Exh. A4. p. 279), it is quite evident that not only does he believe
    Trueman was reprised against for his protected communications, but reforms in the system are
    obviously needed.
35. Enclosure (2) are statements of Trueman's subordinates describing racism, dereliction of duty,
    favoritism, etc., in addition to other relevant evidence reflecting Trueman's military records were
    falsified resulting in his placement into the Navy's mental health system.
36. Obviously, the BCNR's grant of § 1034 financial reimbursement in November 1994 and then its
    denial to protect Trueman under § 1034 in December 1994, is clearly arbitrary and capricious.
    This obstruction of justice issue has also led to the BCNR's failure to accept "newly discovered
    evidence" in which Trueman would prevail on his wrongful discharge claim. These issues are
    prime examples for the need of a private cause of action under § 1034.

expedient hearing to address his wrongful discharge. This wrongful act unduly delay Trueman's due process for over 2 ½ years and once the process could no longer be delay, Trueman's Application denied redress in executive session on July 31, 1996 at the BCNR. In addition to a 2 ½ delay, the BCNR intentionally failed to introduce evidence provided by Trueman to establish his discharge was retaliatory and violated (§ 1034).

(2)   In January 1997, Trueman submitted "newly discovered evidence" to the BCNR he obtained after filing suit under the FOIA/PA.[37] In a letter dated March 24, 1998, W. Dean Pfeiffer, notified Trueman that "newly discovered evidence" he provided in January 1997, was not "new evidence". As a matter of fact, Pfeiffer stated: the "Board intends to take no action on the request for reconsideration because the case is still pending in court and any decision by the Board could impact on the judicial proceedings." (Again, the U. S. Justice Department confirmed Trueman's wrongful discharge claim has not be litigated in this matter).

(3)   In late October 1998, Trueman attempted one last time to obtain congressional assistance to obtain an evidentiary hearing and sought the help of Congressman James Oberstar (D-MN). On March 29, 1999, Joseph G. Lynch, Assistant General Counsel, Manpower and Reserve Affairs (supervisory official of the BCNR), refused to answer specific questions posed by Congressman Oberstar which if not answered, clearly establishes Trueman's discharge as retaliatory. However, on Friday, April 2, 1999, the congressional inquiry was unexpectedly halted by Congressman Oberstar's Chief of Staff, Mr. William Richard, thus, Trueman believes that any further attempts to correct his records within the Department of Defense would be futile at this point.

As clearly evident by the above facts, the Navy IG and BCNR have obstructed the administration of justice under § 1034, and these abuses have all been condoned by the DODIG, DOJ and Members of Congress. Thus, if government officials mandated to uphold and enforce §1034 partake in violations of the statute, the federal judiciary must intervene. Hence, in light of all the facts and circumstances, Trueman requests the following relief:

(1)   That: (1), this case be rendered a "case of first impression" and Trueman's malicious prosecution claim be remanded to trial to establish a precedent under § 1034; (2), that Trueman's pending "wrongful discharge" claim be joindered with his malicious prosecution claim and/or, for the Court to declare Trueman's administrative discharge unlawful, ordering Trueman's reinstatement into the Navy at the rank of Chief Petty Officer (E-7)

37.The newly discovered evidence submitted to the BCNR established a prima facie showing that Trueman's admin discharge board, transfer and barring orders were retaliatory. (See App. Brief Exh. H. p. 122).

with full backpay and benefits dating back to the date of discharge;

(2)   That the Court issue Writ of Mandamus to compel the Department of Defense Inspector General to investigate Respondents, et al., for deliberately violating § 1034 (a violation of military law); That "independent investigations" be ordered to determine if: (a), the DOJ negligently failed to perform duties imposed by statute; (b) if the DOJ defrauded public funds to cover-up its negligence in failing to investigate Respondents for violating § 1034 and aided and abetted human right/constitutional right violations under § 1034; (c), to determine the severity and extent of military members whose rights were violated under § 1034 since Congress outlawed mental health referrals in the wake of § 1034 protected activity in 1992; and (d), to determine whether the Navy IG and BCNR obstructed the administration of justice under § 1034 with respect to Trueman's "Application for Reinstatement" under §§ 1034 & 1552;

(3)   That the Feres Doctrine's bar on intentional torts and medical malpractice be declared unconstitutional as it impedes the enforcement of § 1034 and due to its chilling effects on the administration of justice within the U. S. Armed Forces; and, for such other and further relief the Court deems just, equitable and in the best interest of this Nation, its military personnel, and their families from military officials who abuse their powers.

CONCLUSION

As the Guardians of the United States Constitution, [I] pray that this Court will invoke its supervisory powers and address the overwhelming prima facie case of Governmental malfeasance and misfeasance that have been taking place under the leadership of William Jefferson Clinton, Commander-in-Chief, United States Armed Forces in this matter.[38]

Respectfully submitted,

Jeffrey A. Trueman, Pro Se

This 20th day of April 1999.

The Supreme Court denied my Petition by a vote of 9-0. Although I am very disappointed with this decision, I understand

---

38. On a personal note, this Petition is dedicated to all American Veterans and their families who have suffered injustice since Feres has been per se, "the law of the land".

the ramifications if this case had been brought to the public's eye in the wake of 49 years of injustice due to Feres. However, as Justice Scalia pointed out in *Johnson v. United States* in 1987, Congress's inaction regarding this doctrine and its doing little, if anything in the way of modifying it to prevent Constitutional claims is clearly unjust and irrational. Again, allowing such power to military leaders *can and does result in abuse therefore where are the checks and balances on the military?* Again, I hold the United States Congress responsible for the human/constitutional rights violations that are taking place within our military's mental and legal systems simply because they "control" the Armed Forces of the United States and must act to prevent corruption within. Therefore, I must share a quote from one of this nation's greatest military leaders, that I used to close my Article 138 complaint of abuse of power against Captain Broyles, that explains my reasons for refusing to become party to corruption and turn my back on subordinates at NAS Willow Grove:

> "Courage, Competence, Sacrifice, Caring, Selfless service. These are the watchwords for a successful leader. Your personnel must see you sacrifice for them. You must set the moral, ethical, and the physical standards for them. You much always demonstrate your competence to them. Train them, and lead them competently. They must see you put yourself at risk for them. You must be a problem solver for them. You must totally give your loyalty to them and no one else. You must care for them. Remember,... that upon no other institution does America depend more for values and integrity than it does the Armed Forces. That's why I charge each of you to fight for those values, to make them a part of your character, to make them a part of your life."

The above words were spoken by Army General Colin Powell! I hope I have proven my case favorably in the court of public opinion that flagrant violations of human rights in the United States Armed Forces are being openly condoned by officials of the Clinton Administration.

Chapter 7

A Future Patriot Sums it All Up

"And Liberty and Justice for All"

O
n January 17, 1997 as I was preparing for my trip to the Twin Cities to oppose the government's Motion for Dismissal and the Commander-in-Chief William Jefferson Clinton was preparing to lie at the Paula Jones deposition. My son Gage, who was six at the time, asked me if he would have to talk to the Judge. He had spent many nights sitting by me wondering why I was fighting our government. "Of course not," I said, "but if you had to talk to the Judge what would you say?" As his little mind was racing trying to come up with an answer, his eyes got big and he started to sing—

> "I pledge allegiance to the flag of the United
> States of America and to the republic for which
> it stands, one nation, under God, indivisible,
> with liberty and justice for all."

Although my son was only six years old at that time, I knew he was confused as to where his loyalty should rest. Our children are taught to respect authority and to believe in our way of life as a free people because of the *Declaration of Independence and United States Constitution.* I did not want either my son or daughter, who both suffered because of the events in this story, to grow up with a sense of distrust and hatred towards those who will run their government. I explained that there are good people in government service, but if the good people don't weed out the bad ones, our system of justice can never provide equality and justice for all. One injustice placed upon any American citizen by a government official is essentially an injustice to all Americans. Again, as Ben Franklin stated; *"We must indeed all hang together, or, most assuredly we shall all hang separately."*

Hundreds of millions of American young men women and their parents in our nation don't trust those who run our government. According to "Roll Call" on the Internet on Friday, November 27, 1998, 73 percent of American citizens distrust *most of those* who hold the power in Washington! These numbers are astonishing and reflect the perceptions of people such as my family and friends, average Americans and some betrayed veterans. These people have a deep-seated distrust with the approximately two thousand privileged Americans in the Executive, Legislative and Judicial branches of our government, the ones who are supposed to govern this country at our will!

Is it any wonder that our Armed Forces are in serious trouble due to manpower shortages? It amazes me that the government has spent over 265 million dollars of tax money on television commercials in an attempt to recruit our young men and women, and here I am fighting to get back in the military! Those who run our government simply don't get it!

The United States military in 1999 under the leadership of Bill Clinton, a man who "loathed the military" when he was called upon to serve in Vietnam, is in terrible condition. This is unfortunate because military life is a good life for the most part, if one is assigned to work under a true leader rather than a false leader who abuses the trust placed in our leadership.

A Wake Up Call May be on the Horizon

The falling numbers of new recruits has triggered talk among lawmakers to revive the draft. This should be a wake up call. Only ten years ago, when I was a part of the strongest volunteer military force in the history of this nation, our manpower strength for personnel in active duty was over 4 million strong! Politics took center stage and in only ten years, the Congress destroyed the Armed Forces, which now mans only 1.37 million on active duty, not enough to perform all the duties to defend this nation.

Who will pay the price? That's right. The average American family. My question is this: "Why do 220 million Americans with a right under the First Amendment of the United States Constitution to voice its criticism of those who run our nation, remain silent?" Thomas Jefferson stated: "The spirit of resistance to government is so valuable on certain occasions that I wish it to be always kept alive." These are words that we the people must live by with respect to protecting the human rights of our men and women, or we will never again regain the strength of an all volunteer force.

We must hold our elected officials in Congress accountable with a policy of "zero tolerance" to corruption within our military. If we do not do so, somehow, someway, we will all pay the price.

I requested Congressman James Oberstar's office to provide me with the names of Congressman who suggested this outrageous ploy. Not surprisingly, as with almost every other request for assistance and information from the government, I received no response.

Only days after "Roll Call" published its statistics reflecting that 73% of Americans distrust those who run our government, Reuters ran article with the title: "Military's biggest battle is fighting to fill its ranks: Shortages of recruits puts U. S. Mission in jeopardy."

As I read this article, I became disturbed by this report reflecting how U.S. military officials make the rules day-by-day to achieve manpower strengths and feed their political agendas. The issue was the Pentagon's dilemma in trying to make up a shortage of about 35,000 people in the Armed Forces and the effects the shortage of personnel would have on the military's carrying out its assigned missions.

The article went on to say that to prevent dropping its standards, taxpayers would have to spend up to $40 billion, according to Pentagon estimates! Although, $40 billion is only money, the language in the next part of the article was particularly upsetting to me:

"Some lawmakers and analysts suggest a more dramatic alternative; reviving the draft."

The suggestion of reviving the draft was made in light of a statement by an anonymous Congressman:

"[i]f they [the military] can't recruit for a small military of 1.4 million people today, there's big trouble ahead".

It was further reported that as of 1999:

"...for the first time since the draft ended in 1973 the Navy failed to meet its recruiting goals this year, falling nearly 7,000 recruits short and overall, ships are short some 15,000 junior sailors and to top it off, 3,000 more sailors quit this year than the service expected."

Why is this? I spoke with a Navy Recruiter before I submitted my Petition to the United States Supreme Court. The recruiter was preparing to leave the Navy after serving over ten years. Could his decision and similar actions by thousands of other military members indicate that there is a problem with the leadership at the Pentagon and in the White House?

The recruiter said it was difficult for him to paint the Navy as a career worth pursuing to young men and women because he had lost faith in the very government he was serving to protect and defend!

It is time to take a look at one of the causes for this distrust of the military— the Feres Doctrine!

America's mothers and fathers and young men and women we need to serve our country to keep us free, want nothing to do with the military. Service to one's country is hazardous, and I don't mean engaging in combat with foreign enemies. The Reuters article went on to say in part:

"Recently, in the upscale Philadelphia area known as Upper Darby, Costello met with a college sophomore who wanted to join the Navy, and his father. The father refused to shake Costello's hand. And to keep his son out of the Navy he offered the proceeds from the sale of his mother's house."

I was born in Upper Darby Pennsylvania and raised in the Philadelphia area. I understand completely the feelings and reservations of that boy's father! As a father of two young children who may have to deal with the U.S. Government drafting them one day, I too, will do anything in my power to prevent my children from giving their lives for a handful of self-serving individuals we call politicians in Washington D.C.

It is astonishing that the Clinton Military Establishment could throw me out with a perfect record. I am sure there are many hundreds if not thousands of veterans who have suffered similar fates. When will the "vicious cycle" of politics end? I can guarantee this much: Since my kids were born with my blood, and the United States Government considers me mentally unstable and alcoholic and therefore unfit to serve my country, so are they!

The "vicious cycle" I speak about is the passing of the buck whereby injustice to service members and their families are continually passed on to the next political or military official that fills the office, where injustices should have been dealt with to begin with. Secretary of Defense William Cohen spoke at the dedication of the U.S. Female Veterans Memorial and in his speech he pledged that under his command the military would "treat everyone in uniform with dignity and respect" and "hold accountable those who abuse their power."

ABC 20/20 program, *"AN ABUSE OF POWER?"* aired about one year after Secretary Cohen's speech. To date I have not received any phone calls or letters from the Secretary's office or any official under his direction in the Clinton Military Establishment informing me that Cohen was going to hold those who abused their powers as documented in this book accountable. Violations of people's human rights via the military's mental health system continue as the vicious cycle goes on!

On April 20, 1999, the final play of the 99.9 yard drive was called (the petition to the U.S. Supreme Court). The play was executed flawlessly by my entire team. The pass was caught within the boundaries of the end zone, and all watching saw a touchdown. However, after review by the government's own referees (the U.S. Supreme Court), the touchdown was nullified.

"Liberty and Justice for All" must apply to our men and women in uniform. As members of a free society we must demand the United States Congress to ensure a "zero tolerance" approach to corruption and unlawful retaliation by abuse within the military's mental health system. This must be a high priority in the new millennium.

To begin the long road to change, the American people must demand that the *Feres Doctrine's* "incident to service" bar on relief from intentional torts and medical malpractice be completely repealed or reformed. Members of the military must be afforded a private cause of action with a jury under the provisions of the Military Whistleblower Protection Act, if the administrative remedy processes of the Department of Defense are abused. If military officials know they will be held accountable in a federal court for violating §1034, I believe abuse of power will be phased out and true leaders will once again rule the United States Armed Forces.

I am grateful to the wonderful people who have supported me in this journey such as my good buddy Roy, who is still serving in the military reserves. After the Supreme Court denied my Petition to address corruption within the military's medical and legal processes, I lost all faith in the federal government and was on the verge of denouncing my citizenship to start a new life in another country. However, my buddy Roy put a lot of my concerns and feelings of betrayal into perspective. He gave me the strength to carry on the fight to challenge the Feres Doctrine in the Court Of Public Opinion. Roy helped me hold on to my belief that even though our nation is truly in troubled times due to corruption within our federal government, America is a still great nation because of people such as Roy and his family.

The Feres Doctrine: 50 Years of Injustice Begins

In 1946 Congress passed a statute entitled the *Federal Tort Claim Act* (FTCA) that waived "sovereign immunity" from liability in tort (a wrong). The word "tort" is derived from the Latin "tortus" or "twisted" and is a private or civil wrong or injury resulting from a breach of legal duty that exists by virtue of society's expectations regarding interpersonal conduct, rather than by contract or other private relationship.

The FTCA confers exclusive jurisdiction on United States District Courts to hear claims against the United States, for money damages accruing on and after January 1, 1945 for injury or loss of property, or personal injury or death, caused by the negligent or wrongful act or omission of any employee of the government while acting within the scope of his/her office or employment, under circumstances where the United States, if a private person, would be liable to the claimant in accordance with the law of the place where the act or omission occurred.—Public Law, Title 28. Sec. 1346(b).

The Feres Doctrine was born in December, 1947, when First Lieutenant Randolph J. Feres died in a fire in an Army barracks at Pine Camp, N.Y. Believing that the fire was caused by a defective heating plant, his widow sued the United States. Three years later, in 1950, the Supreme Court dismissed her suit. Explaining the majority opinion, Justice Robert Jackson said that members of the armed services may not sue the government for death or injury resulting from activities "incident to service."

In October 1950, three cases, including the Randolph J. Feres case, were heard simultaneously by the United States Supreme Court. The resulting rulings put into place the foundation for the many injustices and abuses that have taken place within our military service. Accountability for intentional wrongs and medical incompetence are allowed to go unchecked as a result. Essentially, what it came down to was the unwillingness by Congress to keep tabs on the military to ensure that those in positions of authority were not abusing their powers.

The cases involved three American families: Bernice Feres, as executrix under the last will and testament of Rudolph J. Feres, deceased; a case filed by Arthur Jefferson, a former member of the U. S. Army and finally, a case filed by Edith Griggs, as executrix of the estate of Dudley Griggs, deceased.

In all three cases, Justice Robert Jackson held that the government was not liable under the Federal Tort Clams Act for injuries to servicemen arising out of or in the course of activity incident to military service.

The 1950 Opinion of Justice Robert Jackson

A common issue arising under the Tort Claims Act, as to which Courts of Appeals are in conflict, makes it appropriate to consider three cases in one opinion.

The Feres case: The District Court dismissed an action by the executrix of Feres against the United States to recover for death caused by negligence. Descendent perished by fire in the barracks at Pine Camp, New York, while on active duty in service of the United States. Negligence was alleged in quartering him in barracks known or which should have been known to be unsafe because of a defective heating plant, and in failing to maintain an adequate fire watch. The Court of Appeals, Second Circuit, affirmed.

The Jefferson case: Plaintiff, while in the Army, was required to undergo an abdominal operation. About eight months later in the course of another operation after plaintiff was discharged, a towel 30 inches long by 18 inches wide, marked "Medical Department U. S. Army," was discovered and removed from his stomach. The complaint alleged that it was negligently left there by the army surgeon. The District Court, being doubtful of the law, refused without prejudice the Government's pretrial motion to dismiss the complaint. After trial, finding negligence as a fact, Judge Chestnut carefully reexamined the issue of law and concluded that the Act does not charge the United States with liability in this type of case. The Court of Appeals, Fourth Circuit, affirmed.

The Griggs case: The District Court dismissed the complaint of Griggs' executrix, which alleged that while on active duty he met death because of negligence and unskillful medical treatment by army surgeons. The Court of Appeals, Tenth Circuit, reversed and, one judge dissenting held that the complaint stated a cause of action under the Act.

The common fact underlying the three cases is that each claimant, while on active duty and not on furlough, sustained injury due to the negligence of others in the armed forces. The only issue of law raised is whether the Tort Claims Act extended its remedy to one sustaining "incident to the service" what under other circumstances would be an actionable wrong. This is the "wholly different case" reversed from our decision in Brooks v. United States.

There are few guiding materials for our task of statutory construction. No committee reports or floor debates disclose what effect the statute was designed to have on the problem before us, or that it even was in mind. Under these circumstances, no conclusion can be above challenged, but if we misinterpret the Act, at least Congress possesses a ready remedy.

We do not overlook considerations persuasive of liability in these cases. The Act does confer district court jurisdiction generally over claims for money damages against the United States founded on negligence. It does contemplate that the Government will sometimes respond for negligence of military personnel, for it defines "employee of the Government" to include "members of the military or naval forces of the United States," and provides that "'acting within the scope of his office or employment' in the case of a member of the military or naval forces of the United States, means acting in line of duty." Its exceptions might also imply inclusion of claims such as we have here. 28 U.S.C. Sec. 2680(j), 28 U.S.C.A Sec. 2680(j) excepts "any claim arising out of the combatant activities of the military or naval forces, or the Coast Guard, *during time of war*" (emphasis supplied), from which it is said we should infer allowance of claims arising from non-combat activities in peace. Section 2680(k) excludes "any claim arising in a foreign country." Significance also has been attributed in these cases, as in the Brooks case, to the fact that eighteen tort claims bills were introduced in Congress between 1925 and 1935 and all but two expressly denied recovery to members of the armed forces; but the bill enacted as the present Tort Claims Act from its introduction made no exception. We also are reminded that the Brooks case, in spite of its reservation of service-connected injuries, interprets the Act to cover claims not incidental to service, and it is argued that much of its reasoning is as apt to impose liability in favor of a man on duty as in favor of one on leave. These considerations, it is said, should persuade us to cast upon Congress, as author of the confusion, the task of qualifying and clarifying its language if the liability here asserted should prove so depleting of the public treasury as the Government fears.

This Act however, should be construed to fit, so far as will comport with its words, into the entire statutory system of remedies against the Government to make a workable, consistent and equitable whole. The Tort Claims Act was not an isolated and spontaneous flash of congressional generosity. It marks the culmination of a long effort to mitigate unjust consequences of sovereign immunity from suit. While the political theory that the King could do no wrong was repudiated in America, a legal doctrine derived from it that the Crown is immune from any suit to which it has not consented was invoked on behalf of the Republic and applied by our courts as vigorously as it had been on behalf of the Crown. As the Federal Government expanded its activities, its agents caused a multiplying number of remediless wrongs-wrongs which have been actionable if inflicted by an individual or a corporation but remediless solely because their perpetrator was an officer or employee of the Government. Relief was often sought and sometimes granted through private bills in Congress, the number of which steadily increased as Government activity increased. The volume of these private bills, the inadequacy of congressional machinery for determination of facts, the importunities to which claimants subjected members of Congress, and the capricious results, led to a strong demand that claims for tort wrongs be submitted to adjudication. Congress already had waived immunity and made the Government answerable for breaches of its contracts and certain other types of claims. At last, in connection with the Reorganization Act, it waived immunity an transferred the burden of examining tort claims to the courts. The primary purpose of the Act was to extend a remedy to those who had been without; if it incidentally benefited those already well provided for, it appears to have been unintentional. Congress was suffering from no plague of private bills on the behalf of the military and naval personnel, because a comprehensive system of relief had been authorized for them and their dependents by statute.

Looking to the detail of the Act, it is true that it provides, broadly, that the District Court "shall have exclusive jurisdiction of civil actions on claims against the United States, for money damages...." This confers jurisdiction to render judgment upon all claims. But it does not say that all claims must be allowed. Jurisdiction is necessary to deny a claim on its merits as matter of law as much as to adjudge that liability exists. We interpret this language to mean all it says, but no more. Jurisdiction of the defendant now exists where the defendant was immune from suit before; it remains for courts, in exercise of their jurisdiction, to determine whether any claim is recognizable in law.

For this purpose, the Act goes on to prescribe the test of allowable claim, which is "The United States shall be liable... in the same manner and to the same extent as a private individual under like circumstances..." with certain exceptions not material here. It will be seen that this is not the creation of new causes of action but

195

acceptance of liability under circumstances that would bring private liability into existence. This, we think, embodies the same idea that its English equivalent enacted in 1947 (Crown Proceedings Act 1947) expressed; "Where any person has a claim against the Crown after the commencement of this Act, and, if this Act has not been passed, the claim might have been enforced, subject to the grant...." of consent to be sued, the claim may now be enforced without specific consent. On obvious shortcoming in these claims is that plaintiffs can point to no liability of "private individual" even remotely analogous to that which they are asserting against the United States. We know of no American law which ever has permitted a soldier to recover for negligence, against either his superior officers or the Government he is serving. Nor is there any liability "under like circumstances," for no private individual has power to conscript or mobilize a private army with such authorities over persons at the Government vests in echelons of command.

The nearest parallel, even if we were to treat "private individual" as including a state, would be the relationship between the states and the militia. But if we indulge plaintiffs the benefit of this comparison, claimants cite us no state, and we know of none, which has permitted members of its militia to maintain tort actions for injuries suffered in the service, and in at least one state the contrary has been held to be the case. It is true that if we consider relevant only a part of the circumstances and ignored the status of both the wronged and the wrongdoer in these cases we find analogous private liability. In the usual civilian doctor and patient relationship, there is of course a liability for malpractice. And a landlord would undoubtedly be held liable if an injury occurred to a tenant as the result of a negligently maintained heating plan. But the liability assumed by the Government here is that created by "all the circumstances," not that which a few of the circumstances might create. We find no parallel liability before, and we think no new one has been created by, this Act. Its effect is to waive immunity from recognized causes of action and was not to visit the Government with novel and unprecedented liabilities.

It is not without significance as to whether the Act should be construed to apply to service-connected injuries that it makes '... the law of the place where the act or omission occurred' govern any consequent liability. This provision recognizes and assimilates into federal law the rules of substantive law of the several states, among which divergencies are notorious. This perhaps is fair enough when the claimant is not on duty or is free to choose his own habitat and thereby limit the jurisdiction in which it will be possible for federal activities to cause him injury. That his tort claims should be governed by the law of the location where he has elected to be is just as fair when the defendant is the Government as when the defendant is a private individual. But a soldier on active duty has no such choice and must serve any place or, under modern conditions, any number of places in quick succession in the forty-eight states, the Canal Zone, or Alaska, or Hawaii, or any other territory of the United States. That the geography of an injury should select the law to be applied to his tort claims makes no sense. We cannot ignore the fact that most states have abolished the common-law action for damages between employer and employee and superseded it with workman's compensation statutes which provide, in most instances, the sole basis of liability. Absent this, or where such statutes are inapplicable, states have differing provisions as to limitations of liability and different doctrines as to assumption of risk, fellow-servant rules and contributory or comparative negligence. It would hardly be a rational plan of providing for those disabled in service by other in service to leave them dependent upon geographic considerations over which they have no control and to laws which fluctuate in existence and value.

The relationship between the Government and members of its armed forces is 'distinctively federal in character', as this Court recognized in United States v. Standard Oil Co.,... wherein the Government unsuccessfully sought to recover for losses incurred by virtue of injuries to a soldier. The considerations which lead to that decision apply with even greater force to this case: '... To whatever extent state law may apply to govern the relations between soldiers or others in the armed forces and persons outside them or nonaffiliated governmental agencies, the scope, nature, legal incidents and consequences of the relation between persons in the service and the Government are fundamentally derived from federal sources and governed by federal authority'. No federal law recognizes a recovery such as a claimants seek. The Military Personnel Claims Act,... now superseded... permitted recovery in some circumstances, but it specifically excluded claims of military personnel 'incident to service.'"

This Court, in deciding claims for wrongs incident to service under the Tort Claims Act, cannot escape attributing some bearing upon it to enactments by Congress which provide systems of simple, certain and uniform compensation for injuries or death of those in armed services. We might say that the claimant may (a) enjoy both types of recovery, or (b) elect which to pursue, thereby waiving the other, or (c) pursue both, crediting the larger liability with the proceeds of the smaller, or

197

(d) that the compensation and pension remedy excludes the tort remedy. There is as much statutory authority for one as for another of these conclusions. If Congress had contemplated that this Tort Act would be held to apply in cases of this kind, it is difficult to see why it should have omitted any provision to adjust these two type of remedy to each other. The absence of any such adjustment is persuasive that there was no awareness that the Act might be interpreted to permit recovery for injuries incident to service.

A soldier is at peculiar disadvantage in litigation. Lack of time and money, the difficult if not impossibility of procuring witnesses, are only a few of the factors working to his disadvantage. And the few cases charging superior officers or the Government with neglect or misconduct which have been brought since the Tort Claims Act, of which the present are typical, have either been suits by widows or surviving dependents, or have been brought after the individual was discharged. The compensation system, which normally requires no litigation, is not negligible or niggardly, as these cases demonstrate. The recoveries compare extremely favorably with those provided by most workman's compensation statutes. In the Jefferson case, the District Court considered actual and prospective payments by the Veterans' Administration as diminution of the verdict. Plaintiff received $3,645.50 to the date of the court's computation and on estimated life expectancy under existing legislation would prospective receive $31,947 in addition. In the Griggs case, the widow, in the two-year period after her husband's death, received $2,695, representing the six months' death gratuity under the Act of December 17, 1919, as amended..... It is estimated that her total future pension payments will aggregate $18,000. Thus the widow will receive an amount in excess of $220,000 from Government gratuities, whereas she sought and could seek under state law only $15,000, the maximum permitted by Illinois for death.

It is contended that all these considerations were before the Court in the Brooks case and that allowance of recovery to Brooks requires a similar holding of liability here. The actual holding in the Brooks case can support liability here only by ignoring the vital distinction there stated. The injury to Brooks did not arise out of or in the course of military duty. Brooks was on furlough, driving along the highway, under compulsion of no orders or duty and on no military mission. A Government owned and operated vehicle collided with him. Brooks' father, riding in the same car, recovered for his injuries and the Government did not further contest the judgment but contended that there could be no liability to the sons, solely because they were in the

Army. This Court rejected the contention, primarily because Brooks' relationship while on leave was not analogous to that of a soldier injured while performing duties under orders.

We conclude that the Government is not liable under the Federal Tort Claims Act for injuries to servicemen where the injuries arise out of or are in the course of activity incident to service. Without exception, the relationship of military personnel to the Government has been governed exclusively by federal law. We do not think that Congress, in drafting this Act, created a new cause of action dependent on local law for service-connected injuries or death due to negligence. We cannot impute to Congress such a radical departure from established law in the absence of express congressional command. Accordingly, the judgments in the Feres and Jefferson cases are affirmed an that in the Griggs case is reversed.

Judgments in the Feres and Jefferson cases affirmed; judgment in the Griggs case reversed.

Mr. Justice DOUGLAS concurs in the result.

Appendix III

Lessons Learned

A guide to preventing unlawful reprisals

Warning: The information in this section should not be construed as legal advice.

The following information is based on my experience seeking vindication within the Department of Defense and federal courts. I challenged the deprivation of my First and Fifth Amendment rights to protected speech and due process of law in seeking vindication after being subjected to false claims of mental illness and a wrongful discharge.

Knowing I had a long battle to fight challenging the constitutionality of the *Feres Doctrine*, I worked in the legal system starting in 1996 and obtained a degree as a legal assistant/paralegal to obtain credibility in discussing these lessons learned.

Since I started this project in January 1994, I have spent thousands of hours doing research while pursuing my own defense in the lawsuit I discuss in the book. Although I have learned much from trial and error, I am still in the dark about the legal system. Not only is the legal system complex, it is also expensive to litigate a case. Additionally, litigation requires a long-term commitment and is a frustrating process, especially when the defendant is the United States government. For every penny you have, the government has the equivalent of a thousand dollars.

Being a litigant in a lawsuit is no cake walk. It takes a lot of patience, especially if you are fighting for changes in the system and not for financial gain. This brings me to another lesson learned: **"Believe in your cause!"**

Although the price of fighting the government can be substantial, as an average citizen you can obtain justice against the government if you believe in the cause you are fighting, You must be mentally prepared for delays and the long process it takes getting a case to court. If you are in the military, the Feres Doctrine and qualified immunity technical factors can sidestep the rights you would normally have as a U.S. citizen. Having your rights violated in the military and trying to vindicate yourself is a major uphill battle.

The Ultimate Lesson Learned

Being unprepared and unknowledgeable of the field I was playing on cost me years of stress and hardships that I could have avoided. What I should have done from the moment I decided to do something about the abuses in my department was to research the laws and understand just how far the laws would protect me. The ultimate lesson I've learned is that because of the Feres Doctrine, **I should never have placed "duty, honor, country" over that of my own self-interests.**

Knowledge is Power!

If you want to protect your rights, you must understand how the power structure in the system operates and to whom each official in the system is accountable. Lodging a complaint against a superior, especially a commanding officer in the United States Armed Forces, is not well received by the Pentagon. Individuals in a command position are assigned a position of public trust by the Pentagon. The Pentagon doesn't like to look bad in their choice of leadership. The Pentagon and the U.S. Government do not hesitate to spend millions of taxpayers' dollars to cover up intentional and deliberate abuse of power and other government malfeasance in order to keep it out of the eyes of the public. Command integrity must be preserved at all costs, and if that means taking down individuals by placing false and detrimental information in one's service record, this can be easily achieved.

Therefore, before the laws are reformed to provide a military member full protection of their rights (such as affording a "private cause of action" under § 1034), think hard before proceeding with an issue that could affect your career or family. Obtaining justice in the military for the rank and file man and woman depends on whether a person who is superior in rank will keep their word to subordinates when presented with a problem.

Politics is the name of the game. Since the Pentagon is overseen by civilians appointed by each sitting President, there is a vicious cycle. Stonewalling and delay tactics are used during each presidency and once a new administration is placed into power, those who abused their powers are gone, so it is easy to point the finger at them and then brush the issue under the carpet.

Legal Terms you Should Know

There are thousands of legal terms and legal decision in the American system of jurisprudence. Following are some terms you should be aware of. Additionally, go to your local courthouse and spend some time in the law library doing research about potential problems one is faced with in the Armed Forces. Lawyers go to the law library as well, and maybe you will find a connection!

Scope Of Employment. The range of activities encompassed by one's employment; acts done while performing one's job duties.

Due Process Of Law. I once thought that our rights and our freedoms from being victimized by the government as American citizens are *absolute*. Due process of law ensures these rights. Due process is divided into "substantive" and "procedural" elements.

Due process is derived from the Fifth Amendment of the Constitution, which provides that no person shall be deprived of life, liberty, or property without due process of law.

Substantive due process relates to whether a law is rational and relates to legitimate goals passed by legislative bodies. **Procedural** due process guarantees procedural fairness in situations in which the government would deprive one of property or liberty. Procedural due process requires notice and a right to a fair hearing prior to deprivation of liberty or a Constitutional right.

Essentially, due process is the exercise of judgment by those whom the Constitution has entrusted with the unfolding of the process.

When a service member brings forth a claim of fraud, waste and abuse in the public's trust, no retaliatory action should be taken. In the military, however, you can be denied a fair hearing under due process of law if for any reason an administrative separation process is initiated against you to silence your claims. The reality with the Feres Doctrine and qualified immunity is that anyone can be railroaded out of the military through legally established processes such as the administrative discharge board, without an opportunity to defend one's self.

Understanding due process can help you defend your rights in the case of reprisal. "Arbitrary and capricious" action by commanding officers in the military is cited as follows:

> "When a military correction board fails to correct an injustice clearly presented in the record before it, is acting in violation, of its mandate, and such a violation, contrary to the evidence, is arbitrary and capricious one. *Eye v. United States*, 1975, 512 F.2d 1383, 206 Ct.Cl. 388.

Personal Advocate: When a military member files a protected communication under military grievance procedures, a third party should be assigned to monitor the process. If you ever decide to proceed through the grievance system in the military, it would be wise to obtain this protection to head off potential reprisals. A good starting point would be to call the nearest military legal service office and ask for guidance in obtaining this right. Chances are, if you believe a superior is abusing his/her power, that person is not going to inform you of this crucial right. Take it!

Detrimental to good order and discipline: This legal classification is a "death wish" to any military member and can only be invoked by the member's military commander. Essentially, when an installation command makes the determination that a member is "detrimental to good order and discipline," the career of that member is over. Individual commanders hold the power of

204

a god to control good order and discipline at their commands. Because this legal determination is a military decision, federal courts will not intervene. This classification is an abusive commander's best damage control tool because once invoked, the system takes it at face value. There is no reprieve.

Personnel Action: Any action taken on a member of the Armed Forces that affects or has the potential to affect that military member's current position or career. Personnel actions include a promotion; a disciplinary or other corrective action; a transfer or reassignment; a performance evaluation; a decision on pay, benefits, awards, or training; and any other significant change in the duties or responsibilities inconsistent with the military member's current rank.

Chilling Effect: In law this term refers to the consequences of a policy or practice which discourages the exercise of a legal right. A chilling effect occurs when persons perceive the possibility of sanctions or reprisals if their rights are exercised. For example, the use of a psychological evaluation resulting in charges of mental instability can discredit a grievance filed against a superior officer and discourage military personnel from exposing corruption.

Immunity: A right or exemption from a duty or penalty; a favor or benefit granted to one and contrary to the general rule.

Official Immunity: A personal immunity accorded to a public official to shelter him or her from liability in case of a claim that someone has been injured by his actions that were the consequence of the exercise of his official authority or duty.

Immunity is a complicated legal issue. However, as cited in the case of *Harlow v. Fizgerald*, 457 U.S. 800, 818, 102 S. Ct. 2727, 2738, 73 L.Ed.2d 396 1982):

> "Qualified immunity protects government officials
> performing discretionary functions from personal liability
> for money damages insofar as their conduct does not violate
> clearly established statutory or constitutional rights of

which a reasonable person would have known").
Furthermore, the Supreme Court has noted that qualified
immunity protects "all but the plainly incompetent or those
who knowingly violate the law." *Malley v. Briggs*, 475 U.S.
335, 341…"

As you can see, qualified immunity is not always defensible. With the added power of the Feres Doctrine, however, in the military breaking the qualified immunity barrier is a tough road to travel, and proving intentional abuse of power is very costly.

Injunction: An order prohibiting a party from acting in a particular way or requiring a specific action by a party. An injunction allows a court to minimize injury to a person or group until the matter can otherwise be resolved. Or an injunction may prevent injury altogether. One reality to understand is that the federal courts are very reluctant to intervene in military decisions. However, if an official action by a military official is so blatantly wrong and abusive, you should seek an injunction to prevent any unlawful personnel action from taking place. For example, if you have ten-year track record of outstanding performance and behavior and then, all of a sudden it is claimed that you have a mental problem, this is the time to seek a lawyer and obtain a court injunction.

I recommend that if you believe an unfavorable personnel action is about to occur (such as being sent to a mental hospital), seek an injunction. Don't wait until the action occurs because once an unfavorable personnel action is set into motion, it is difficult to defend against it. The word of a military commander is given great deference by the Pentagon and the courts. You need to be able to prove to a federal judge that the unfavorable personnel actions took place in the wake of a protected communication. Although the courts give great deference to military decisions, filing an injunction may compel a abusive official to back off.

Statute: A written law enacted by a legislative body. A statute declares, requires, or prohibits something. For example, the Military Whistleblower Protection Act (hereinafter called the "Act") is a written law which makes it illegal to threaten or take unfavorable personnel actions against a member who lawfully communicates fraud, waste or abuse to an IG or Member of Congress.

Intentional Tort: A wrongful act knowingly committed that interferes with the interests of another in a way not permitted by law. I believe that being ordered for a psychological and alcohol dependency screening purposely done to discredit and prevent due process of a legitimate claim of fraud, waste and abuse falls within the category of intentional tort. This is why one needs a lawyer to research the facts to show a *prima facie* case of intentional misconduct.

Statute of Limitations: Any law which fixes the time within which an individual must take judicial action to enforce his or her rights. After the statute of limitations has passed, one's claim can be barred forever. Essentially, from the moment you feel that a wrong has been taken against you, the clock starts running. Each type of tort has a different time period in which action can be brought. Some statutes run for two years, some for only months. Again, a lawyer must be retained to preserve your rights and stop the statute from running (toll) in your claim.

Precedent: A previously decided case which is recognized as authority for the disposition of future cases.

Doctrine of *Stare Decisis*: A doctrine based on the Latin term, *stare decises*, meaning to stand by that which was decided. This doctrine describes the American legal system in which courts "are slow to interfere with principles announced in the former decisions and often uphold them even though they would decide otherwise were the question a new one. Although *stare decisis* is not inviolable, our judicial system demands that it be overturned only on a showing of good cause. Where such good cause is not shown, it will not be repudiated."[39] The U.S. system of justice is based on past court decisions and statutory law. Without

---

39. Steven H. Gifis, Associate Professor of Law, Rugers University, Barron Educational Services, Inc. 288 U.S. 38, 94 Black Law, 4th edition.

acknowledging the showing of good cause, the system allows former case law and statutory laws to stand as they are.

The Complexity of the American System of Justice

When I began my quest for justice, I could not have imagined the difficulties I would eventually face in the American judicial system. I did not realize that no matter how strong a case to prove reprisals and constitutional right violations may be on its face, the legal system is not simple. With statutory laws and case laws that set precedent in our legal system, you may need to cite thousands of cases heard that present similar issues. Again, this is where a good lawyer is your best bet!

Be a Part of Your Quest

One thing that has worked for me has been to take an active part in dealing with my own crisis. Obtaining sworn statements and researching and collecting evidence relevant to the issue at hand have not only given me peace of mind, they have also saved me a tremendous amount of money. I have actively participated in the collection of evidence and the preparation of my own affidavits and have saved substantial amounts of money. Essentially I have performed the duties of a paralegal in my own case. On average, a paralegal is paid around $60 per hour, and lawyers are paid from $100 to $150 per hour depending on their expertise. Some rates are even higher! Litigation is a costly avenue. Obtaining personal knowledge and assisting your attorney will benefit you in the end. Don't call your attorney with every question you may have. Attorneys have other clients, and even a telephone call to your attorney costs money! Research the issue yourself, and then ask.

In my case, I averaged about two hours per day over the past five years in my own case. This is a conservative estimate, but I am sure that I saved substantial amounts of money in attorney fees and costs.

Time Is on Their Side

One reality that I have learned throughout my quest is that the passage of time will hurt your case. The key word is "fresh!" Keep things "fresh" and moving as swiftly as possible. A good lawyer will do this for you, but always go with your gut feeling if you think your attorney should be responding to newly discovered evidence or filing motions and letters on your behalf. Remember when fighting the government that time is their best weapon. Everything moves on in time, including people and memories. Also, it has been recognized by the Supreme Court that fighting the military is a difficult fight to undertake, considering that military officials are scattered all over the country and even the world. The Pentagon has always known that the playing field is not level. The government relies on time to break people down and cover up wrongful acts of its officials.

Keep Involved But Don't Be Too Pushy

By not being more forceful with my attorney than I was, my case was delayed by almost three years. My cases were filed late, and I lost my chance to address the issues of false arrest, false imprisonment and malicious prosecution claims. When you sign a retainer agreement or agree to a contingency fee, make sure you find out immediately the statute of limitations in your particular situation. If you pass the time limit set in the statute of limitations that applies to your case, your claims are barred forever.

If the attorney you hired is procrastinating to a point that you feel lack of action could jeopardize your case, seek other legal counsel. Realize, however, that military cases are not always money makers for attorneys, and they may be reluctant to take them on.

The Military's Grievance System

You may hear that once a person joins the service he or she has no rights. This is false. The truth is that all military personnel have

209

the *right* to present any legitimate grievance to their command without the *fear of intimidation, reprisal, or harassment.*

From the start of my ordeal, I had to learn day by day information about my rights which the military did not inform me about. Unfortunately for me, my fight was one of trial and error, the only guide I had. For example, from the moment I filed my February 1993, grievance, I should have been assigned a personal advocate to ensure that reprisals did not occur. This did not happen, although it was Broyles' obligation to assign me a personal advocate.

When things like this happen and your rights are not fully protected, these improprieties must be pointed out immediately to higher authority and to your lawyer. When I started the grievance process I was naive and trusted my commanding officer. If I had to do it again, the first step I would take would be to obtain a personal advocate (a third party), who could have been a witness to the many issues of legal and medical misconduct that took place in my case. Then I could have had a witness to testify in support of an injunction preventing my admission into a military hospital. Also, I think a sworn affidavit of a third party would have helped me immensely in filing an injunction to prevent my placement in the military's mental health system.

Being on active duty provides the opportunity for you to obtain free legal representation from a military lawyer. This is a positive, especially for lower ranking members who may not have the money to obtain civilian counsel. It is important to be given legal advice from the beginning phase of your dispute and a military lawyer can provide initial advice for your case.

If a dispute develops that cannot be settled by your military attorney and the situation gets hot and heavy, realize that although military lawyers are court appointed officers under the U.S. Constitution, they are still military officers who are controlled by rank.

It May not be Safe to Utilize the Military's Chain Of Command

As a military member, you have the right to circumvent the chain of command if you feel that your concerns will not be given fair consideration.[40] I think that using the chain of command is the right thing to do, but there are unfortunate consequences if your commander is not a true leader. A true leader never jeopardizes the safety and well-being of military members and keeps his or her word to subordinates.

I believe that the chain of command should be used initially to express one's concerns of fraud, waste, or abuse. Report your concerns to your next superior. If that person blows off your concerns or threatens you, it is time to stop proceeding through the chain. You can then show the DODIG, and a court of law if need be, that you attempted to correct the problem at the lowest level and your concerns were ignored. You must be able to show that management was made aware of the problems but failed to address them. Only you as the person facing this dilemma can make the decision about when to move outside the chain of command.

When you present a problem to your immediate superior, the initial reaction of this supervisor will reveal the whole story in most instances. If corrective action is taken with respect to your concerns you are in luck. Chances are, you have a "true leader" above you. If no corrective actions is taken, and you are treated unfairly in any way, you can be certain that the seed of reprisal has been planted and that your actions from that point on will be watched closely.

Watch also for the deceptive superior who in the beginning of a dispute may appear to be on your side but is just collecting information to build a defense countering your claims of improprieties. If your immediate superior is a person of genuine integrity and honor, you will see corrective action being taken

---

40. As provided for in the Military Whistleblower Protection Act, Public Law Title 10. U.S.C. Sec. 1034

211

immediately. Good leaders do not wait to correct problems that are affecting the morale and well-being of their subordinates. However, if the weeks pass by and no action is taken, there will probably be trouble ahead if you persist with the grievance.

After you notify your immediate superior of the problems and believe that your disclosures have been met with negative results or that threats of unfavorable personnel actions have been initiated (e.g. being transferred to another position or department), this is the time to stop proceeding through the chain. Relax. Play the game, Keep 'em guessing! When I presented issues of abuse of power, gross mismanagement, etc., to Feener, his reaction was "So what?" He told me that the problems I had reported were his concern and not mine. At that time, I should have informed Feener that if he did not want to correct the problems then maybe my Congressman would.

By informing Feener of this both orally and in writing, I would have satisfied the requirement for protection under the "Act." He would then have been aware of the fact that a possible protective communication to a Member of Congress was being initiated. I did not do this with Feener, nor did I do it with Rumery, although I should have.

An important aspect in proving reprisal is to be able to show that supervisors in your chain of command were made aware of your intentions to file a protective communication under the law but did not act. Don't count on a Congressman to help you, but be sure your superior(s) know you are not going to put up with their abuses. You do not, of course, have to go any further with a complaint, but if you do you are covered under the law.

Obtain Written Statements from Others

When an issue seriously affects the personnel or unit readiness, I recommend not going forth with a complaint unless you have supporting statements of others. If the issue affects the morale of others, people will participate with you in trying to correct the problem. They did in my case, in some instances, and they will in yours if they want change. If they don't, stop the process. The problem in my case was that my witnesses were deprived of telling their side of the story because I allowed the chain of command to become too deeply involved in the conflict. I knew my chain was corrupt, but I still allowed the administrative system in place to correct the problems, to takes its course as required by military regulations. The truth of the matter is that criticism of a superior officer by a subordinate is conduct not always welcomed at the top of the chain. If you are a supervisor and people are complaining to you about abuses, to protect your interest you should get these complaints in writing and make sure they are notarized by a notary public. These statements should be made immediately after an incident occurs. This is essential because from the moment the incident occurs to the time one can make it to Court (if need be), people scatter all over the world in the military, and memories fail. It is credible testimony to be able to say "I documented the incident immediately after it occurred" rather than saying, "I think" or "I believe" when the time comes to fight your case in within the administrative processes or in court. You should know the facts, and the best way to preserve facts is by swift documentation.

If those you lead or work with are hesitant to submit a sworn statement—stop! As a supervisor you must also protect your career and interests. If the problems are not serious enough for others to sign and swear out an affidavit, maybe they are frivolous issues to begin with.

Timing Is Everything When It Comes to Reprisals

Although it would require a book to explain every form of reprisal that may arise from exposing a wrong, here are some that could be included: transfers to dead-end assignments, intimidation and harassment, falsification or placement of misleading detrimental information in your records. Be on the lookout after a complaint is filed because reprisals usually occur immediately after the chain of command has been challenged.

From my experience, I would say that the reprisal which hurts the military member who pursues a grievance the most is falsification of the member's performance evaluation. The route to the top in the military is paved by what is in the performance evaluation. This is why manipulation of the process is so common, and "payback" for a complaint is undertaken and supported by a reporting senior or commanding officer. Although you can challenge and submit a rebuttal to a performance evaluation, once the evaluation is signed by the commanding officer, the word of that individual will be supported by a higher authority. Civilian courts also give great deference to military decisions. The courts look at the military as a way of life completely separate from that of the civilian world.

If you have always received good evaluations and then, after a grievance is filed, your next evaluation does not reflect your true performance but contains detrimental information—watch out. This is a definite indication that major trouble has begun, and the beginning of a structure discharge may be at hand. If your annual performance evaluation is coming up at the time of a conflict with a superior, don't say anything until this official document is signed and finalized. Furthermore, if you are up for transfer or reenlistment, hold off on your complaint.

The Act includes a sixty-day time frame to report fraud, waste and abuse or the claim does not have to be investigated. However, showing that you were concerned for your career is a valid justification for filing the complaint after you are transferred. This is especially true if the problems are severe and are of possible importance to the public. Additionally, when you transfer to a new command, don't talk about your legal dispute with your former command. According to the Act, a complaint to the DODIG and the person making it is confidential. You should not receive any harassment at your new command.

In my case, the exemplary performance evaluation I received six weeks prior to my grievance contradicted any claims of mental shortcomings or alcohol abuse. Unfortunately, this evaluation carried no weight in the rebuttal phase in which I pointed out reprisal. Remember, one must show a *prima facie* case (on its face) that the unfavorable actions taken cannot be supported by evidence. If I had proceeded with my grievance prior to signing my last evaluation, the evaluation would definitely not have reflected a 4.0 sailor.

Qualify For Protection Under the Act As Soon As Possible

If you feel your concerns will not be properly addressed by the chain of command, then it is time to obtain protection under the Act. As you have seen with the handling of my case by the Inspectors General, proceeding through the process to remedy retaliatory actions is not always fair and just. Justice in any case depends on the integrity of the investigator assigned to your case. If that person is honorable and just, your problems and the entire situation may be handled properly. However, reprisals in the wake of an IG complaint are common.

If a case must be filed in a federal court of law because it cannot be properly remedied within the system, you must prove to a reasonable judge (military discharges are not heard by a jury, although they should be, to outrage the public), that your versions of events are more credible than that of your opponent.

The "Act" did not protect me because by the time I tried to use it, the damage was already done and too many people in the medical and judicial systems in the Navy were involved with blowing off my issues of corruption. This protected avenue under law should be initiated immediately after the next superior in one's chain of command fails to address a subordinate's concerns. The hidden clause that the Pentagon does not want you to know is that if you do not report directly to the DODIG, protected status will not be granted under the law.

Always report fraud, waste and abuse to the DODIG first! Here's an illustration to give you an idea as to how things change without warning. During my research in preparation for the filing of my Petition for Writ of Certorari, I found on the DODIG website in October 1998 that a communication to *any* departmental Inspector General *now* qualifies as a protected communication under the law. It is important to keep up on changing developments within the system.

The Process to Report Fraud, Waste, Abuse and Unlawful Reprisals

Although it is the policy of the United States Armed Forces that all military personnel have the *right* to present any legitimate grievance to their command without the *fear of intimidation, reprisal, or harassment*, the reality is that no laws on the books will protect the rights of military personnel from retaliation if those in a position to stamp out fraud, waste and abuse within the Department of Defense condone such abuses. If I could do it all over again, I would take better measures to protect my own rights. For starters, I would have filed the claims of improprieties immediately with the Hotline of the Department of Defense Inspector General rather than using the Article 138 process.

The Mission Of The DODIG Hotline

The Hotline is the military member's best protection to prevent unlawful reprisals for upholding one's duty to country in reporting fraud, waste, abuse and mismanagement within the Armed Forces of the United States of America.

The Hotline's primary responsibility is to receive and evaluate concerns and complaints by military members regarding issues of fraud, waste, abuse and mismanagement. The Hotline is configured into teams that are available Monday through Friday from 8 a.m. to 4:30 p.m. (EST). Hotline operations and procedures are set forth in the following publications: (1) DOD Directive 7050.1, January 4, 1999, "Defense Hotline Program;" (2) DOD Instruction 7050.7, December 14, 1998, "Defense Hotline Procedures;" and (3) DOD Instruction 7050.8, December 14, 1998, "Defense Hotline Quality Assurance Review Program."

You can file a complaint with the Hotline in several ways: (1) facsimile transmission, (2) U.S. Postal Service, and (3) email at hotline@dodig.osd.mil. I do not recommend email, however, since confidentiality is not guaranteed. The mailing address of the Hotline is:

Defense Hotline
The Pentagon
Washington, DC 20301-1900
Telephone (703) 604-8567 (DSN prefix is 664)
Toll-free number (800) 424-9098

With the Internet, information can be gathered quickly within the Department of Defense by typing "keyword" at www.defenselink.mil. This site provides information about the functions of the DOD and may be helpful in obtaining the information you need.

When you file an initial complaint of fraud, waste and abuse, be sure to inform the DODIG that you do not want your identity disclosed. As a good friend of mine who is a veteran and attorney once said, "Always keep them guessing!"

What Should Be Reported

According to the Military Whistleblower Protection Act, you should be willing to report the following situations that are protected communications: (1) Violations of law, rule, or regulation; (2) Substantial and specific danger to the public health or safety, contract and procurement irregularities; bribery and acceptance of gratuities; (3) Significant case of mismanagement; (4) Conflicts of interest; (5) Travel (TDY/TAD) fraud; (6) Military Reprisals (violations of Whistleblower Protection Act involving service members); (7) (Violations of Whistleblower Protection Act involving Defense contractor employees and non-appropriated fund employees); (8) Improper referrals of military personnel for mental health evaluations; and (9) Gross waste of funds (file with the Hotline.)

The law prohibits unfavorable personnel actions from taking place against a military member in the wake of protected communications, and this too, is a reportable issue that the Hotline will also address.

217

As defined by §1034, a ***protected communication*** is:

"(a) Any lawful communication to a Member of Congress or an Inspector General.

(b) A communication in which a member of the armed forces provides information that the member reasonably believes evidences a violation of law or regulation, including sexual harassment or unlawful discrimination, mismanagement, a gross waste of funds or other resources, an abuse of authority, or a substantial and specific danger to public health or safety, when such communication is made to any of the following:

> "(1) A Member of Congress, an IG, or a member of a DOD audit, inspection, investigation, or law enforcement organization.
>
> (2) Any other person or organization (including any person or organization in the chain of command) designated under component regulations or other established administrative procedure to receive such complaints."

Upon receipt of complaint by the Hotline pertaining to an issue of fraud, waste and abuse, your case will be assigned a case number, and Hotline will forward your complaint to the your respective Departmental IG. The complaint next undergoes a preliminary inquiry to determine if investigation of the claim is warranted.

You should be aware that Departmental Inspectors Generals report to the highest ranking uniformed official in each military department. In other words, the "rule of law" can be obstructed by the "rule of rank" thanks to the Feres Doctrine. If you believe your Departmental IG is not acting on relevant evidence or is not questioning witnesses who observed improprieties, this must be reported to the Hotline. As provided by the law, an inquiry into the complaint must be completed within 180 days. If for any reason the Departmental IG assigned to the case cannot complete their inquiry within the 180 days, the IG must give reasons to the

DODIG. You should also be receive notification for the delay. Be sure to obtain a copy of the letter explaining the reasons for the delay. To obtain information from your case file, you will have to file a request under the provisions of the Freedom of Information Act (FOIA), Public Laws, United States Code Title 5, Section 552 and the Privacy Act (PA), and Title 5, Section 552a (g)(5). These laws allow you to obtain documents which the government has created such as investigative reports. The Privacy Act allows you access to your own personal records. According to the FOIA/PA, an individual who requests information under this law, is to be provided an *initial response within ten working days!* If you don't receive a response, *appeal this immediately* to the next superior in the command's chain, also known as the Initial Denial Authority (IDA). If the IDA refuses to act on an appeal, you have the legal right to file a lawsuit in federal district court to compel release of documents the government maintains.

At the conclusion of the investigation(s), a report will be provided with the results of all specific facts of wrongs alleged in the complaint, relevant documents acquired during the investigation and *summaries of interviews conducted.* You should receive this report within 30 days of the completion of the report. MAKE SURE YOU GET THIS REPORT. You will have to file a FOIA/PA to obtain this document.

Stay Alert to Changes in Both Law and Regulations

An important piece of advice pertaining to the process is to always check to see if the Act has changed. Keep up on this stuff, because another sneaky way for those who abuse their powers to get away with their wrongs is by simply claiming that you did not file a complaint on time. All legal claims in our system of justice are time sensitive. Filing a complaint too late will deprive you justice no matter how meritorious your claim may be.

If Unfavorable Personnel Actions Are Initiated

According to the law, the Office of Special Inquires at the DOD is the primary official tasked with investigating reprisal/unfavorable personnel actions in the wake of a military members protected communications to the Hotline. As defined by §1034, a *"personnel action"* is:

> "Any action taken on a member of the Armed Forces that affects or has the potential to affect that military member's current position or career. Such actions include a promotion; a disciplinary or other corrective action; a transfer or reassignment; a performance evaluation; a decision on pay, benefits, awards, or training; referral for mental health evaluations under DOD Directive 6490.1; and any other significant change in duties or responsibilities inconsistent with the military member's rank."

In the event that unfavorable personnel actions are initiated against you, it is a good idea to establish a "trial notebook" from the beginning of your ordeal. Documentation is critical. From the date of my discharge until my "Application for Reinstatement" was reviewed, two and one-half years went by. You need to be able to show that you kept "contemporaneous" notes. Your retaliators will not remember the specifics as to how they reprised against you. Set up the notebook any way you wish, but keep correspondence which you send and receive in chronological order and date stamp all correspondence received from the opposition.

Reality Dictates Justice

A problem today is that without question the DODIG is undermanned, and their case loads continue to grow. Between 1985 and 1998, 175,000 Hotline complaints were filed! I spoke with Marcia Campbell, the Chief, DODIG Special Inquiries Division after the pathetic handling of my case prior to Shea's involvement. She said, "You can't expect us to uncover every wrong because we are undermanned and over burdened!"

If You are Wrongfully Discharged

If you are discharged after engaging in a protected communication, obtain a civilian attorney as soon as possible. In the application be sure to state that your discharge resulted from an activity protected under §1034. Submit your application to the Board for the Correction of Military Records (BCMR), in accordance with Title 10 U.S.C. §1552, the required administrative remedy under public law that must be followed prior to filing suit in federal district court or the federal court of claims. Under the statute, the BCMR has 180 days to act on the application or it is considered an exhaustion of administrative remedies under §1034. Be certain that your attorney keeps communications open with the BCMR so that the 180-day provision will be met.

The BCMRs do not have to hold an evidentiary hearing, but a discharged veteran's presence at the hearing is important. It is up to the BCMR to decide, but when you are not there to defend yourself, you know what can happen as I proven in my case!

If you face involuntarily or wrongful discharge from the United States Armed Forces as a direct result of §1034 reprisals, the following additional guidance is provided:

- ☐ Obtain sworn affidavits from co-workers, peers, and superiors if possible, stating that they believe you were discharged for engaging in protected activity under federal law; include their reasons;

- ☐ Obtain any severance pay due to you;

- ☐ If you are undergoing physical therapy or have an existing medical condition, request a medical board before your discharge and then obtain your benefits from the VA for "service connected disabilities." Remember that if you receive disability payments from the VA, your severance pay will be deducted in full before your payments begin;

- ☐ Obtain a certified copy of your service record before leaving the military, and request your "C" file. This file contains your medical records and every single medical event that took place in your career and request a microfiche copy of your official record held in Washington D.C.

☐ Obtain your G.I. Bill educational benefits and buy into the program if not already signed up;

☐ Obtain your transitional identification which grants you access to any military installation in the world for a period of two years following your discharge date;

☐ Communicate with your creditors, as they will give you some time to sort out your difficulties;

☐ Obtain your unemployment benefits (this should help for six months) and speak to your Veterans Representative at your unemployment office. Visit your nearest VA hospital or clinic and seek counseling to ensure all facts and circumstances leading to your discharge are documented;

☐ Obtain an attorney to help you file your wrongful discharge claim under §§1552 & 1034 of Title 10 immediately;

☐ Utilize government's benefits under the welfare program until you can focus and find yourself a job to support your family;

☐ For credit reasons, if you must file bankruptcy, find a job that was similar to the one you had in the military so that you can obtain financing for a VA home loan;

☐ Finally, always keep the faith that the stand you took in the public's trust is honorable and although there will be times in the struggle, especially when you receive confusing and frustrating information from the government, it will be frustrating and painful. However, don't ever double guess yourself that exposing corruption in the Armed Forces was anything but the right thing to do, because one day down the road a family member or friend may be protected because of your courage to do the right thing!

☐ And most important, keep the lines of communication open with your spouse or significant other, and always surround yourself with people who truly care for you!

Preserving Your Financial Losses for Exposing Corruption

An important issue to understand is that if you decide to voice your concerns of corruption and then are discharged, financial compensation for enlisted members differ from that of officers. When a enlisted military member is vindicated and placed back onto active duty, if the case calls for this, that person will be compensated only for the number of months left on their enlisted contracts. This is why it is important if you are intending to transfer or reenlist to hold off on filing a Hotline complaint. Any money you make in the civilian world after discharge will be calculated into the total amount due to the member if back pay is received. If you are an enlisted member and lose your career in retaliation for your complaint, vindication may take many years. Even if you are eventually vindicated by a military correction board or a federal court and the discharge board's actions were considered arbitrary and capricious, my former attorney advised me that the former member will receive back pay only for the amount of time left on their contracts at the time the discharge took place. Officers, on the other hand, can retrieve back pay to the day they were dismissed, due to their indefinite status, as they serve at the pleasure of the President.

As an example, suppose that I had been vindicated and reinstated on active duty. Instead of receiving six or more years of back pay, I would only receive four months back pay because when I was discharged, I had only four months left on my enlisted contract. Therefore, instead of my family and I receiving $150,000 in back pay and benefits, we would only have received about $10,000. Offset this with money I made as a civilian and I would probably have received nothing!

My advice to any enlisted member who proceeds with a grievance against a superior is to reenlist before you file your grievance if possible. At the very least, make sure you have sufficient time on your contract left so when you are vindicated years later, you will receive substantial back pay for your courageous efforts!

Suggestions You Can Make to Your Members of Congress

You can probably readily see that the provision that an enlisted member is only granted whatever amount of time left on their contract for back pay reasons is fundamentally unfair. A reprisal is a reprisal, and the detrimental effects are the same no matter who you are.

Congress should be placed on notice about this financial injustice. Additionally, there should be a *safety net mechanism* to ensure that unlawful reprisals arising from the lawful actions of military members end in the military. Each family member of the victim of reprisal should be equally compensated along with the service member because everyone who is victimized by an abusive leader in the military equally suffers the same amount of injustice. Reasonable compensation is not allowed, and something must be done to make affected persons whole again.

The federal government spends millions to defend military officials who abuse their power, and pays out substantial settlements to keep lawsuits out of court, such as in Keller's case. Somehow, compensation in addition to back pay must be written into the Act to provide reasonable compensation to family members of servicemembers who are victims of a retaliatory discharge. If the law were changed, funds to pay for compensation could be taken from the pension checks of those who abuse their powers. Putting the "liberty interests" of this privileged class at stake might serve as a deterrent to those who feel they can abuse their powers and get away with it due to the Feres Doctrine.

Some Final Advice

In my journey I found an organization which helps people such as myself: The Government Accountability Project (GAP) in Washington, DC. This organization played a crucial part in my obtaining the opportunity to share my story with 20/20. GAP can be reached at (202) 408-9855. This nonprofit organization exists to provide assistance and or guidance to government officials who expose fraud, waste and abuse. If they cannot help, they can probably refer you to another organization for assistance.

Another way to protect yourself is to provide your story to the national press, especially if high-ranking military members are violating the requirements of their public offices and the public's trust! Keep the news media informed of your situation, and if your story of abuse shocks the conscience of an editor or reporter, you may be afforded the opportunity to tell your story to the nation.

It took me four years of trying to get the national media to help me regarding to the military's misuse of the psychological evaluation. Don't lose confidence that in the long run, the media just might want to hear what you have to say!

It is my hope that the above suggestions will prevent unlawful reprisal from taking place against another military member in the future. However, the system is the system and until Congress acts to reform or repeal the incident to service bar regarding intentional torts and medical malpractice to prevent unlawful retaliation, justice will depend wholly on the integrity of your commanding officer.

I believe that *VERPA* (Veterans' Equal Rights Protection Advocacy) will become a force in the future to protect the human/ constitutional rights of honorable men and women who refuse to become a party to corruption within our Armed Forces. VERPA's address is PO Box 3213, Duluth, MN 55803; email address is tverpa@aol.com.